Theory and methods
in the social sciences

THEORY AND METHODS IN THE SOCIAL SCIENCES

Textbook for First Year Social Scientists

Stein Ugelvik Larsen (ed.)

SOCIAL SCIENCE MONOGRAPHS, BOULDER

DISTRIBUTED BY COLUMBIA UNIVERSITY PRESS, NEW YORK

2002

Original: *Teori og metode i samfunnsfaga*
Det Norske Samlaget

Translation: Per O. Storli
Language consultant: Peter Cribbs

Layout: Rusaanes Bokproduksjon AS

Financial support: Bergen University Fund and
MUNIN: Marketing Unit for Norwegian International Non-Fiction

Contents

Introduction

Stein Ugelvik Larsen

The main goal of this book is to familiarize students at an early stage of their studies with some of the central theses and theories which comprise the most fundamental thinking in the social sciences. Through the linking of method- and theory-learning to concrete, classical 'covering laws', students will become acquainted with the way theories are formulated and used to explain the phenomena of social life. The book therefore aims to be useful to social science students in the first phase of their studies.

The introductory phase may, however, be the most difficult for students entering an academic discipline. At an early stage in their studies students should therefore be given an appreciation of some of the central concepts in what is to become their field of study. But one cannot reasonably expect this to be an easy task. New students are not familiar with relevant concepts and ways of thinking, and the panorama to be surveyed is rather complicated. To facilitate the use of the book, all the 15 laws it introduces are presented in condensed form and written according to a similar pattern. It is hoped that this will make it easier for students to understand and compare the theories, even though they deal with very different themes and originate in different academic disciplines.

In the social sciences, as is in all scientific disciplines, disagreements arise from time to time regarding different aspects of the theoretical status of the disciplines concerned. There may be different positions, each stressing one point rather than another, and different views regarding the ways in which the theories should be used in research and in teaching. Even so, there is always fairly widely agreed that theory as such should have a prominent place in the curriculum. Without a firm grip on theory, the other aspects of methodology are likely to seem rather superficial. Statistical techniques and guidelines for the gathering and analysis of data are valid for scientific disciplines in general, but they can only be really useful if anchored in scientific problems, i.e. in the understanding of, and the search for theory. This book therefore endeavors to make the teaching of theory important and relevant, and to raise the general level of theoretical sophistication within the social sciences.

Structure of the chapters

As already mentioned, all the chapters will follow the same pattern, the aim being to give a systematic and comparable presentation of all laws and theories. The reader should recognize the basis on which evaluations are made and discern the similarity of the theories, even though they cover different fields. I believe this is a very useful way of acquiring a knowledge of theory, because:

1) the reader learns to think in theoretical terms and comes to know why this is important.
2) acquaintance is made with many of the central laws and theories within, or closely connected to, the social science disciplines.
3) comparison of theories is made easier, the pattern of analysis being the same.

All the chapters in this book originate in the seminar series *Law and Structure*, a long-standing activity organized at the Department of Comparative Politics, at the University of Bergen. During this seminar we have discussed and analyzed the selected laws according to the same principles used in their presentation here.

Each contribution starts with the *original formulation* (1) as written by the theory's author, in the original language. However, since a theory is often the basis of an entire book or is hidden between the lines, it is not always easy to identify the crucial sentences that constitute the theory. The theory's original formulation is followed by a *brief explanation* (2) which provides the reader with an initial outline of what is to be analyzed.

This is followed by a presentation of the theory's *background* (3), where the author discusses the person or persons behind the theory and the historical context in which it originated. The intention is to provide a background to the theory from the perspective of the history of science. Many social science theories have arisen within specific social or academic contexts and these contextual dependencies are interesting to compare. But in most cases theories develop and break away from the contexts of their origins and become laws capable of general application to phenomena far removed from those that inspired them.

The next consideration is *formalization and precise definition* (4). Any theory laid down in a quotation will often have be vague and ambiguous in meaning, and in this section the author will elucidate the core and the true logic of the theory. Here the relevant variables are brought into focus and their mutual inter-connections explained. Several laws and theories are simplified by means of figures, simple illustrations and/or mathematical formulae. The formalization results in greater precision once the verbal language of the original formulation has been "left aside". But here the balance between logical simplification and loyalty to the original formulation is often far from straightforward.

In the section *Generality and testability – Critique* (5) the author deals with the question of whether or not the theory can have been deduced from a more *general* theory. In other words, does there exist a theory on the "higher level", from which the theory in question can have been deduced? And if so, are there other theories with which the theory under discussion might usefully be compared? The point of such questions is to draw attention to the appearance of possible new paradigms (cf. the article on Thomas Kuhn - chapter 4). In this way we can perhaps acquire a basis for the discovery of new and more general theoretical perspectives. The generality discussion therefore involves an important future-oriented perspective. Concerning *testability*, the author discusses the extent to which the theory can be verified or falsified. Can the theory, such as it has been formulated and formalized, be tested against empirical evidence, and what kind of challenges would such testing involve? In the social sciences the term *operationalization* is applied to the definition of the variables employed when the theories are tested against empirical evidence. Thus operationalization is the concrete operation performed to ascertain whether the hypothesis accords with the facts. A high degree of innovation is often required to find a reasonably adequate operationalization, and this will vary from one theory to another. Operationalization is therefore no simple process, but rather an important theoretical challenge which is often accorded insufficient attention in courses on methodology.

Empirical assessment – Conclusion (6) offers a critical survey of some of the central findings made by researchers on the basis of the theory in question. The aim of this section is to present empirical results that support the theory, as well as those that do not, and to contrast these with each other. In the *conclusion* the author attempts to summarize how matters stand with the theory today. Here the author presents instances of empirical tests which study the theory from various angles, thus giving the reader an impression of how the theory has been fruitful as a source of deductions which have been tested and empirically proven as "right" or "wrong".

Finally, each chapter includes a list of *literature* (7), containing the works referred to by the author and the most important texts used by the founder of the theory.

Fundamental theories and discipline-delimited theories

Part I of the book covers theories relating to the fundamentals of social science, while Part II presents theories specific to the disciplines in question and which reflect the normal disciplinary divisions at Norwegian and foreign educational institutions. Viewed as a whole the book thus provides a survey, not only of theories relating to particular disciplines, but of theories fundamental to all "human" sciences. A capable social scientist must be well acquainted with both. Divisions between various social science disciplines might well have been created artificially, on the basis of distinctions that in many cases have arisen from fortuitous, historical events. The growth of knowledge in a discipline is, however, frequently as much a result of specialization in a particular field as of fruitful influence from other disciplines.

The first two theories presented in Part I deal with the preconditions for growth in science in general, and apply in principle to *all* types of scientific activity. Nils Gilje presents the background for the breakthrough of modern science in his discussion of the Weber/Merton thesis (chapter 1), whereas Harald Grimen deals with Kuhn's theory of scientific revolutions (chapter 2). In both chapters the basis for the explanations is provided in terms of the social, i.e. the contextual preconditions for breakthrough and growth. Both theories are empirically testable, but their contents are different.

The two theories that follow – on the hermeneutic circle (chapter 3) and the thesis of finitism (chapter 4) – concern the given limits for the growth of knowledge. David Doublet shows how understanding and interpretation are unavoidably conditioned by social foundations and linked to given historical contexts. The hermeneutic circle asserts that we are unable to transcend historical prejudices, and that there are inner dynamics operative between a statement and the recipient who has to decode it. Likewise, in his discussion on finitism Harald Grimen explains that all concepts are socially conditioned. A precondition for an adequate/correct interpretation of a concept is the fixed relationship the interpreter has to the social environment in which this concept is used. If an adequate interpretation is to be produced, one can neither "step into" nor "step out of" the social context. Therefore, both these laws/theses represent a critical attitude to the question of how new knowledge might possibly be insulated from the social circumstances to which we belong.

The hysteresis thesis (chapter 5) and the self-fulfilling prophecy (chapter 6) raise the problem of how to test theories about society without being influenced by preexisting knowledge. Gaute Torsvik shows how, in all social contexts – as well as in the natural sciences – history can be a disturbing force which makes it difficult to explain social phenomena. Jan Erik Karlsen deals with 'self-fulfillment' and how knowledge of theories among the individuals concerned constitutes one of the conditions behind the theory. E.g. when people know how a bank crisis occurs, they look for early warnings that a crisis might be forthcoming and act in ways that make the bank go bankrupt, even though the bank was solvent before the run to withdraw deposits started. Both theories therefore raise the question of how explanations of social phenomena should take hysteresis, and self-fulfillment into consideration in their basic formulations.

The two last chapters of Part I deal with problems relating to social experiments within the social sciences. Ole Jacob Broch discusses the placebo effect (chapter 7) and the important difficulties that arise when experimental results are to be separated from other unintended effects. When new medicines are tested out, both an experiment group and a control group receive substances, although what the control group receives is a totally inert preparation, and nobody in either group knows who has received what. Even so, the latter preparation generally has an effect which is referred to as placebo. Tom Colbjørnsen takes the so-called Hawthorne experiment (chapter 8) as his starting point, and demonstrates how individuals involved in a social experiment (workers in an industrial enterprise) change their behavior due to their participation in the experiment. These theories both bring to light the difficulties inherent in social experiments and the particular requirements researchers have to impose in order to gauge effects on the dependent variable.

As already mentioned, Part II presents some of the classics of the various social science disciplines. The economist Jan Erik Askildsen analyzes the assumptions required for the validity of Adam Smith's 'invisible hand' within free-market theory (chapter 9). The geographer Peter Sjøholt discusses the assumptions required for different types of agriculture in different areas on the basis of von Thünen's isolated state theory (chapter 10). In relation to both theories a matter of great importance in all theoretical analysis becomes clear, namely the distinction between the assumptions behind the theory and the theory itself (the relationship between independent and dependent variables).

The political scientist Thor Øivind Jensen goes into the problems that arise in the distribution of important welfare benefits within a society. Hart's inverse health care law (Chapter 11) states that all welfare reforms suffer from an inherent weakness, whereby those who are in greatest need of the available benefits receive the least of them – in stark contrast with the aim of the reforms. A corresponding negative tendency is demonstrated by the social anthropologist Ørnulf Gulbrandsen in his discussion of the exploitation of "common lands" (chapter 12). These are often over-exploited and ruined since, for reasons of rational self-interest, people strive to maximize their own personal benefit. These two theories belong to different branches of the discipline but are similar in being empirical theories and perhaps deducible from more general theories: Hart's inverse health care law from the so-called Matthew principle ("For to every one who has will more be given, and he will have abundance; but from him who has not, even what he has will be taken away." Mt 25.29) or the status-theory, and the Tragedy of the Commons, either from marginal utility theory, or the free-rider problem.

The sociologist Knud Knudsen discusses Durkheim's classical suicide hypothesis (chapter 13) and demonstrates how the thesis is based on a more general theory concerning strong and weak social integration. In many methodology textbooks this thesis is presented as a prime example of the falsification of theories by means of a wealth of empirical tests. The theory combines macro-sociological comparisons (between countries, regions, professions, religious groups etc.) and micro-relations (suicides within families, in specific areas etc.). It is a widely held belief that suicide is a clearly identifiable act which is easy to compare across various kinds of borders and populations. The analysis therefore encourages the formulation of larger-scale theories.

The last two chapters concern theories that relate to voting research. The political scientist Lars Svåsand analyzes cross-pressures (chapter 14), and the media researcher Helge Østbye focuses on effects of opinion-leadership (chapter 15). Both theories are general, empirical and falsifiable. They both demonstrate that neither cross-pressure nor opinion-leadership can be measured directly, but only established through indirect observation. This is also a central point in the concept of a law or a theory: they are not tested directly, but only indirectly through the deduction of hypotheses, and from them the operationalized, empirical tests. Only in this way can the presence of cross-pressure and opinion-leadership be proven and explained .

The concept of theory: structure and empirical generalization

It is no easy task to give an unambiguous definition of theory, such as the concept is now used in social science. However, there are at least two different ways of describing the nature of a scientific theory:

1 The process-oriented definition, i.e. what kind of function a theory has in scientific work.
2 The delimitation definition, whereby scientific theorizing is distinguished as one special activity among the many in which scientists engage.

In the process-oriented definition the theory is the guiding principle that governs the search for stable relationships. It is the final point under which singular observations are subsumed, and in terms of which different research results are organized according to major explanations. Thus, theories provide answers to many and various isolated phenomena. According to this definition a theory provides a general explanation for many questions that arise from isolated observations.

In the process-oriented definition the various steps from theory and hypothesis to test illustrate how subsumption of the particular to the general is brought about. A theory comprises an arsenal of different hypotheses, i.e. contentions about how certain relationships appear within a society. Hence it is possible to infer from the theory, i.e. formulate, many different hypotheses, all of which share the same theory as their common basis.

Furthermore, a hypothesis comprises an arsenal of options for deducing tests that examine what empirical reality must look like if the hypothesis is to be falsified/verified. This way of defining theories implies that the theory is not subject to direct testing, the object of testing being the hypotheses inferred from the theory. The procedure is based on the assumption that a theory is a statement on a general level, and that the hypothesis a concrete statement deduced from the theory.

The process-oriented theory definition:

THEORY (comprising an arsenal of concrete hypotheses)

$\downarrow$

HYPOTHESES (comprising an arsenal of empirical tests)

$\downarrow$

TESTS (applied to empirical examples; answer: yes or no – true or false)

A theory can be *true or false*, this being determined through the derivation of concrete hypotheses (deduction), these again being tested against empirical evidence. A theory can be *fruitful or unfruitful*, the classification here depending on its potential for the deduction of interesting and different hypotheses, these in turn being testable against the empirical knowledge available.

An example of the process-oriented definition is provided by the studies on suicide by the French sociologist Emile Durkheim (cf. chapter 13). Durkheim tried to answer the question why suicide was more frequent in Denmark and Sweden than in Norway, and less frequent among Catholics and Jews than among Protestants. Observations from suicide statistics required answers which took all the actual variations into account. Durkheim had to organize all the questions which the observations raised under just a few principal answers, thereby according the single observations a definite meaning. His isolated observations are what we have called tests. The general answers sought are what we refer to as hypotheses. Durkheim found several such hypotheses to furnish the precise answers he was looking for.

Which such an arsenal of hypotheses Durkheim continued his search for a general theory under which all the hypotheses could be brought into line. This resulted in the social integration theory: he found that social deviations and social commonality varied according to the degree of strong/feeble attachments and socially meaningful/not meaningful human relationships. The theory could furnish answers concerning several kinds of deviation, such as suicide, criminality, divorce etc. From the general theory we can thus deduce several hypotheses concerning social deviation or social solidarity/commonality. If we consider the theory 'true' or probable, this is due to its being confirmed by many separate observations. It follows that a good theory will furnish confirmative answers to our questions when we observe different features of social life. Moreover, a good theory will also be an instrument for predicting what will happen in future: the theory is applicable to past, present and future alike.

The "look" of a theory can vary considerably. An entire book can be 'the theory'. The theory may also take the shape of a mathematical formula or an abbreviated sentence. In social science we also frequently see authors using the terms *theory* and *model* indiscriminately. There are also cases where a concrete hypothesis is discussed, where the theory is not given in plain words, but is tacitly understood to be an underlying precondition.

A theory is a contention concerning the way in which phenomena (all/several of the same type) influence another one (all/several of the same type). In current terminology these "phenomena" are called variables. The accepted formulation is that the independent variable accounts for the change (effect) in/on the dependent variable: when the dependent variable Y changes, this is due to a change in the independent variable X. *Change in X results in change in Y: $X \rightarrow Y$.*

In many other cases the term theory is used to refer to a sentence that expresses something abstract as opposed to something concrete. A person may be described as a "theoretician", meaning that the person referred to is not of a practical turn. This type of common usage is not what is meant by theory here.

A theory is therefore an instrument of thought used to introduce order into a vast and complex reality. The theory is related to reality – our empirically established knowledge – by means of the hypotheses and tests set up to show what reality will be like if the theory is 'true'. We often employ the terms *deduction* (inferring "downwards" from the general to the particular) and *induction* (inferring "upwards" from the particular to the general). In classical logic we learn how the deductive inference functions by combining two premises and a conclusion. In practical logic it is not always easy to ascertain which are the correct/reasonable deductions. The basis of correct/reasonable deduction and correct/reasonable generalization may indeed be just an understanding that prevails among the majority of scientists belonging to a certain discipline. The agreement may also be of a temporary character, disagreement in scientific circles will therefore arise as to what is a correct/reasonable deduction, and what is a correct/reasonable generalization. But it is generally accepted that theory plays a primary role in the provision of answers to questions arising from the study of particular phenomena of social life.

The second definition of theory is intended to *delimit* theories from other statements. In the history of science this is close to the so-called *demarcation principle*, delimiting – "demarcating" – science and non-science. It was the Austrian-British philosopher Karl Popper who suggested this definition in debate with the so-called Vienna Circle, the members of which held that a dividing line between science and non-science could be drawn by testing theories against reality. In this much there was agreement between the Viennese philosophers and Popper. It is the test criterion that delimits scientific theories from non-science such as normative statements and speculations.

Disagreement arose around the various views held on the status of theories as final truths. Popper maintained the impossibility of determining the truth of a theory, even if it has been confirmed by means of tests correctly inferred from that same theory. Later, new hypotheses may be deduced from the theory in question, which new tests fail to verify. Hence we can never establish conclusively that a theory is true, only that it is false. There are no final truths, although we can at least establish conclusively when a statement is incorrect or false. In Popper's view the task of science is thus the invalidation (falsification) of theories, not the establishment of 'ultimate' truth.

According to the delimiting definition, a scientific theory is therefore a general statement liable to falsification against reality. This falsification is effected through the process outlined above: theory, falsifiable hypothesis and test.

Theories, laws, theses and effects

The contributors to this book use various terminology in discussing the various theories. In one chapter they are termed 'theses', while elsewhere they are called 'laws', and in some contexts they are referred to as 'effects'. The varying use of terminology is a result of our wish to present the theories as they are discussed in the international literature and in keeping with the way they are expressed in the original formulation. For example, the two-step hypothesis (chapter 15) has most frequently been referred to in social science as a *hypothesis* and only on rather rare occasions as a theory.

The reader should not be confused by the terminology employed. All chapters deal with theories which are general, but which differ somewhat with regard to empirical testing and falsification. Some of them would easily be accommodated by the definitions of theory given above, whereas others have a somewhat less defined status as empirical theory, which is particularly true of the theories dealt with in the first section, e.g. the hermeneutic circle (chapter 3) and the hysteresis theory (chapter 5). Both of these chapters deal with the general difficulties met with in attempts to draw unambiguous conclusions about empirical social conditions. They cannot so easily provide a basis for the deduction of empirical tests, although this too could be possible. This applies also to the chapters on finitism (4) and the self-fulfilling prophecy (6). Some may take the view that it would be more appropriate to describe Hart's inverse health care law as an empirical generalization, rather than a theory in the strict sense of the word. This somewhat uncertain use of terminology shows that the theory concept is in fact not so clearly delimited as I may have suggested above. Nonetheless, all chapters deal with theories, laws, theses or effects of direct relevance for social science and which can, in principle at least, be tested against empirically established knowledge.

In the last chapter of the book the editor tries to open up for a broad discussion on how to arrive at new perspectives on both the 'discovery' of the nature of theories and on 'how to play' with existing theories while introducing the four incompatible hypotheses. He also points to the difficult, but very important distinction between assumptions behind the theory and the theory proper. This is thus an invitation for the theory-minded social scientists to penetrate into the difficult, but very stimulating task of 'concrete' theoretization.

PART I

Theories on Foundations of the Social Sciences

1
The Weber-Merton Thesis Protestantism and the Breakthrough of Modern Natural Science

NILS GILJE

1. Original quotation

Die Ausgeprägte Vorliebe der protestantischen Askese für den durch mathematische Fundamentierung rationalisierten Emprismus ist bekannt [...]. Die bevorzugte Disziplin alles puritanischen, täuferischen und pietetistischen Christentums war demgemäss die *Physik* und warden demnächts andere, mit gleichartiger Methode arbeitende mathematisch-naturwissenschaftliche Disziplinen (Weber 1969[1904-1905], pp. 232-33).

The Puritan complex of a scarcely disguised utilitarianism; of intramundane interests; methodological, unremitting actions; throroughgoing empiricism; of the right and even the duty of libre examen; of anti-traditionalism – all this was congenial to the same values in science (Merton 1970 [1938], p 136).

Ascetic Protestantism helped motivate and canalize the activities of men in the direction of experimental science. This is the historical form of the hypothesis. (Merton 1968, p. 589)

The generic hypothesis under discussion holds that at a time in Western society when science had not yet become elaborately institutionalized, it obtained substantial legitimacy as an unintended consequence of the religious ethic and praxis of ascetic Protestantism. (Merton 1984, p. 1093)

 NILS GILJE

2. Translation and brief explanation

(First quotation:)
The decided propensity of Protestant asceticism for empiricism, rationalized on a mathematical basis, is well known [...] The favourite science of all Puritan, Baptist, or Pietist Christianity was thus physics, and next to it all those other natural sciences which used a similar method, especially mathematics. (Weber 1996 [1904–05] pp. 232–33)

The central point of the Weber-Merton thesis as presented in the four versions given above is the contention that there exists a particular value affinity between ascetic Protestantism (e.g. Puritanism, Anabaptism and Pietism) and the new experimental sciences which gradually emerged during the 17th century. According to Max Weber (1864-1920) who formulated the first version of the thesis, ascetic Protestantism had a particular predilection for the new physics. The background was the firm belief of ascetic Protestants that God and his intentions could be recognized only through his Creation. God reveals himself not only in the Holy Scriptures, but also in the Book of Nature (*Biblia naturae*). The new natural sciences could therefore be understood as a means of seeking "God in Nature". The investigation of Nature means interpreting God's handwriting, or finding the way to God. Some of the most important scientists thought that it was possible to come to know the "meaning" of the world through empirical understanding of the divine laws governing Nature. In Protestant circles experimental natural philosophy therefore obtained high prestige and religious sanction: the exploration of the creation is a contribution to the glorification of God. On this background ascetic Protestantism might also be said to motivate prospective participants for scientific research. Only in the natural sciences B and not in the speculations of Scholasticism or in Humanist philology B was it possible to grasp God's Creation physically and begin to unravel what he intended with the World (cf. Weber 1992, pp. 182-183; Weber 1989, pp. 16-21).

Weber also stressed the point that the ascetic Protestant and the naturalist had one more set of values in common: both were worldly ascetics who shared the firm belief that the world could be mastered in a methodically controlled way. In Weber's view there was an unambiguous "elective affinity" between the ethics of ascetic Protestantism and the spirit of the new natural sciences.

The so-called "Merton thesis" was formulated by the American sociologist Robert K. Merton (born 1910) in his classic study *Science, Technology and Society in Seventeenth Century England (= STS)*, published in 1938. One of the purposes of the work was to establish whether Puritan ethics had a similar affinity to the spirit of science as to the spirit of capitalism. *STS* can therefore be regarded as a continuation of a research program originally developed by Weber. Merton's monograph is an explicit attempt to test out Weber's incidental remarks concerning ascetic Protestantism and natural science (Merton 1970, pp. 59-60; Rattansi 1990, p. 351). Like Weber, Merton emphasizes the point that the Puritan ethos conferred a new religious significance and legitimacy upon science. Puritan ethics and practice also rendered an important contribution to the institutionalizing of the new sciences. An impetus of this kind was hardly to be found in other religious denominations (Merton 1970, pp. 86-102).

The most exciting part of Merton's study is perhaps his attempt to establish the existence of a particular harmony between the values of Puritanism and the new natural sciences. In analyzing the works of scientists like Boyle, Newton, Ray, Wallis and Watkins, Merton tried to bring to light the motives that had made them engage in science. The result of this research is both impressive and challenging. Merton found a "point to point correlation" between the ethos of Puritanism and "the avowed attributes, goals and results of scientific investigation" (1970, p. 90). In Merton's view the new sciences embodied "patterns of behavior which are congenial to Puritan tastes. Above all, it embraces two highly prized values: utilitarianism and empiricism" (1970, p. 92). This argument was to be of great importance to Merton: it is precisely the combination of rationalism and empiricism that is so characteristic of Puritan ethics, and this combination also made up "the essence of the spirit of modern science" (Merton 1970, p. 92).

Merton denies – as did Weber – any intention of presenting a full explanation of the connection between Puritanism and science. In Merton's perspective both were components in a complicated system of mutually dependent factors. It is therefore totally erroneous to consider religion as the independent and science as the dependent variable (cf. Merton 1970, pp. 104-105).

3. Background

At the beginning of the 17th century it was a widespread view in radical Protestant circles that a reform of the Church must be followed by a reform of the sciences, and that traditional authorities had to give way. In the view of many Protestants of the time the Aristotelian tradition was equally destructive to the Church and the sciences: "Neither science nor the Church need a Pope" (Samuel Hartlieb). In this respect the Weber-Merton thesis expresses the attitudes and views of prominent naturalists of the period (cf. Cohen 1990; Hill 1965; Hooykaas 1972; Webster 1976, 1986). This does not mean, however, that the *theologians* of ascetic Protestantism had any intention to do away with the traditional world view or to promote a scientific conception of nature. Both Weber and Merton realized that many 16th century Protestant theologians had no particularly positive attitude to the new sciences (with Melanchthon and Calvin as possible exceptions), no more than they took a positive stand towards early-modern capitalism. In this case, we can talk about a more or less contingent concurrence of values. The legitimation potential of ascetic Protestantism was thus an unintended consequence of its theory and practice. The reformers did not *intend* to help bring about the scientific revolution (Weber 1923, p. 359; Merton 1970, pp. 74 and 100).

Both Weber and Merton emphasized the fact that the ethics and practice of ascetic Protestantism have lost much relevance for modern science. Just as triumphant capitalism, once it had established itself, no longer needed the support of Protestantism, so modern science developed an ever-stronger ethos of self-generation, which has to a large extent freed itself from religious values (cf. Weber 1992). Moreover, Merton analyzed the ethos of modern science in several works, i.e. the norms arising from values like universalism, communism, disinterestedness, and organized scepticism (cf. Merton 1968, 1973, 1976).

In Weber's work the thesis is integrated into a wider program for a new sociology of religion and is related to assumptions of a long term "disenchantment of the world" (*Entzauberung der Welt*): a complete "disenchantment of the world" would mean that there are in principle no magical, mysterious, or incalculable powers at work in Nature (cf. Weber 1989, p. 13). Ascetic Protestantism was an important contributor to this process. The enmity of Protestantism against magic thus paves the way for a natural alliance with the new sciences. Both movements share the assumption of a constant and intelligible order inherent in Nature. The book of Nature is written in a mathematical language and contains universal laws which exclude magic powers. According to Weber the Protestant disenchantment of the world opens for a secularized and rationalized world picture, thus creating an important precondition for experimental science.

Robert K. Merton is already one of the classics of sociology. For most of his career he has worked at Columbia University. Lewis Coser has appropriately called Merton "our foremost manufacturer of sociological thinking caps" (Coser 1975, p. 9). Many of Merton's sociological concepts and theories have become standard features of scientific culture: manifest and latent functions, social dysfunctions, self-fulfilling prophesies, status sets and role sets, the Matthew effect, the Thomas theorem, "theories of the middle range", sociological ambivalence etc. As we shall see, Merton's later concepts and theories can shed light on the problems he raises in *STS*.

STS was Merton's first extensive monograph. Based on his 1935 doctorate thesis it was first published in the journal *Osiris: Studies on the History and Philosophy of Science* in 1938. For a number of reasons the monograph was little known before it was republished in 1970 (cf. Cohen 1990; Merton 1990). Merton's article "Puritanism, Pietism and Science" (1936) was, therefore, the point of departure for much of the early discussion of the Weber-Merton thesis.

Merton is still professionally active, and today is considered as one of the founders of the sociology of science. Among his most important works we can mention the following: *STS* (1970), *Social Theory and Social Structure* (1968), *The Sociology of Science, Theoretical and Empirical Investigations* (1973), and *Sociological Ambivalence and other Essays* (1976). Merton is perhaps best known for his numerous articles, of which some of the most widely read are: "Science and the Social Order" (1938), "The Self-Fulfilling Prophecy" (1948), "Social Structure and "nomie" (1949), "Singletons and Multiples in Scientific Discovery: A Chapter in the Sociology of Science" (1961), "The Matthew Effect in Science" (1968).

The Weber-Merton thesis is an interesting example of what Merton has termed "multiple scientific discoveries", meaning that there is a tendency for different researchers to arrive at the same results at approximately the same time and independently of one another (1973, pp. 343-370). In a series of minor works published in the 1930s, Dorothy Stimson investigated (independently of Merton) the connection between Puritanism and 17th century science. She proposed the theory

that Puritanism was an important factor, hitherto little regarded, in making conditions in England favorable to the new philosophy heralded by Bacon and in promoting the type of thinking that helped to arouse interest in science and to create a ready reception for the work of the geniuses produced in that century (Stimson 1990, pp. 151-152).

At around the same time the historian of literature Richard F. Jones was arguing in favor of a similar thesis in the important work *Ancients and Moderns: A Study of the Rise of the Scientific Movement in Seventeenth-Century England* (1961, originally published in 1936). Weber, Merton, Stimson and Jones can be said to have arrived at more or less the same conclusions, even though their work was based on different methods and different data (Merton 1948, p. 1091). This case of multiple discoveries is in itself an interesting phenomenon in the sociology of science.

The Weber-Merton thesis can also be regarded as a "Phoenix phenomenon" in the history of ideas: some theories and hypotheses – such as Durkheim's law of suicide, Weber's Protestant ethic thesis and the Weber-Merton thesis – appear to be immortal, even though they are subjected to severe criticism. In revised and rejuvenated forms they rise from the ashes and see one renaissance after the other (Merton 1961, 1984). Consequently, the Weber-Merton thesis forms an integral part of a more or less permanent scientific controversy in the fields of sociology and history of science. It can thus be regarded as an interesting case of what has been called studies of scientific controversies (cf. Engelhardt and Caplan 1987).

Up to the mid-1960s the Weber-Merton thesis aroused only slight interest. To some extent, research in the history of science seemed to support some of Merton's empirical findings, but showed little interest in his theoretical and sociological intentions. The thesis appeared to be more or less exhausted. However, towards the end of the 1960s the situation changed radically, above all due to new approaches in the history of science and culture pioneered by Christopher Hill (1965), R. Hooykaas (1972) and Charles Webster (1974, 1976). In many respects these studies supported Merton's conclusions and gave rise to an intense discussion among historians of science and sociologists. The debate took yet another turn in the 1980s. This time it was the aspect of the Weber-Merton thesis dealing with Pietism which was exposed to criticism (Becker 1984, 1991). This criticism forced Merton to stand forth, and he made a new and sophisticated theoretical contribution to the discussion (1984).

In the 1980s it became increasingly clear that the so-called Weber-Merton thesis is not, in the strict sense of the word, one thesis, but contains several logically and empirically independent theses. Per se, even the Merton thesis contains radically different assumptions concerning the relationship between Puritanism and science. (Abraham 1983, Zuckerman 1989, Ben-David 1991). It therefore requires some elucidation and theoretical clarification.

4. Formalization – precise definition

In an attempt to give a precise presentation of the Weber-Merton thesis it might be useful to say something about what it does *not* attempt to say. Neither Weber not Merton contended that early-modern science was an exclusively Protestant business. Weber pointed out that "the first basis of modern science originated from *Catholic* areas and heads" (Weber 1987, p. 324). It cannot be claimed that Puritanism created modern science, nor that Protestantism did so in a wider sense. The natural sciences of the 16th and 17th centuries were developed by researchers professing different Christian faiths, taking as their points of departure knowledge established by Greeks, Arabs, Jews and others (Merton 1970, pp. 86-102).

Nor is the Weber-Merton thesis a theory in the sociology of knowledge which implies that in some way ascetic Protestantism determined the cognitive contents of the new natural sciences. Both Weber and Merton have rejected this kind of speculative *Wissenssoziologie* (Weber 1989; Merton 1945, 1973).

The Weber-Merton thesis contends that ascetic Protestants would be more inclined to study natural sciences and to consider experimental research a vocation than were members of others denominations (Merton 1970, p. 111). Merton claimed that this hypothesis could be tested through an investigation of the confessional attitudes of members of the Royal Society: "If Puritanism was as closely linked with science as we have been led to suspect, then the composition of this pioneer group [Royal Society, NG] should reflect this linkage" (Merton 1970, p. 112). Even though the Puritans were, according to Merton, but a relatively small minority of the English population, they accounted for 62% of the members of the original Royal Society (1970, p 114). Similar research done on continental scientific communities and academies appears to confirm this tendency, as did Merton's research on Pietism, based on secondary sources (1970, pp. 119-127). In what follows, this Puritanism/Pietism thesis will be referred to as W-M 1.

Sometimes Merton seems to think that W-M 1 can be presented as a testable empirical deduction from a more general hypothesis (cf. the title of chapter VI in *STS*: "Puritanism, Pietism and Science: Testing an Hypothesis"). There are several versions of the general hypothesis, which was already very cautiously formulated in 1936, in Merton's article "Puritanism, Pietism and Science":

> It is a thesis of this study that the Puritan ethic, as an ideal-typical expression of
> the value attitudes basic to ascetic Protestantism generally, so canalized the inter-
> ests of seventeenth-century Englishmen as to constitute an important *element* in
> the enhanced cultivation of science (1936, p. 1).

This thesis claims that *Puritan* ethics canalized the interests of *Englishmen* towards science. With a view to Pietism, Merton formulated a similar general hypothesis. This is possible because "the ethical principles of Puritanism and Pietism are almost identical" (Merton 1970, p. 124). Because Merton regarded W-M 1 as well corroborated, he considered it legitimate to advance the more general thesis, which will subsequently be referred to as W-M 2.

Another important problem which is formulated in *STS* springs from Merton's original analysis of the new value orientation in 17th century England. Taking as his base 29 120 biographical reports in the Dictionary of National Biography, he was able to show that a dramatic change in the attitude towards science and other intellectual activities took place from the 1640s onwards. At the same time as Puritan radicalism fastened its grip on cultural institutions following the English Revolution, a growing interest in "experimental philosophy" can be noted, together with a higher status enjoyed by science. This situation involves changes in attitudes and new cultural orientations which, during the second half of the 17th century, resulted in naturalists rising to the top of the intellectual hierarchy. These empirical findings were also underpinned by other types of data (Merton 1970, pp. 38-54). The final conclusion of *STS* points to this aspect of the thesis: "On the basis of the foregoing study, it may not be too much to conclude that the cultural soil of seventeenth century England was peculiarly fertile for the growth and spread of science" (Merton 1970, p. 238).

The conclusion is very much along the same lines as W-M 2: the new religious ethics and practice progressively established in England in the second half of the 17th century created a framework of conditions favorable to the development of science. This historical hypothesis can, however, be given a more precise sociological formulation. The change is clearly expressed in Merton's preface to the 1970 edition of *STS*, where he states that Puritanism "happened to advance the institutionalization of science by providing a substantial basis for its legitimacy" (Merton 1970, p xvii). This is also the central message in "The Fallacy of the Latest Word: The case of Pietism and Science" from 1984: "Ascetic Protestantism, including Pietism, served to legitimate a nascent and slightly institutionalized science (...)" (Merton 1984, p.

1096). This *institutionalization* thesis, explicitly present both in Weber and in the early Merton, will subsequently be referred to as W-M 3.

It should be stressed that neither of the theses presents Puritanism as indispensable or absolutely necessary for the progressive establishment (or institutionalization) of natural science in this period. As emphasized by Merton, other *functionally equivalent* ideologies might have conferred an equivalent legitimacy on science. There is nothing in Merton's work to justify a contention that only ascetic Protestantism could be vested with such a function: "*As it happened*, Puritanism provided major (not exclusive) support in that historical time and place. But that does not make it indispensable" (Merton 1970, xviii).

From an historical perspective it is easy to understand that scientific research in the 16th and 17th centuries had to contend with many obstacles (cf. the trials of Servetus, Bruno and Galileo). Religious and political authorities often took a stand hostile to *libre examen*; there was a widespread fear that science would undermine the traditional world-view and could lead to atheism. The intellectual elite at the universities were mostly Scholastics and Humanists. In this group there could hardly be many seriously interested in experimental research and natural science. They rejected out of hand the idea that the new natural sciences should be given a status equal to that of their own disciplines (or even surpassing them). The new sciences could therefore not expect any immediate support from traditional academic authorities. However, in the 1640s the English Revolution put all established authorities under pressure. In this situation natural science received unexpected and perhaps unintended support from the Puritan ideology. It is also a fact that this ideology included elements of Francis Bacon's utilitarianism and Utopian ideas (cf. Webster, 1974, 1976). In this way the new natural sciences were invested with some sort of *religious* legitimacy.

5. Generality and testability. Critique

There is no doubt that W-M 1 is the thesis most vulnerable to attack. Merton's attempt to test the thesis by means of an analysis of Puritan influence among early members of the Royal Society is faced by several problems. Already in the 17th century there were controversies concerning the definition and delimitation of the notion of "Puritanism", as is still the case among today's historians. The term has been used in a wide sense as well as in a restricted one. "Puritanism" may be interpreted as meaning the highly heterogeneous religious and ideological movement which was to become the dominant force in the English Revolution and which held an important position in political and intellectual life up until the Restoration of the 1660. But "Puritanism" may also be understood as meaning the fundamentalist religious elite constituting the "vanguard" of the English Revolution, and which was totally banned from public life after 1660. Practically none of Merton's Puritans belongs to this group. In many situations he uses the term "Puritan" in such an open and comprehensive way as to cover almost all of English Protestantism. As pointed out by Michael Hunter, Merton establishes "a generalized connection between religious and intellectual trends which is indisputable because it is so vague" (Hunter 1981, p. 113).

Several researchers have tried to test out W-M 1, the most thorough research being that carried out by Lotte Mulligan. Taking as her starting point 162 members of the Royal Society who were older than 16 in 1642, and thus old enough to take sides in the civil war, she found that only 38 supported Parliament, whereas 85 were Royalists (the rest of the members could not be confessionally defined). Consequently, Mulligan arrived at a conclusion quite different from Merton's:

> The typical background of a science enthusiast in the 1660s was not middleclass, mercantile, puritan, politically radical, unacademic or utilitarian. Rather, our typical Fellow was a royalist, Anglican, university-educated gentleman (Mulligan, 1973, p.108).

One may of course discuss how significant such statistical data are. In the 17th century the Royal Society had many passive members not engaged in research. It is possible that Mulligan's test would have been more sensitive (and meaningful), had the selection been confined to the "hard core". Out of the ten most active members (Robert Boyle, Jonathan Goddard, Henry Oldenburg, William Petty, John Wilkins, Lord Brouncker, Walter Charleton, John Evelyn, Sir Robert Moray and Christopher Wren) the first five had sided with Parliament in the Civil War; a fact that might indicate a stronger "Puritan" influence among the *researchers* than Mulligan assumes (cf. Brooke 1991, p. 114).

There is much, however, to indicate that Merton over-emphasized the *Puritan* ethos. It is probable that a moderate and broad-minded Anglican ideology, the so-called "Latitudinarianism", played a far more important role than Merton assumed. This religious ideology, which enjoyed strong support from the 1660s onwards, may be characterized by a will to compromise and religious tolerance, and after the Restoration it became a safe harbor for many former Radicals. John Wilkins

(1614-1672) is often considered its foremost spokesman (Shapiro 1970). During the Civil War he was a moderate supporter of Cromwell and Parliament. As head of Wadham College in Oxford he took in several scientists of pronounced Anglican and Royalist sympathies. After 1660 his "Club for Comprehension" included many former sectarians and radicals. In 1668 England's most famous Copernican was appointed Bishop of Chester, ending his career as court chaplain of Charles II. Would it make sense to label Wilkins as "Puritan"? He might perhaps be said to have been a moderate Puritan in the 1640s, but it would definitely be wrong to classify him as a Puritan after the Restoration.

Several researchers have suggested that in many contexts the term "Puritan" might well be substituted by "Anglican" (Jacob and Jacob 1980). From an empirical point of view there is reason to believe that in the 17th century a great number of religious and secular ideologies contributed to the legitimation of scientific activity and to motivate students towards scientific research. It is, however, a rather impossible task to determine precisely the relative weight of these "isms", the problem being further complicated by the fact that, as time passed, the relation between these factors was subject to change. Even so, we can assume that Protestant values held a dominant position in this complex. Much of the criticism of the Weber-Merton thesis might probably have been different, had Merton used the term "Protestant ethics and practice" instead of "Puretan ethics and practice".

Merton himself has characterized W-M 2 as a thesis belonging to "a middle-range level". If "Puritan" is replaced by "Protestant", then much of the research in the history of the sciences of the 17th century turns out to support the thesis. Even though there are strong empirical counter-arguments, the thesis still enjoys considerable support. However, from a sociological and philosophical point of view several objections to W-M 2 should be mentioned: Merton never claimed Puritan ethics to be an independent variable on which science was dependent, thus avoiding any strong claim involving cause and effect. It is therefore unclear whether in Merton's opinion there is something more than a correlation between the ethics of Puritanism and the spirit of science, and what this "something" could possibly be. From an empirical point of view it is always difficult to determine *what* motivates people towards scientific research. Both Weber and Merton claimed Puritan ethics to be a very important factor, but even in the cases of natural scientists with a clearly Puritan orientation it is problematic to determine whether or not it was their *religious conviction* that led them towards science. Merton himself realized this problem:

To what extent did the old Puritans turn their attention to science Y because this interest was generated by their ethos, and to what extent was it rather the other way, with those having entered upon a career in science Y for whatever other reasons, subsequently finding the values of Puritanism congenial to them? (Merton 1970, p. xxviii)

Merton recognized both processes as real, but found it difficult to make any precise statement about the strength of their interdependence. In principle, one might also imagine both Puritan ethics and the spirit of science as conditioned by the same social and economic circumstances, which would be the core of a Marxist critique of the Weber-Merton thesis.

On one point it is absolutely necessary to revise both W-M 1, W-M 2 and W-M 3. There is no reason to believe, as Weber maintains, that *physics* was the preferred discipline among ascetic Protestants. Among Puritans and, more generally, Protestants, neither physics nor mathematical natural sciences held any unique position. Walter Pagel (1985), Piyo Rattansi (1990) and Charles Webster (1976, 1982, 1986) have shown that many Protestants took a particular interest in medicine, chemistry (alchemy), biology, metallurgy and "practical" sciences. In fact, the one discipline dominated almost exclusively by Protestants was chemistry: Libavius, Jean Beguin, Daniel Sennert, Nicaise Le Febvre, Nicholas Lemery and John Boyle were all Protestants. During most of the 17th century also "occult" disciplines held a strong position in these circles. Against this background there is reason to question the range of Weber's thesis of a Protestant *Entzauberung der Welt*. For many 17th century naturalists astrology, alchemy, natural magic and natural science went hand in hand. Even Newton listened to Pan's flute (cf. McGuire and Rattansi 1966; Webster 1982).

6. Empirical assessment – conclusion

Historians of religion as well as of science have criticized Merton's (and Weber's) contention that the ethical principles of Puritanism and Pietism were more or less identical (Merton 1970, p. 124). It is highly doubtful whether Pietism can be regarded as the continental equivalent of Puritanism. The attitude of Pietism to the natural sciences was probably more skeptical and negative than was that of Puritanism. This criticism has been put forward particularly by Georg Becker (1984, 1991). However, we have little knowledge as to the part played by religion in the legitimation and institutionalization of experimental research in Lutheran and Calvinist Europe. This controversy cannot, therefore, be regarded as definitely solved in favor of Becker (cf. Merton 1984).

Much of the recent discussion of the Weber-Merton thesis opens for comparative perspectives. We have reason to believe that natural scientists met with more severe limitations to their activities in Catholic Europe than in 17th century England. For instance, John Wilkins had no problem publishing his pro-Copernican essay *Discourse concerning a new planet* in 1640. This would probably have been impossible in Italy or Spain. On the other hand, it is an undeniable fact that researchers with a Catholic background like Galileo, Descartes, Mersenne and Gassendi made important contributions to the mechanization of the world picture and the new "atomism". The question is whether there is something in Catholic culture *functionally equivalent* to Merton's ascetic Protestantism. So far, this is yet another discussion with no definite conclusion.

Other researchers have suggested that the Weber-Merton thesis can be fruitfully studied in the light of Chinese and Arabic history of science. There is a broad consensus that at the end of the Middle Ages Chinese technology had reached a significantly more advanced stage than that of the West. There is also reason to believe that Arabic science (particularly in the fields of astronomy and optics) in the same period was more advanced than Western science (cf. Huff 1993). But already in the 16th century Chinese as well as Arab science seems to be stagnating. How is this stagnation to be explained? Why was scientific development in China and the Arab world unable to adapt itself to the same trend for rationalization that swept the West? Why did these cultures not develop a specifically *modern* science? This problem has perhaps been most clearly formulated by Toby E. Huff :

> Considered altogether, in mathematics, astronomy, optics, physics, and medicine, Arabic science was the most advanced in the world. In different fields it lost the lead at different points in time, but it can be said that up until the Copernican Revolution of the sixteenth century, its astronomical models were the most advanced in the world. Consequently, the problem at hand asks why Arabic science, given its technical and scientific superiority built up over five centuries or so, did not give rise to modern science (Huff 1993, p. 52)

The Weber-Merton thesis, and quite particularly W-M 3, has proved fruitful for the discussion of such problems. It seems clear that neither Confucianism nor Islam have had the same positive legitimating function in their respective cultural areas as Protestantism had in England. This might perhaps contribute to an explanation of why research in the natural sciences never gained a proper *institutional* foothold in traditional Chinese and Arabic cultures. In plain words this means that W-M 3 is still an exciting and challenging hypothesis.

No attempt has been made to test the Weber-Merton thesis in the light of Norwegian or Scandinavian data. In research done on Norwegian Pietism, more precisely the Haugian movement, it has been pointed out that the followers of the popular Norwegian religious leader Hans Nielsen Hauge took an active interest in technological and economic progress, but most probably took no such interest in natural science (Gilje 1997). However, a case of this kind should not be interpreted as a counter-example to the thesis. The Haugians of the outgoing 18th century lacked all cultural or institutional preconditions for science, as was also the case of the Puritan Boers in 17th and 18th century South Africa (De Klerk 1977). Consequently, ascetic Protestantism cannot *per se* channel interest towards the natural sciences, and cannot be treated as an effective cause producing the same effects under all historical conditions. Puritanism and Pietism are relevant variables only in the presence of material and institutional conditions that make research in the natural sciences possible. Once again, it should be stressed that ascetic Protestantism is not an independent variable.

It is still an unsolved question whether Pietism (and, more generally, Protestantism) contributed to the legitimation of natural science in Scandinavia. We know that Tycho Brahe had fairly good working conditions in Denmark. At the beginning of the seventeenth century it was probably more dangerous to be a theologian than an astronomer in Denmark and Norway (Garstein 1953). In this period Protestantism in Norway appears to have had a certain predilection for topographic and natural history research (cf. Peder Claussøn Friis, Erik Pontoppidan et al.). But even concerning questions of this kind we lack final conclusions. The relevance of the Weber-Merton thesis for Scandinavia therefore remains an unsolved question.

In this study we have endeavored to show that the Weber-Merton thesis is problematic for conceptual and empirical reasons. Nonetheless, it is still probable that Protestantism was important in legitimizing research and channeled interest towards science, but it is difficult to prove this on an empirical basis. In any case, the W-M 1 is highly questionable.

W-M 2 and W-M 3 can still be considered plausible and fruitful hypotheses. Admittedly, here as well we need more precise definitions and modifications, but these versions of the thesis still generate important questions, and hold a central position in most recent discussions concerning the relation between religion and science. The problems concerning the institutionalization of scientific research, explicitly expressed in W-M 3, have proved to be a stimulating approach in comparative sociology of science and in history of science.

It was of course clear to Merton that the history of science did not begin with the Reformation. Even so, it is possible that he attached too much importance to religious factors in his attempt to explained the institutionalization of science in England and, more generally, in Europe. To some extent he neglected the role played by the *universities* in the development of modern science. We should not forget that Copernicus, Kepler, Galileo, Brahe and Newton were products of the international university culture. From the very start European universities represented scientific values and a chance to criticize old as well as new ideas. This was the soil in which the new natural sciences could take root.

Although the Weber-Merton thesis has been thoroughly criticized, it has endured surprisingly well. The hard core of the research program remains more or less intact, while less important hypotheses and assumptions have been modified or rejected.

7. Literature

Abraham, G. 1983: "Misunderstanding the Merton Thesis: A Boundary Dispute between History and Sociology", *Isis* vol. 74, pp. 368-387.

Becker, G. 1984: "Pietism and Science: A Critique of Robert K. Merton's Hypothesis", *American Journal of Sociology* vol. 89, pp. 1065-1090.

Becker, G. 1991: "Pietism's Confrontation with Enlightenment Rationalism: An Examination of the Relation between Ascetic Protestantism and Science", *Journal of the Scientific Study of Religion* vol. 30, pp. 139-158.

Ben-David, J. 1991: *Scientific Growth. Essays on the Social Organization and Ethos of Science*, University of California Press, Berkeley/Los Angeles/Oxford.

Brooke, J.H. 1991: *Science and Religion. Some Historical Perspectives*, Cambridge University Press, Cambridge.

Cohen, I.B. (ed.) 1990: *Puritanism and the Rise of Modern Science. The Merton Thesis*, Rutgers University Press, New Brunswick and London.

Coser, L. (ed.) 1975: *The Idea of Social Structure,* Harcourt, New York.

De Klerk, W.A. 1976: *The Puritans in Africa: A Story of Afrikanerdom*, Penguin, Harmondsworth.

Engelhardt, H.T. and A. L. Caplan 1987: *Scientific Controversies*, Cambridge University Press, Cambridge.

Garstein, O. 1953: Cort Aslaksøn. Studier over dansk-norsk universitets- og lærdomshistorie omkring 1600, (Cort Aslakssøn. Studies in Danish-Norwegian Learning about 1600), (in Norwegian), Lutherstiftelsens forlag, Oslo.

Gilje, N. 1997: "Hans Nielsen Hauge and the Spirit of Capitalism", in *Philosophy Beyond Borders* (eds. Ragnar Fjelland et al.), SVT Press, Bergen.

Hill, C. 1965: *Intellectual Origins of the English Revolution*, Oxford University Press, Oxford.

Hooykaas, R. 1972: *Religion and the Rise of Modern Science*, Scottish Academic Press, Edinburgh.

Huff, T.E. 1993: *The Rise of Early Modern Science. Islam, China and the West*, Cambridge University Press, Cambridge.

Hunter, M. 1981: *Science and Society in Restoration England*, Cambridge University Press, Cambridge.

Jacob, J.R. and M. J. Jacob 1980: "The Anglican Origins of Modern Science: The Metaphysical Foundations of the Whig Constitution", *Isis* vol. 71, pp. 251-257.

Jones, R.F. 1961: *Ancients and Moderns: A Study of the Rise of the Scientific Movement in Seventeenth-Century England*, Washington University Press, St. Louis.

McGuire, J.E. and P.M. Rattansi 1966: "Newton and the 'Pipes of Pan'", *Notes and Records of the Royal Society* vol. 21, pp. 109-134.

Merton, R.K. 1936: "Puritanism. Pietism and Science", *Sociological Review* vol. 28, pp. 1-30.

Merton, R.K. 1938: "Science and Social Order", *Philosophy of Science* vol. 5, pp. 321-337.

Merton, R.K. 1945: "Sociology of Knowledge", in G. Gurvitch and W. Moore (eds.): *Twentieth Century Sociology*, Philosophical Library, New York, pp. 366-405.

Merton, R.K. 1948: "The Self-Fulfilling Prophecy", *Antioch Review* (Summer), pp. 193-210.

Merton, R.K. 1961: "Singletons and Multiples in Scientific Discovery: A Chapter in the Sociology of Science", *Proceeding of the American Philosophical Society*, vol. 105, pp. 470-486.

Merton, R.K. 1968: *Social Theory and Social Structure,* Free Press, Glencoe, Illinois.

Merton, R.K. 1970: *Science, Technology and Society in Seventeenth Century England*, Fertig, New York.

Merton, R.K. 1973: *The Sociology of Science: Theoretical and Empirical Investigations*, University of Chicago Press, Chicago.

Merton, R.K. 1976: *Sociological Ambivalence and Other Essays*, Free Press, New York.

Merton R.K. 1984: "The Fallacy of Latest Word: The Case of 'Pietism and Science'", *American Journal of Sociology*, vol. 89, pp. 1091-1121.

Merton, R.K. 1990: "*STS:* Foreshadowings of an Evolving Research Program in the Sociology of Science", in I. Bernhard Cohen (ed.): *Puritanism and the Rise of Modern Science. The Merton Thesis*, Rutgers University Press, New Brunswick and London, pp. 334-373.

Mulligan, L. 1973: "Civil War Politics, Religion and the Royal Society", *Past and Present*, vol. 59, pp. 92-116.

Pagel, W. 1985: *Religion and Neoplatonism in Renaissance Medicine*, Routledge, London.

Rattansi, P. 1990: "Puritanism and Science: The 'Merton Thesis' after Fifty Years", in Jon Clark et al. (eds.): *Robert K. Merton. Consensus and Controversy,* Falmer Press, London/New York/Philadelphia, pp. 351-371.

Shapiro, B. 1968: "Latitudinarianism and Science in Seventeenth-Century England", *Past and Present*, vol. 40, pp. 16-41.

Shapiro, B. 1970: *John Wilkins 1614-1672: An Intellectual Biography*, University of California Press, Berkeley.

Stimson, D. 1990: "Puritanism and the New Philosophy in 17th Century England" (1935), in I. Bernard Cohen (ed.), *Puritanism and the Rise of Modern Science*, pp. 151-159.

Weber, M. 1923: *Wirtschaftsgeschichte von Max Weber*, (ed. S. Hellmann and Palyi), Duncker & Humbolt, Munich.

Weber, M. 1987: *Die protestantische Ethik II. Kritiken und Antikritiken* (ed. By Johannes 'Winckelmann), Gütersloher Verlagshaus, Gütersloh.

Weber M. 1989: *Max Weber's 'Science as a Vocation'* (ed. by Peter Lassman and Irving Velody), Unwin Hyman, London.

Weber, M.1992: *The Protestant Ethic and the Spirit of Capitalism* (translated by Talcott Parsons), Routledge, London and New York.

Webster, C. (ed.) 1974: *The Intellectual Revolution of the Seventeenth Century*, Routledge and Kegan Paul, London.

Webster, C. 1976: *The Great Instauration: Science, Medicine and Reform 1626-1670*, Holmes & Meier, New York.

Webster, C. 1982: *From Paracelsus to Newton: Magic and the Making of Modern Science*, Cambridge University Press, Cambridge.
Webster, C. 1986: "Puritanism, Separatism, and Science", in D. Lindberg and R. Numbers (eds.): *God and Nature. Historical Essays on the Encounter between Christianity and Science*, University of California Press, Berkeley, pp. 192-217.
Zuckerman, H. 1989: "The Other Merton Thesis", *Science in Context*, vol. 3, pp. 239-267.

2
Kuhn's Theory of Scientific Revolutions

HARALD GRIMEN

1. Original quotation

[...] the successive transition from one paradigm to another via revolution is the usual developmental pattern of mature science. (Kuhn 1970, p. 12)

2. Brief explanation

Kuhn's object of investigation is mature sciences, in which researchers share common presupposition or *paradigms*. Immature scientific disciplines are *pre-paradigmatic*, divided into rival schools based on different world-views. At different historical times some disciplines have overcome this phase, and the researchers have arrived at an agreement concerning the basic premises of their disciplines. Their disciplines have matured. Consensus about fundamental assumptions is a sign of maturity. Thereafter, scientific development follows a characteristic pattern: it alternates between periods of revolution and periods of stability.

For Kuhn, parallels between political and scientific development justify the use of the term "revolutions" to describe certain phases of scientific development. Scientific revolutions are non-cumulative episodes "in which an older paradigm is replaced in whole or in part by an incompatible new one" (Kuhn 1970, p. 92). Political and scientific revolutions exhibit genetic as well as structural similarities.

Genetic similarities concern the way in which revolutions are brought about: political revolutions are triggered by a feeling in part of the society that established institutions no longer solve the problems they were created to solve. Scientific revolutions start when some researchers feel that an established theory is no longer valid for research into a specific aspect of nature, where this theory had previously indicated a direction. In both cases a sense of crisis is a prerequisite for revolution.

Structural similarities concern the developmental patterns of these revolutions. Political revolutions aim at changing institutions in ways which these same institutions do not permit: old institutions must thus be replaced by new ones. In the interim period between old and new institutions a society will lack political control. An increasing number of people feel alienated vis-a-vis the established institutions. The result is a crisis, and there is broad support for a restructuring of society. Society is divided into competing sides: those who defend the old regime confront those who want to establish a new one. The result is polarization and dissolution of normal politics. The participants disagree about the political framework within which political change should take place and be assessed, and they do not recognize a common supra-institutional framework. They must therefore resort to propaganda and often to force. Revolutions are episodes outside normal institutions and normal politics, periods when politics is not conducted with normal means.

Paradigm shifts are characterized by similar features. The option between different paradigms is, on the social level, an option between incompatible or incomparable social conventions and, on the theoretical level, between incompatible or incomparable expectations. The choice is not determined by normal scientific criteria. Such criteria are dependent on controversial paradigms, and are not convincing for those who do not share the paradigm. When paradigms are used in debates about paradigm shifts, they acquire a circular role, each group referring to its paradigm to defend its own paradigm. Paradigm shifts are not brought about by observations and logical arguments alone. The premises which the two parties in a paradigm controversy share are not sufficiently extensive and robust to make such arguments convincing. Nor are there, in paradigm shifts, standards recognized by all sections of the relevant group (Kuhn, 1970, p. 94). Revolutions are extra-institutional events, periods in which science is carried out by unusual means. To explain revolutions we have to investigate the use of propaganda techniques, as well as observations and logical arguments.

3. Background

Thomas S. Kuhn (1922-94) was professor of the philosophy and history of science at MIT, after having lectured at Harvard, Princeton and Berkeley. He had studied theoretical physics, but became interested in the history of science at an early stage in his career. He published four books: *The Copernican Revolution: Planetary Astronomy and the Development of Western Thought* (1957), *The Structure of Scientific Revolutions* (1962, new edition 1970), *The Essential Tension* (1977), and *Black-Body Theory and the Quantum Discontinuity, 1894-1912* (1978). *The Structure of Scientific Revolutions* is his best-known and most-discussed book, today ranking as a standard reference work.

Kuhn belongs to the so-called post-empiricist trend in the theory and history of science. This trend originated in the 1950s, partly as a reaction to logical empiricism. Later, the post-empiricists debated with representatives of another trend, critical rationalism (Popper and his followers). Central names in post-empiricism are N. R. Hansson, S. Toulmin, M. Hesse and P.K. Feyerabend, perhaps also I. Lakatos and L. Laudan. Toulmin's book *The Philosophy of Science* (1953) is often regarded as the starting point for the tradition. These thinkers differ in many respects and often enter into discussion with one another. But they share certain ideas which identify them as belonging to the same tradition:

1 They are, more or less, *relativists*, either doubting or totally rejecting the idea of trans-historical, universal criteria for rational belief and action. They also reject the idea of clear-cut and a-historical dividing lines between scientific activity and knowledge on the one hand and non-scientific activity and other kinds of belief on the other, believing instead in epistemic continuity between scientific knowledge and other opinions. On this point Lakatos and Laudan differ from the others, and cannot categorically be characterized as post-empiricists.

2 They are *methodological contextualists* and adherents of a historical orientation in the study of the sciences. What science is, has to be understood in the light of the historical contexts within which research is carried out and its results are evaluated. The demarcation line between science and non-science is context-bound and historical.

3   They profess an *action orientation* and reject the view that we can obtain realistic pictures of what research is via accomplished research results. Instead, they stress the importance of historical studies of scientific practices, criticizing earlier philosophy and history of science for having disregarded this point.

4   Their view regarding the relation between *theory* and *observation* implies the rejection of the assumption that theory-language and observation-language are radically different. It is impossible to describe observations without being influenced by theoretical assumptions. Observation sentences are "theory laden" (Hansson, 1969, p. 306), a view which also Popper shared. Many of them tend towards a constructivistic conclusion: the world and its structures are shaped by our theories about them. If our theories change, so too will the world's structure, at least the world as we perceive it.

5   They are *semantic holists*, basing themselves on a particular philosophy of language about the sense and reference of the terms used in constructing theories. The sense of each and every term is determined by the total theoretical context of which the term is a part, and the sense determines the reference of the term. If we change parts of a theory, the sense – and, consequently, the reference – of each term will change (meaning-variance). Theory changes imply global shifts: we shift meanings, references and world-views.

6   In their studies they take as their starting point units more *comprehensive* than single theories: constellations of theory, methodologies, values, metaphysical presuppositions, ideas about the legitimacy of problems and solutions and the like. Paradigms, research programs and background theories are examples of units more comprehensive than single theories.

Kuhn fitted into this picture. He defined himself as a historian of science. In an autobiographical comment he stated that he was drawn from physics to the philosophy and history of science when he discovered that science, as encountered in historical source material, appeared to be an activity very unlike "the one implicit in science pedagogy and explicit in standard philosophical accounts of scientific method" (Kuhn, 1977, p. 4).

4. Formalization – precise definition

Kuhn distinguished between different phases in the development of a discipline. Disciplines are constituted by professional specialists within delimited special fields. Changes take place simultaneously on a social and a theoretical level: new paradigms emerge out of theoretical and social chaos. They result in a new group structure which will cement theoretical orientations, until expectation crises in the relation between paradigm and experience create new theoretical chaos. The paradigms, as well as the groups on which they are based, then dissolve. The motivational force will be research understood as expectation-guided activity, for which the paradigm is the horizon of expectations. Changes occur when expectations are systematically and irreparably frustrated.

Kuhn's theory is presented in schematic outline in the table on the next page (modified in accordance with Brante 1980).

In the *pre-paradigmatic* phase an academic discipline is divided into competing schools. The specialists lack common views and methods. They lack a common paradigm or horizon of expectations. There is no agreement as to what sort of phenomena is studied. Before Newton, in optics there was disagreement about what light really *is*: light was perceived as particles emanating from physical objects, as modifications of the medium between the physical objects and the eye, and as an interaction between the medium and an emanation from the eye. There were no unanimously recognized observations which all researchers felt bound to explain, nor standard methods obligatory for all. In the absence of a paradigm all facts are equally relevant, and data gathering is much more casual than in later research. The pre-paradigmatic phase has no common metaphysics (understanding as to what kinds of phenomena are studied), no common methods, nor generally recognized observations which everybody tries to explain, and no common criteria for data relevance. Data gathering is unsystematic and casual, and attempts are continuously made to build up the discipline from the very fundamentals. Kuhn termed such disciplines *immature*.

At different times in history this changed in some scientific disciplines. Their professionals arrived at common views, often due to one school gaining hegemony in the field. The disciplines entered a *paradigmatic* phase: astronomy with Ptolemaeus' *Almagest*, geometry with Euclid's *Elements*, physics with Aristotle's *Physics*, optics with Newton's *Optics*, the theory of electricity with Franklin's *Electricity*, chemistry with Lavoisier's *Chemie*, geology with Lyell's *Geology*. These works defined legitimate problems and methods for researchers. They were sufficiently *unprecedented* to distract an enduring group of researchers from competing modes of research, and *open-ended* enough to furnish problems to investigate. Kuhn termed research results exhibiting these two characteristics "paradigms". Using this term he is able to state that "some accepted examples of actual scientific practice B examples which include law, theory, application, and instrumentation together B provide models from which spring particular coherent research traditions" (Kuhn, 1970, p.10).

Phases	Theoretical level	Sociological level
Pre-paradigmatic period	No common paradigm. Disagreement as to which kind of phenomena is studied by the discipline. No common, recognized observations or standard methods. Unsystematic data gathering.	Many competing schools or institutions existing side by side. Poor communication between members of the discipline. Books are the most important communication media.
Paradigm establishment	Exemplary research achievement occurs. Agreement about legitimate problems methods, and solutions. Agreement about fundamental metaphysical questions	Beginning professionalization. Specialized journals, associations and scientific societies established. Specialist conferences arranged. Journal articles become the most important communication media
Normal Science	Research as paradigm articulation, "mopping-up" operations and "puzzle-solving". The aim of research is not theoretical innovation or discovery of new types of phenomena.	Textbooks, university disciplines. The discipline gains control over its own socialization of new members.
Anomalies	Expectation crisis: New phenomena emerge that do not fit into the paradigm.	Incipient critique and discussions of fundamentals. First signs of communication deficiency between researchers.
Crisis	The paradigm is watered down and developed in several versions. Extraordinary research. Everything is subject to trial. Philosophical discussions and attempted development of new theories.	Polarization in the research community, hard critical discussions, incipient loyalty shift from the old to the new.
Revolution	Alternative paradigm emerging and old rejected.	Conversions, large groups of researchers shift loyalty, professional civil war, old journals closed and new ones emerging
New Paradigm	General recognition of new exemplary research achievement, new agreement on "the fundamentals". New problem perception, new solutions, new methods.	New publications, new-profiled old journals, new socialization, new group structure, new persons gaining authority, adherents of the surpassed paradigm marginalized and disappear.

In the paradigmatic phase communication between researchers is facilitated, because they can take the fundamentals for granted. The discipline becomes professionalized, journals are founded, and specialized education is provided. In this phase scientific development alternates between periods of *normal science* and *revolutions*.

In periods of normal science a paradigm is taken for granted. Agreement exists about the fundamentals of the scientific discipline. A study of the paradigm prepares beginners for membership in the community. Because everybody learns the basic ideas and techniques from the same concrete models, the ensuing practice of individual scholars will rarely lead to controversies on fundamentals. Researchers are committed to the same rules and standards: "the commitment and the apparent consensus it produces are prerequisites for normal science, i.e., for the genesis and continuation of a particular research tradition" (Kuhn, 1970, p. 11).

A paradigm obtains status because it solves, better than do its competitors, problems viewed by a group of researchers as acute, even though it does not solve every problem. From the start it gives but "a promise of success discoverable in selected and still incomplete examples" (Kuhn, 1970, pp. 23-24). Normal science is the attempt to honor the promise, enlarging the knowledge of the facts emphasized by the paradigm, by increasing the accordance between facts and predictions and by articulating the theoretical ideas implied by the paradigm.

Kuhn characterizes normal science alternatively as "mop-up work", paradigm articulation and puzzle-solving .

"Mopping-up" operations fill the career of most researchers. These are attempts to force nature into the relatively rigid categories of the paradigm. The activity is not aimed at discovering new types of phenomena. What does not fit in, is often neglected. The aim of the researchers is not to create new theories, and they are often intolerant vis-a-vis new theories set up by others. Normal science is aimed at the specification of the phenomena already visible in the light of the paradigm. This is an activity with a drastically narrowed field of vision. This is however not a defect, but essential for scientific development. By highlighting a group of relatively narrow problems the paradigm enables researchers to study in depth a fragment of nature in a way which otherwise would have been quite unimaginable.

Articulation means making measurements and predictions more precise and exact (for instance by developing new instruments), finding new fields where predictions might be proven true, clarifying notions, doing away with ambiguous formulations as well as formulating in a clearer way problems which at first could just be dimly perceived:

"These three classes of problems – determination of significant fact, matching facts with theory, and articulation of theory – exhaust, I think, the literature of normal science, both theoretical and empirical" (Kuhn, 1970, p. 34). Such work takes most of the researchers' time, and without a paradigm defining problems and promising enduring solutions their all-out efforts would not be imaginable.

Kuhn also compares normal science to *puzzle-solving*. A puzzle has solutions which we know we can find by trying to make the pieces fit into each other, until the result is a true copy of the picture already at hand. If the solution is not found, the fault lies in the person who fails to find it, not in the puzzle. The puzzle-solver and not the puzzle is to be blamed. Likewise, the paradigm offers researchers the criteria for picking out solvable problems. The community accepts such problems as scientific and exhorts its members to exert themselves to solve them. A reason why normal science progresses is the concentration of the members of a research community on problems whose solutions nothing but their own incapacity can prevent them from finding: "Failure to achieve a solution discredits only the scientist and not the theory" (Kuhn, 1970, p. 80). Researchers are motivated by the belief that they can solve puzzle problems hitherto not solved by anybody.

Normal science is "a highly determined activity, but it need not be entirely determined by rules. That is why (...) I introduced shared paradigms rather than shared rules, assumptions and points of view as the source of coherence for normal research traditions. Rules (...) derive from paradigms, but paradigms can guide research in the absence of rules" (Kuhn, 1970, p. 42). Normal science is practiced with a relatively dogmatic attitude. It is the period of the anonymous toilers. Their stern dogmatism is functional, allowing detailed investigations as well as impeding the abandonment of fertile ideas before their potential has been exhausted.

Nevertheless, *anomalies* will often occur, that is, phenomena which are not possible to incorporate in the paradigm: "Discovery commences with the awareness of anomaly, i.e. with the recognition that nature has somehow violated the paradigm-induced expectations that govern normal science" (Kuhn, 1970, pp. 52-53). Paradigms are horizons of *expectations*. Often something occurs which frustrates expectations. New theories normally emerge after a period of professional uncertainty, created by anomalies that steadfastly resist all attempts to solve them. Crises come about when the paradigm proves incapable of solving problems highlighted by this same paradigm. The emergence of many different versions of the same theory is frequently a sign of crisis, and "by proliferating versions of the paradigm, crisis loosens the rules of puzzle-solving in ways that ultimately permit a new paradigm to emerge" (Kuhn, 1970, p. 80).

Not all contradictory evidence to a theory will of necessity cause a crisis. There is no theory free from contradicting evidence. But now and then anomalies are registered, which clearly "call into question explicit and fundamental generalizations of the paradigm" (Kuhn, 1970, p. 82). If an anomaly is perceived as more than an ordinary puzzle-problem, the scientific discipline can be thrust into a *crisis*, and the anomaly is recognized as a serious problem. The best researchers of the discipline use increasingly more time trying to solve this anomaly, and "if it still continues to resist, as it usually does not, many of them may come to view its resolution as *the* subject-matter of their discipline. For them the field will no longer look quite the same as it had earlier" (Kuhn, 1970, pp. 82-83, italics by Kuhn).

The speciality's answer to the crisis is *extraordinary research*. In order to solve the problem different versions of the paradigm are tested out, the result being that it is watered down and in the end nobody any longer knows on which premises it is based. The rules governing normal scientific research become looser, and research resembles that of the pre-paradigmatic phase. New attempts are continually made to create new theories. Researchers often discuss the philosophical fundamentals of the discipline: "The proliferation of competing articulations, the willingness to try anything, the expression of explicit discontent, the recourse to philosophy and to debate over fundamentals, all these are symptoms of a transition from normal to extraordinary research" (Kuhn, 1970, p. 91). There is a gradual breakdown of communication and general consensus.

Research balances between rigid dogmatism and disintegrating scepticism. In Kuhn's view both dogmatism and scepticism are functional, but at different times. Normal science is the period of dogmatism, securing for the paradigm the possibility to show its potential. In this phase sceptics are quickly defined out. Extraordinary research is the period of sceptics, guaranteeing the admittance of new ideas. Dogmatists then very quickly lose their audience.

There are three ways of solving a crisis: 1. Anomalies may be incorporated in the old paradigm. 2. They may be considered impossible to solve and ignored. 3. Suggestions for a new paradigm may gradually gain acceptance in the scientific discipline concerned. Even so, the old paradigm is not rejected until a promising alternative is found.

Paradigm shifts are not cumulative, but mean reconstruction of scientific disciplines based on new ideas. Such a rebuilding can change the most basic theoretical generalizations, and many of the methods. In the period between an old and a new paradigm there is a great B but never complete B overlap between the problems possible to solve on the basis of the old paradigm, and those requiring a new line of thought. But there will also be decisive differences in the ways problems are perceived and solved. Frequently the persons creating the ideas embodied in the new paradigm are young or new researchers in the field, because they are less bound by the old ideas. Gradually, a struggle between the adherents of the old paradigm and the adherents of the new develops. The new paradigm is accepted only after thorough resistance, on a background of old expectations. The struggling parties often misunderstand each other, even though they may be using the same words: "Communication across the revolutionary divide is, inevitably, partial" (Kuhn, 1970, p. 149). The debate is often based on propaganda, not on factual or logical arguments.

Once the transition is accomplished, the researchers have changed their view of the research field, the methods and the aims of their discipline. What has been brought about is a revolution comparable to a visual gestalt shift. Visual gestalt shifts represent "a useful elementary prototype for what occurs in full-scale paradigm shift" (Kuhn, 1970, p. 85).

Paradigm shifts imply a shift of world-views, comparable to a religious conversion: "I would argue [...] that in these matters neither proof nor error is at issue. The transfer of allegiance from paradigm to paradigm is a conversion experience that cannot be forced" (Kuhn, 1970, p. 151). Old words acquire new meanings and refer to new phenomena. Researchers see new things, develop new instruments and search in new places, and they discover something new when they look with new instruments at phenomena which they have already seen before: "It is as if the professional community had been suddenly transported to another planet where familiar objects are seen in a different light and are joined by unfamiliar ones as well" (Kuhn, 1970, p. 111). The new paradigm and the old are not comparable, and give rise to different kinds of practice. The transition is not fully explainable on the basis of observations, experimental results and logical arguments. It is to some extent irrational and non-cumulative.

The scientific discipline gradually slips into a period of new normal science. New puzzles are to be solved, new "mopping-up" operations to be accomplished. And this period will last until new anomalies once again drive the discipline into a crisis. If the rebuilding of the discipline is unsuccessful, it will vanish and disappear.

5. Generality and testability. Critique

Kuhn's theory has been the object of much criticism, and not all of it can be dealt with here. I shall first mention four ways in which the theory cannot be tested. Then, I shall show how, in principle, it can be tested, and how, in practice, it may be difficult to test.

First, the theory is neither a recipe for provoking scientific revolutions, nor for the construction of new paradigms. Kuhn's aim was not the forging of such a theory. Therefore, the theory cannot be tested through research practice, as it has not been formulated in order to originate any particular type of practice.

Secondly, the theory cannot be used to predict scientific development, i.e. to predict when established paradigms will collapse, what will be the contents of new paradigms, or when they will emerge. New paradigms are constellations of ideas comparable to mutations. Most mutations are pernicious and vanish. Sometimes mutations survive, because they offer the individuals carrying them advantages in certain environments. Nothing can be said about what mutations will emerge in the future, nor about which ones will survive, or for how long. We have no theories enabling us to predict scientific innovations or the viability of a paradigm. There is good reason to believe that we are incapable of making such theories.

Thirdly, the theory does not admit that external observers – seeing a paradigm confronted by a phenomenon it cannot explain – can make a certain statement as to whether or when the paradigm will collapse. The importance of the anomalies is a question of the importance attributed to them by the researchers themselves. The status of the anomalies is subject to change following their interpretation by the researchers, and attempts to predict developments based on the relationship of paradigm and anomalies alone are subject to the subjectivity principle, i.e. they have to be based on the categories, interpretations and views of the researchers involved. Nor does the theory say anything about how many anomalies a paradigm can endure without ending in crisis. Some paradigms can endure many, others few. Crisis does not come about on the sole basis of the number of anomalies registered. They occur when researchers regard one or more anomalies as sufficiently intricate and threatening to what they believe in.

Fourthly, the theory says nothing about how quickly or how often revolutions will occur. It is possible that two great discoveries could be close to each other in time, resulting in two quick revolutions, without this contravening Kuhn's theory. The theory offers only a small probability that this will occur, but it does not exclude it.

Nevertheless, the theory can be tested as a theory about past development in the history of the sciences. In mature sciences we find, with regular intervals, historical episodes (revolutions) with almost total replacements of central theoretical and methodical presuppositions. It would be a hard blow to the theory if we were unable to point out such episodes. The theory is incompatible with continuous scientific development, and also with continuous revolution without traceable non-revolutionary intervals. We can test out the theory following the development of scientific disciplines which Kuhn termed mature, and see if we can find revolutions and non-revolutionary periods following each other in the way the theory predicts.

In mature scientific disciplines we also find mono-paradigmatic periods, i.e. periods governed by one single paradigm. In such periods research has a particular character (normal science). The theory is incompatible with a discipline being permanently split into rival schools, each with its own basic presuppositions. We can test out the theory by looking at a scientific discipline in periods of normal science, to ascertain whether or not the activity conforms to the pattern described by Kuhn.

The theory may, perhaps, also be tested as a theory about what type of research is most efficient. In Kuhn's view the most efficient kind of research is normal science, because this type of research, being a kind of dogmatically guided activity with a limited, but detailed field of vision, necessarily leads to crises of expectations and, consequently, to theoretical change. Letting a hundred theoretical flowers flourish at the same time is less efficient, because it would impede a steadfast, collective and detailed scrutiny of nature. This kind of theory testing requires, however, long-term perspectives and clear efficiency criteria, which most probably we do not have.

There are nowadays more researchers than ever before engaged in normal science. Specialization is increasing, a fact to be inferred from the great quantity of ever more specialized journals and disciplines. Due to more researchers and increasing specialization there is an increasing number of individuals in a position to concentrate intensely on narrowly delimited problems. This may result in the periods between the revolutions becoming shorter, because the theoretical potential of a paradigm is more quickly exhausted, the paradigms thus getting a shorter life before the outbreak of a crisis.

In practice the theory is, however, difficult to test out, being built, as it is, on vague concepts.

The paradigm concept is vague. Masterman found that in *The Struc-*

ture of Scientific Revolutions, Kuhn had used the concept in 21 different ways (Masterman, 1970, p. 61). Kuhn replied in the 1970 edition of the book. He there distinguished between paradigms in a wider and a more narrow sense. In his words paradigms in the wider sense are disciplinary matrices, consisting of four elements that form a unity and function together:

1 *Symbolic generalizations*, defined as formal elements or such as are easy to formalize, e.g. Newton's second law: $f = m \cdot a$. Such expressions are points of reference for logical and mathematical techniques, functioning partly as laws of nature and partly as definitions.

2 *Metaphysical assumptions* or beliefs in special models, e.g. that gas molecules behave like small elastic billiard balls in random movement. Such assumptions furnish researchers with preferred or legitimate metaphors and analogies, and help them define "what will be accepted as an explanation and as a puzzle-solution [...]" (Kuhn, 1970, p. 184).

3 *Values*, e.g. that predictions must be precise and preferably quantitative, that theories should be simple, consistent, credible and in harmony with other theories. Such values are shared by groups larger than the specialist groups, but may be interpreted differently by different groups.

4 *Exemplary research achievements* are concrete problem solutions presented to students in lectures, laboratories, examinations or in the final chapters of textbooks. They are examples which show how to do the job: "Scientists solve puzzles modeling them on previous puzzle-solutions [...]" (Kuhn, 1970, p. 189). Kuhn reserves his paradigm concept for such research achievements, which are paradigms in the narrow sense.

It is an open question whether Kuhn's answer makes it easier to test out the theory. In practice it is still difficult to decide when we are facing one or more paradigms. And the theory also faces other difficulties.

Kuhn contended that paradigms can be both *incomparable and incompatible*. If two paradigms are incomparable, they cannot be incompatible, and vice versa. To make them incompatible at least one statement in the one must contradict a statement implied by the other, i.e.

incompatibility is defined by reference to the law of non-contradiction. In that case they must refer to one and the same phenomenon. Two incomparable paradigms cannot, however, refer to one and the same phenomenon. Kuhn's semantic holism entails that the terms used in two paradigms cannot refer to the same phenomena, and that the statements contained in two paradigms cannot contradict each other. But then it is difficult to understand why a partial and reciprocal agreement can be found between the adherents of new and old paradigms, and how historians like Kuhn can understand earlier paradigms (Shapere 1980).

It is difficult to identify the social groups that uphold paradigms. Kuhn localized the paradigms on different social levels, and gives no precise criteria for delimiting the groups. He sometimes defined a research community as a group that shares a paradigm, and sometimes tried to establish independent criteria for the identification of such communities. He sometimes stated that the entire science of physics has one common paradigm, and sometimes that a group upholding a paradigm is acting within the limits of a narrowly delimited speciality, with no more than approximately a hundred members worldwide. This makes the concept of revolution lack precision: does it make sense to talk of revolutions involving no more than some hundred geographically scattered actors?

6. Empirical assessment – conclusion

The most important conclusions to be drawn from attempts to test Kuhn's theory seem to be the following:

It is highly improbable that there ever were episodes as dramatic as Kuhn's revolutions. The changes of theories and concepts are probably less total than he claims. What is left are sequences of greater or smaller concept modifications, distinguished only by differences of degree. This may destroy the particular element in Kuhn's theory (Toulmin 1970, p. 45). Kuhn is also barely aware of all that survives the revolutions, his paradigms being "packages" which are accepted or rejected in their entirety. But in the research process the participants may agree on some levels and disagree on others, a fact not easily compatible with Kuhn's model of thought (Alexander 1982, p. 26).

When Kuhn maintained that in some scientific disciplines the transition from the pre-paradigmatic to the paradigmatic phase took place in Antiquity or in the Renaissance he failed to notice that in those periods there existed no social groups equivalent to our research communities capable of bearing paradigms and dedicating themselves to a strictly disciplined normal science. A sociological condition for applying his theory to those periods is missing, and Kuhn probably made himself guilty of presenting us with an anachronism: he illegitimately transferred to the past the social structure of science in our times.

Kuhn exaggerated consensus in non-revolutionary periods. Most disciplines are always more fragmented into different theory traditions than what seems inferrable from Kuhn's analysis of normal science.

His theory probably cannot satisfactorily explain how a new consensus is brought about after a revolution. Without a theory of consensus formation a decisive link between two central elements in Kuhn's picture is missing: the theory of dissent (incomparable paradigms) and the theory of consensus (normal science). He is often criticized for his inability to explain the transition from normal science to crisis (from consensus to dissent), because he failed to show why apparently innocent puzzle problems suddenly become menacing anomalies. But the central problem is his inability to explain the transition from crisis to normal science. As soon as disagreement arises, it is nearly impossible to see how Kuhn can fetch the rabbit back to the hutch (Laudan 184, p. 17).

Several attempts have also been made to apply the theory to the social sciences and the arts (e.g. Friedrichs 1970, Ritzer 1975), but with little success. Eckberg and Hill present a survey of 14 attempts to find sociological paradigms, resulting in 12 different views as to what are the fundamental paradigms. Their conclusion is that in sociology we often find research not founded on models taken from other research, and sometimes short-lived traditions or research based on a single theoretician. But we seldom observe comprehensive puzzle-solving. The relevant literature offers few instances of the solving of an important puzzle-problems, according to Eckberg & Hill (Eckberg and Hill 1980, p. 131). In short, normal science is missing. This makes it difficult to use Kuhn's theory of scientific development, since the theory presents development as continuous transitions between periods of normal science and revolutions. The social sciences and the arts are, probably, multi-paradigmatic. There are always several theory traditions existing side by side. This is, in Kuhn's view, atypical for mature scientific disciplines. The logical conclusion should then be either that the social sciences are immature sciences, or that they belong to a kind of science which cannot be grasped by Kuhn's way of thinking.

In a more recent work (Kuhn 1991, p. 24), Kuhn states that the transition from the pre-paradigmatic to the paradigmatic phase might already be taking place in psychology and economics, but he gives no evidence to support his statement. However, in his opinion such a transition cannot be expected in disciplines which have social and political systems as their objects of study. Such systems lack the stability which characterize the phenomena of nature. If the object of study is in a state of constant change, it is rather improbable that researchers will arrive at an agreement of the kind typical of normal science.

7. Literature

Alexander, J.C. 1981: *Theoretical Logic in Sociology* vol. 1, University of California Press, Berkeley.

Barnes, B. 1982: *T.S. Kuhn and Social Science*, Macmillan, London.

Brante, T. 1980: *Vetenskapens struktur och förandring*, (Structure and change in Science) Doxa, Lund.

Friedrichs, R.W. 1970: *A Sociology of Sociology*, The Free Press, New York.

Gutting, G. 1980: *Paradigms & Revolutions*, University of Notre Dame Press, London.

Hacking, I. (ed.) 1981: *Scientific Revolutions*, Oxford University Press, Oxford.

Hansson, N.R. 1969: *Perception and Discovery*, Freeman, Cooper, & Co., San Francisco.

Johannessen, K.S. 1985: *Tradisjoner og skoler i moderne vitenskapsfilosofi*, (Traditions and schools in modern theory of science) Sigma, Bergen.

Kuhn, Th. 1957: *The Copernican Revolution: Planetary Astronomy and the Development of Western Thought*, Harvard University Press, Cambridge, Mass.

Kuhn, Th. 1970: *The Structure of Scientific Revolutions*, The University of Chicago Press, Chicago.

Kuhn, Th. 1977: *The Essential Tension*, The University of Chicago Press, Chicago.

Kuhn, Th. 1978: *Black-Body Theory and Quantum Discontinuity*, 1894-1912, Oxford University Press, Oxford.

Kuhn, Th. 1991: "The Natural and Human Sciences", in D.R. Hiley, J.F. Bohman and R. Shusterman (eds.): *The Interpretive Turn*, Cornell University press, Ithaca and London.

Lakatos, I. and A. Musgrave (eds.) 1970: *Criticism & The Growth of Knowledge*, Cambridge University Press, Cambridge.

Laudan, L. 1984: *Science and Values*, University of California Press, Berkeley.

Masterman, M. 1970: "The Nature of a Paradigm", in Lakatos, I. and A. Musgrave (eds.): *Criticism and the Growth of Knowledge*, Cambridge University Press, Cambridge.

Radnitzky, G. 1968: *Contemporary Schools of Metascience*, Scandinavian University Press, Göteborg.

Ritzer, G. 1975: *Sociology: A Multiple Paradigm Science*, Allan & Bacon, Boston.

Ritzer, G. 1981: *Toward an Integrated Sociological Paradigm*, Allan & Bacon, Boston.

Shapere, D. 1981: "Meaning and Scientific Change", in Ian Hacking (ed.): *Scientific Revolutions*, Oxford University Press, Oxford, pp. 28-59.

Toulmin, S. 1953: *The Philosophy of Science*, Hutchinson, London.

Toulmin, S. 1970: "Does the Distinction between Normal and Revolutionary Science Hold Water?", in Lakatos, I. and A. Musgrave (eds.): *Criticism & the Growth of Knowledge*, Cambridge University Press, Cambridge.

3
The Hermeneutic Circle
On Limits for Interpretation and Conditions for Understanding

DAVID R. DOUBLET

1. Original quotation

Der Zirkel darf nicht zu einem vitiosum, und sei es auch zu einem geduldeten, herabgezogen werden. In ihm verbirgt sich eine positive Möglichkeit ursprünglichsten Erkenntnis, die freilich in echter Weise nur dann ergriffen ist, wenn die Auslegung verstanden hat, dass ihre erste, ständige und letzte Aufgabe bleibt, sich jeweils Vorhabe, Vorsicht und Vorgriff nicht durch Einfälle und Volksbegriffe vorgeben zu lassen, sondern in deren Ausarbeitung aus den Sachen selbst her das wissenschaftliche Thema zu sichern. (Heidegger, Martin 1927, p. 312).

Die Hermeneutik [...] ist daher nicht etwa eine Methodenlehre der Geisteswissenschaften, sondern der Versuch einer Verständigung über das, was die Geisteswissenschaften über ihr methodisches Selbsbewusstsein hinaus in Wahrheit sind und was sie mit dem Ganzen unserer Welterfahrung verbindet (Gadamer, Hans-Georg 1960).

2. Translation and brief explanation

We should not allow the circle to be degraded to one which is vicious, even if it is one which is merely tolerated. In this circle lies hidden a positive possibility of primordial cognition which, it is true, can only be caught when interpretation has realized that its rst, unchanging and ultimate task is not to let sudden impulses or popular notions dictate its aim, its cautions, and what it antici-pates, but to secure the scientic theme through the working-out in terms of the things themselves. (Heidegger 1927, p. 312)

Hermeneutics [...] is therefore not a methodology of the spiritual disciplines, but an attempt to reach an understanding concerning the real nature of spiritual/moral disciplines which transcends their methodologic self-awareness, and what links them to the totality of our world experience. (Gadamer, Hans-Georg 1960).

The word hermeneutics originates from the Greek *hermeneutikos*, meaning the art or doctrine of interpretation. What makes hermeneutics different from other doctrines of interpretation is that it involves more than rules or principles for the interpretation of text: In the for-mulation of Gadamer and Heidegger – new-hermeneutics – the text emerges as a *means of communication* between sender and recipient. According to Gadamer the *written* text needs a particular approach es-sentially different from forms of oral communication. (In modern times technology has given rise to types of text which are located at the point of intersection between written and oral expression, e.g. e-mail and "chat"). Whereas in oral forms of communication, the sender and recipient are present in the same room at the same time, and thus able to eliminate possible misunderstandings and errors of interpretation, *writing* on the other hand is a one-way communication with only one party present.

In a way one could say that hermeneutics is a method of interpreta-tion for the recipient of one-way communication. Thus the recipient does not confine his attention to the communication received, but reads the text in terms of *who* sent it, the *circumstances* surrounding it and, not least, when it was made. All these factors make up the historical and social background which is decisive in discovering the meaning of what is communicated. Hermeneutics is thus a doctrine of interpreta-tion which views the overall historical and social perspective as meth-odologically crucial.

This overall perspective is the *framework* into which the text inter-preter places the text. The framework comprises, among things, norms, value assessments, language rules (cf. Max Weber's concept "verste-hen", or Karl Popper's "situational logic"). One can assume either that a given text is in harmony with the general system of values that ap-plied when the text was shaped, or alternatively, that it breaks with that system. But in both cases the text is understood on the basis of the overall framework surrounding the author at the time the text was written. At the same time, interpretation brings these older norms into confrontation with the overall framework of values, the norms and language nuances belonging to the age in which the *text interpreter* lives. Thus the overall hermeneutic perspective comprises *the norms and values of the past as well as those of the present*. However, the hermeneutic method is not confined to the study of texts alone. In many ways hermeneutics is an excellent instrument for interpreting any cultural manifestation. Also scientific theses must therefore be understood in the light of the interpretation we give to them.

3. Background

We can speak of hermeneutics from a variety of standpoints: theological, philosophical, legal, reformatory and romantic. As a method of interpretation, hermeneutics plays a particularly strong part in the fields of theology and law. These disciplines are termed *dogmatic*, because researchers are not at liberty to take a stand of their own, but are bound not only by the theme itself, but also by an authorized *view* of the theme. The theologian is bound by the authorized understanding of the dogmas, and the judge by the legislator's understanding of the laws, so-called authentic law interpretation. Hermeneutics as an interpretational method is known primarily from older times, which were dominated by a hierarchic world view, i.e. before Descartes (1596-1650) and Copernicus (1473-1543). This was a time when science, thought and philosophy were dictated by the Church and the aristocracy.

The concept of the *hermeneutic circle* can be traced back to Schleiermacher (1768-1834). For Schleiermacher the hermeneutic circle referred to a necessary method of *practical* interpretation used in work relating to classical texts such as Plato's Dialogues and the New Testament. After Schleiermacher, hermeneutics as a scientific method is found particularly in 19th century German historicism. The aim of German historicism was to single out what was specifically German in the fields of language, law and culture.

The early 19th century saw the development of a new orientation focused around phenomenology in German scientific circles, which was oriented towards hermeneutic method and the understanding of culture. The central names here are Heidegger (1889-1976) and Gadamer (born 1900). It was Heidegger who shaped hermeneutics and the hermeneutic circle as a general philosophical method, which could in principle be detached from the narrow concerns of text reading. Due to the ideological connection between hermeneutics and German nation building, and not least to Heidegger's open support of the Nazi regime, it was not until the 1960s that problems of this kind could once again be seriously discussed.

The classical theory of knowledge

Heidegger and Gadamer represent a radical departure from the classical theory of knowledge. The starting point for this theory is the question whether or not it is possible for man to acquire reliable knowledge of the external world. According to classical theory, established knowledge must first be subjected to *critical analysis*, whereafter an analysis has to be made of the limits and possibilities of human cognition. Not least, un-equivocal intersubjective criteria have to be found regarding what is reliable knowledge and what is not. Such intersubjective criteria enable those in full command of their senses to understand a matter in the same way.

A feature of consistent reasoning is that the point to be proven cannot be part of the argument, for if it were it would involve arguing in a circle. Scientific knowledge should be inferred either by deduction from axioms or by induction based on certain premises. Such reliable scientific methods provide ever-increasing, cumulative knowledge, of the objective world. This cumulative knowledge view was particularly stressed in the scientific program laid out by Auguste Comte (1789-1857) in his *On Positive Philosophy*, but above all in the manifesto of the logical positivists of the Vienna Circle in the 1920s.

Context, circularity and prejudice

The hermeneutic method refutes the possibility that man can free himself from his historical, cultural and scientific background – from his context. The contention that man is thus bound up in the context of his traditions breaks radically not only with the epistemological program of the logical positivists, but also with the entire modern philosophy of knowledge in the tradition initiated by Descartes. In Heidegger's view, the belief that science has freed itself from tradition is in itself merely a product of scientific tradition. Scientific cognition is merely a model that helps us to understand reality. The value of this model is, according to Heidegger, *equal* to that of any other way of conceiving reality, e.g. to that of the religious perception of reality.

Seen from the perspective of the classical theory of knowledge, the hermeneutic circle involves two remarkable features, the first being the *circle concept* and the other the *prejudice concept*. Classical theory of knowledge avails itself of elementary logical thought on the inadmissibility of conclusions being circular, e.g. in a definition of the word "worker" we cannot use the word "work" ("a worker is someone who works"). However, this circularity acquires an epistemologically positive value in hermeneutics, for it is precisely this circular structure ("the pendulum movement") that makes it possible to understand the interaction of individual cognition with the social and historical context. According to the neo-hermeneutic school, individual cognition must *of necessity* be related to social and historical circumstances.

In hermeneutic thinking, a positive and constructive value is ascribed also to the concept *prejudice* (predisposition, fundamental attitude). This represents a radical departure from the philosophical programs of Descartes and Kant, who both stressed the necessity that, in his search for truth, man should free himself from prejudice.

Legitimate court decisions

The notion *prejudice* or *préjugé* is taken from legal jargon. Prejudice denotes a "decision" made before the beginning of legal proceedings, and before the legitimate decision is made in court. There are two aspects of court decisions in particular that guarantee their legitimacy and characterize their logic. Firstly, there is the *contradiction principle* meaning that the issue should be elucidated from all sides. Secondly, there is the principle that a person charged in a criminal case should be considered *innocent until judgement has been passed.* In terms of law the notion of prejudice violates both of these principles. "A decision" made prior to trial in court, i.e. a "judgement" passed in advance, is no lawful decision. It is, in short, illegitimate according to our normal sense of justice.

According to Kant, legitimate cognition is a result of judicial procedure, whereas illegitimate cognition is set forth independently of argumentative procedure (Doublet 1989, p. 26). When Heidegger and Gadamer point out that human cognition is, on the whole, existent *prior* to the argumentative procedure, i.e. as "prejudice", the implication is that what has traditionally been characterized as illegitimate cognition is in fact inevitable (and must, therefore, take part in the legitimate procedure). This implies a critique of the traditional theory of knowledge and the theory stating that human cognition is based on inter-subjective argumentative procedures. In Heidegger's and Gadamer's view the fundamental cognition, the real judgement, exists before the procedure as such. The hermeneutic circle thus fundamentally breaks with the optimistic view of knowledge characteristic of classical epistemology.

Moreover, argumentation as an intersubjective instrument suitable for true cognition is downgraded. The individual is not primarily of an argumentative nature, one's opinions and points of view being dictated rather by tradition. The hermeneutic circle thus contends that knowledge is not something acquired by man through different procedures, but something we already possess *before* starting our logical, epistemological procedures. A similar type of argument is put forward by the philosopher Karl Popper in his rejection of the inductive method. Popper points out that we have the theory already, *before* we start searching for proofs. Therefore there is no logically tenable way for us to induce from empirical knowledge to theory (Popper and Eccles 1977).

Even so, the idea of the hermeneutic circle is not necessarily pessimistic about the possibility of knowledge, but merely somewhat skeptical ("Gelassenheit") towards the endeavor of the natural sciences and other conquerors of reality to force the world into mathematical and scientific formulae.

4. Formalization – precise definition

In addition to *circle* and *prejudice* the most essential notion in hermeneutic thought is the relationship between *totality and part*. This relationship involves reciprocal conditioning and may be explained as a hermeneutic pendulum or circle movement.

In the figure below we have tried to illustrate the pendulum movement using as an example the interpretation of a written text. The parts consist of words used to form sentences, which in turn are used to form chapters, and in the end into a book as a totality. The interpretation moves "forward" word by word, but to catch the sense of what is being read there must at the same time be a "backwards" interpretation. E.g. the first word of a poem has no meaning viewed alone, as little as has the first line. The text interpreter must therefore work his way gradually through the text, see the words in their context and make this context appear reasonable in the light of the totality which, in its turn, is determined by the language rules, values and standards valid in the society in question. All interpretation occurs within a circle, i.e. a social and historical context.

Consequently, a reading of the part requires a search for the totality, and through a description of this totality we conceive the part in a more complex way. It is, in short, a question of understanding something on the basis of the context, which enriches and widens our knowledge of the particular parts. And vice versa: the deeper our knowledge of the particular parts within a particular contextual frame, the greater our ability to impart nuances to this frame. Here, according to Heidegger and Gadamer, a circular movement is taking place between totality and part, although this movement is hermeneutic rather than logical. This means that knowledge is not necessarily broadened, but that its character alters with each circular movement of the understanding (see fig. below).

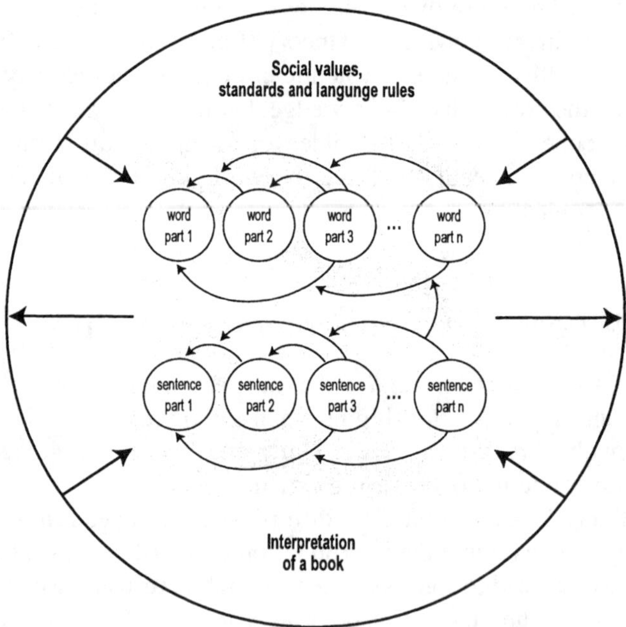

Fig. 1. Interpretation seen as pendular movement between totality and part

New law

It is not feasible to interpret word by word without having a reflexive attitude to the outer as well as to the inner totality of the text. In jurisprudence, new laws are created on the basis of tradition and, not least, in terms of how tradition is understood. In some contexts the establishment of new laws is, to a large extent, entrusted to jurisprudential authorities. But new laws will also be expressions of practical experience and of the dominant values that have been shaped by continuous historical processes. Inherent in this situation are the three fundamental hermeneutic concepts: *precondition or prejudice*, the interplay between *totality and part* and the hermeneutic *circle*.

Dynamics

The dynamics inherent in the totality-part relation cause the hermeneutic circle to be not only *circular*, but also a *spiral* with a dynamic time dimension. This illustrates, e.g., how a notion changes its meaning from one century to another, but how these shifts in meaning remain coherent. The part-totality relation constitutes the basis of how meanings shift.

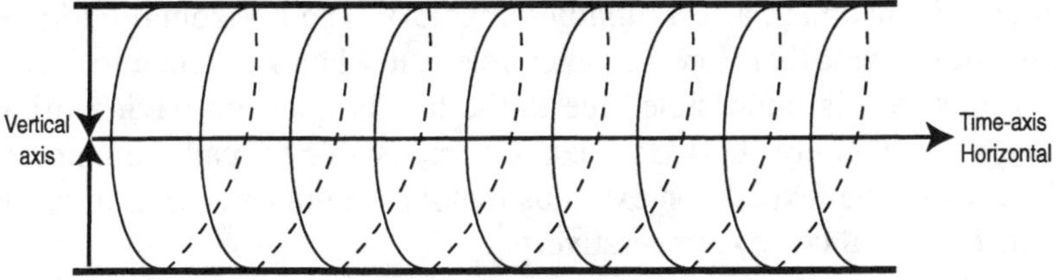

Fig. 2. The hermeneutic circle seen as a dynamic process

In the figure, interpretative movement is illustrated by a horizontal time axis indicating how each new interpretation incorporates interpretative elements from the past. According to this, what is "present" in one instance of interpretation becomes "past" at a later time, without any rupture occurring. The *vertical movement* takes place within the framework of the present, and shows the interplay between totality and part. Viewed in terms of these two interpretative axes, the concepts of precondition, totality/part and the hermeneutic circle ("the spiral") make up the total interpretation. The circular form in the figure should be conceived as a "cylinder" enveloping the interpretation process. It is not subject to change over time and does not widen or narrow, meaning that interpretations arrived at towards the right of the time axis are not "better" or "more general" than interpretations to the left, only different.

The figure is applicable to interpretations of current law in practical court decisions. In a concrete situation the interpretation is influenced by tradition/prejudice as well as by the parts that compose the totality. This amounts to saying that the interpretation of a concrete fact takes into consideration shifts of meaning which occur continually in all societies. Therefore, the hermeneutic circle does not end as a closed circle, but has the structure of a dynamic spiral, demonstrating that new meanings/cases involve existing prejudices, but also carry new prejudices into the future. A parallel train of thought is to be found in Anthony Giddens' theory of the "use" and "reproduction" of social structures (Giddens 1979).

In the juridical context, the vertical interpretative movement takes place between the fact (the phenomenon under consideration) and the rule of law (the laws in force). These two factors are fixed by means of the interpretation of rules and the freezing of the judicial fact. In its horizontal dimension the interpretative movement allows us to regard any particular understanding of a legal decision, or of the words of which it is made up, as essentially temporary. The horizontal interpretative movement therefore becomes relevant when reference to a rule (subsumption) is impossible, due to the law in question having originated in another era. This fact makes it impossible to read the inherent sense out of the textual context, thus making an interpretation in terms of the historical context imperative.

The *horizontal structure* gains importance when in a legal provision words and expressions are used that had a different sense at the time the law was promulgated, both contextually and for the legislator. At the time when the Norwegian constitution was written, the term "borgere" ("citizen") (Art. 50 of the Norwegian Constitution, promulgated 1821) was understood, both contextually and by the legislative authority, as designating a restricted group of male Norwegian citizens. But by the time woman were given the right to vote the term "citizen" had acquired another meaning, applicable to both sexes. The question was then raised whether or not a constitutional amendment was needed to give women the right to vote. Platou (1915, pp. 205-206) held the view that such an amendment was necessary, since the meaning of the citizen concept had to be understood against the background of its contextual meaning, which at the time of promulgation referred to men only. This view reflects a lack of understanding of the fact that a legal provision may change its character due to such things as court practice and general social evolution. We cannot just go back along the horizontal time axis in search of the original sense of the words employed by the legislator, but must also consider as essential interpretative factors the evolution that has taken place along this time axis concerning the understanding of these words. E.g., the concept "lewd literature" has another meaning today, both socially and in legal terms, than it had at the time of the Mykle trial, and this is so regardless of the 1988 amendment to the relevant provision in the *penal code*.[1]

The *vertical structure* of the interpretation model describes the relationship between the legal provision (part) and context (totality). In Gadamer's view a legal provision does not primarily refer to the factual circumstances which it is intended to regulate, since these factual circumstances are not subsumed under the legal provision until the meaning of the rule in question has emerged through interpretation. The question then arises: what does the legal provision refer to, if not to the factual circumstances it is intended to regulate? The answer is that the legal provision refers to the context or totality of which it is a part.

A 1906 provision stipulated that a certificate was needed to navigate a steamship. The Supreme Court went on to apply this rule to motor vessels, which it clearly could not have done if the assumption had been that the provision referred to steamships only.[2] In refuting such an assumption the basis chosen for the *application of the provision* was its context, i.e. its reference framework. In terms of legal dogmatics this is called an "extended interpretation", meaning that what the legal provision refers to is not the objects expressly stated in the provision, but a certain type of legal regulation of an area of life, which in this case proves somewhat more complex than any strictly literal understanding of the text would assume it to be.

This point can be illustrated by the following simple example: the provision concerning "legal complaint interest", as used in § 28, section 1 of the Administration Act, is not interpreted and understood before the lawyer can convey knowledge of the context of the regulation. In this case the regulation must be interpreted on the basis of the concept of "legal interest" of the Civil Dispute Regulation, § 54 (Frihagen 1992, pp. 236-42, particularly s. 237; Eckhoff 1992, pp. 528-30). The § 28 Administration Act and the concept of "legal complaint interest" contribute to the understanding of the context within which the legal provision has been placed. Isolated from its context the provision in itself lacks both meaning and reference. Therefore, the lawyer must

---

1   *Norsk Rettstidende* (Norwegian Journal of Law), 1958 9. 479.
2   Statute of April 7th 1906 on the licence to be navigator of a ship, § 4. The judgment is published in *Norsk Rettstidende* 1929, p. 330.

know the context of the provision, the intention of the legislator, and the relevant court practice. The provision refers to a normal *rule of law* understandable only in the wider historical, intentional and normative context of which it is a part.

The vertical circle in the figure above therefore shows the relationship between the legal provision (part) and the relevant context (totality). Of these two factors the provision in itself is static (as long as the law is not amended), while the totality is subject to continuous change. The contextual *change* of the rule caused by time makes up the horizontal structure of the hermeneutic circle.

The static nature of a legal provision is only a qualified truth. As pointed out in the example of the citizen concept as used in the Constitution, the rule of law inferred from the provision may alter, even though the text of the provision does not. And the purpose in focusing on changes in the context of the provision is to draw attention to the fact that these changes may have consequences for our interpretation of the provision. Nonetheless, at the moment of judicial application it is a tacit precondition that the provision be applied "as if" it were static. In applied law, this "as if" view of legal provisions is an essential aspect of the methodology of legal dogmatics.

As a practical method interpretative hermeneutics contributes nothing new to jurisprudence. Hermeneutics can, on the other hand, contribute to jurisprudence *a scientific awareness* of what takes place when laws are actually applied. It is true that in practical jurisprudence the method of legal dogmatics or the theory of legal sources is a necessary and adequate instrument. But insofar as jurisprudence assumes the status of a *science*, it has to develop its own methodological self-understanding, a precondition here being a methodological self-awareness attainable, e.g. by means of the principles of hermeneutic interpretation. Such self-awareness is a necessary precondition for any further development of a science.

5. Generality and testability. Critique

The hermeneutic circle does not express an inherent orderliness, but must be understood as a clarification of the preconditions for the conceptualization of what humans bring into being, i.e. culture in a wider sense. Whereas human reason is, in Heidegger's and Gadamer's view, conditioned by predetermined boundaries, Kant maintained that by means of reason man is always in a position to judge tradition and the socially sanctioned authorities for himself (Kant 1784, p. 35). This being so, Kant believes that reason can transcend the given context in which mankind finds itself. This constitutes a pronounced difference between the hermeneutic project and Kant's transcendental philosophy.

The hermeneutic structure of understanding is therefore not accessible to empirical confirmation and falsification. In fact, the conditions for knowledge cannot be subjected to the same tests that we use to check hypotheses concerning things that are empirically given. The conditions for knowledge belong on a level which is *different* from that of the empirically given objects. The hermeneutic circle presents itself as a level prior to that of cognition; it represents a meta-level.

Does this imply, then, that hermeneutic structures are above any kind of critical analysis? No: to qualify as scientific, methods must be liable to critique and checking. Although the hermeneutic circle is a figure of thought which is difficult to verify or moderate, it is in no way immune to criticism.

The logical critique

The hermeneutic circle is not a logical circle, but a metaphor. Ever since Schleiermacher and the tradition he established, this metaphor has been deemed logically acceptable (Stegmüller 1952). Once it is accepted that the hermeneutic circle does not involve logical circularity, it is possible to employ the notion of the *circle* as a distinguishing feature of the hermeneutic *method*. Thus from a logical point of view there is no question of the hermeneutic method being above logic. From a logical point of view, it will always be possible to analyze any scientific argumentation be means of logic. *Argumentative circularity is, and will always be, circular, regardless of whether the circle involved is termed hermeneutic or not.* A contention that the hermeneutic circle is immune to the principles of logic is, as Stegmhller sees it, an indication of the non-scientific nature of the hermeneutic tradition.

The jurisprudential critique

Reality is in a state of constant change. Gadamer characterizes any attempt to delimit reality as objectivism. The changes are not due to reality alone, but also to the interpreting subject, who ascribes properties to it that do not remain constant. Thus, reality emerges partly as a reflection of the interpreting subject's activity.

In terms of the philosophy of science the most controversial point in

Gadamer's hermeneutic theory is perhaps his view of reality. Following a scientific line of thought, changes in the external world are explicable as the results of the law-like relationships found in nature itself, the task of science being to discover these inherently law-like relationships. Gadamer himself takes the view that there are changes in nature which cannot be traced back to nature itself, but rather to man. Let us examine an example which demonstrates that Gadamer's standpoint is perhaps not so extreme after all.

No reasonable human being belonging to Western culture will doubt that the earth revolves around the sun. With the Copernican world view as one's basis, this is a piece of "objective" scientific knowledge. Nonetheless, we may enjoy the sight of the sun rising, its crossing the sky and its setting in the West, although "scientifically" the truth is the very opposite of these impressions. No one who sits on their terrace at sunset and sees the red sun disappear behind the horizon would ever say "it is beautiful when the earth is at this angle to the sun". To us it makes more sense to contemplate the sun in an "unscientific" manner. This is termed *perspective relativism*, meaning that what we perceive is dependent on our perspective or prejudices.

Perspective relativism plays a role not only in the interpretation and definition of rules of law, but also in the establishment of juridical facts. According to Gadamer, an interpretation is furnished on the basis of internal scientific preconditions. For those who work with law, this implies that juridical activity depends on how the individual lawyer has adapted to established jurisprudence. The lawyer performs his interpretational work on the background of established jurisprudence. The question then arises: is it possible, in terms of Gadamer's strategy, to decide whether or not a particular result of interpretation is juridically acceptable? Would all interpretations be acceptable? If this were the case, jurisprudence would succumb to a relativism incompatible with the claim that there should always be one, and only one, correct solution to a legal question.

This objection to Gadamer has been raised in different quarters, namely the jurisprudential critique which was formulated by Emilie Betti. Betti solves the problem of establishing standard interpretational rules by suggesting a canon which applies for all lawyers if the result of interpretation is to be accepted as juridically adequate.[3] From the per-

---

3   The idea of a canon for juridical thought is, in fact, congruent with the idea of legal sources: a minimum of *intersubjectivity* among lawyers is secured through the establishment of concrete rules as to how legal material is to be interpreted and employed.

spective of legal theory Betti's objection seems to imply an interpretation of law which is closely linked to the legislator, a view which is also called legal positivism. On the other hand, Gadamer's theory in many ways seems to involve a conception of law which is not limited to the legislator and his intentions alone, but which implies a series of value assessments. However, Gadamer's own view is that he does not advocate a relativism in scientific theory that would admit as scientifically acceptable any possible interpretation. The censuring of individual interpretation is, according to Gadamer, implicit in scientific practice itself.

In the view of the present author, this criterion is too vague. When a legal question requires decision, it is not acceptable that there might be as many solutions to it as there are lawyers. The characteristic of legal thinking is that it searches for one single decision. If one ends up with two possibilities, in principle no legal decision has been arrived at. A defense counsel who in a particular case believes on principle that prison, or the judgement itself, are in themselves wrong can therefore, and with advantage, insist on a hermeneutic method.

6. Empirical assessment - conclusion

The hermeneutic circle can be fruitful in the interpretation of anything from literary texts and legal provisions to hypotheses and propositions. For preliminary university examinations students are trained in the interpretation and precise definition of hypotheses. The point of this is to acquire a fruitful ability to "swing" between the totality and the part by using instances from the society and culture to which one belongs. In this respect "good" interpretations mean relevant interpretations.

Just as there is not a fixed number of interpretations of a rule of law, so neither are there any definite procedures for selecting the "best" interpretation. In practical life the decision as to what constitutes the "correct/best" interpretation will be made by a court majority, by an examination board or by whatever happens to be the pertinent assembly, which gives guidance about what can be accepted as "correct interpretations". In fact, not all possible interpretations are equally relevant or valid, since it is the interpretative practice of the group that defines the limits of what is accepted as a valid interpretation. It follows that in jurisprudence for example, possibilities exist to predict the future interpretation of a given fact seen in the light of an existing rule of law. It is a paradox that the great steps forward in the evolution of science have come about when general truths concerning the validity of methods have been broken in some fundamental way (Feyerabend 1978).

Although interpretation cannot be summarized in fixed rules, this constitutes an important part of all scientific practice. There is no avoiding interpretation when one wishes to understand the contents of propositions framed in human language. Scientific propositions expressed in mathematical symbols also need interpretation, even though their variation is far more restricted than in the case of verbal statements. The main point is to achieve the greatest possible awareness for the methodological parts of the hermeneutic circle as an interpretative instrument, and to express them clearly. In doing this one is able to communicate and think with greater clarity in scientific contexts.

7. Literature

Doublet, David R. 1989: *Die Vernuft als Rechtsinstanz* (The Reason as Instance of Law), Paderborn/Oslo.

Eckhoff, Torstein 1992: *Forvaltningsrett* (Administrative Law) (4th ed.), Oslo.

Feyerabend, Paul 1978: *Against Method*, London.

Gadamer, Hans-Georg 1960: *Wahrheit und Methode. Grundzüge einer Philosophischen Hermeneutik* (Truth and Method. Fundamentals of a Philosophy of Hermeneutics), Tübingen.

Giddens, Anthony 1979: *Central Problems in Social Theory. Action, Structure and Contradiction in Social Analysis*, London.

Helmholtz, H. 1903: "Über das Verhältnis der Naturwissenschaften zur Gesamtheit der Wissenschaften" (On the Relationship of the Natural Sciences to the Totality of Science), in *Vortäge und Aufsätze* (Lectures and Essays), Braunschweig.

Heidegger, Martin 1927: *Sein und Zeit* (Being and Time), Tübingen.

Heidegger, Martin 1954: "Die Frage der Technik" (The Question Concerning Technology) (1953), in *Lectures and Essays*, Pfüllingen.

Heidegger, Martin 1972: "sDer Ursprung des Kunstwerkes" (The Origin of the Work of Art), in *Holzwege* (On the Wrong Track), Frankfurt.

Heidegger, Martin 1978: *Metaphysische Anfangsgründe der Logik* (Metaphysical Foundations of Logic), Frankfurt.

Kant, Immanuel 1787: *Kritik der reinen Vernunft* (Critique of Pure Reason) (B-ed.).

Kant, Immanuel 1784: "What is Enlightenment?" in AA VIII.

Platou, O. 1915: *Forelæsninger over Retskildernes Theori* (Lectures on the Theory of the Sources of Law), Kristiania.

Popper, Karl and John C. Eccles 1977: *The Self and Its Brain. An Argument for Interactionism*, New York.

Safranski, Rüdiger 1997: *Ein Meister aus Deutschland* (A master from Germany), Frankfurt.

Stegmüller, W. 1952: *Hauptströmungen der Gegenwartsphilosophie* (Main Currents in Contemporary Philosophy), Vienna.

4
The Finitism Thesis
On Social Roots and Limits
to Knowledge

HARALD GRIMEN

1. Original quotation

This conception of knowledge [i.e. that knowledge is conventional and that it is our decisions and judgements which determine what is to count as conventional, H.G.] is sometimes called ▢nitism. Its core assertion is that proper usage is developed step by step, in processes involving successions of on-the-spot judgements. Every instance of use, or of proper use, of a concept must in the last analysis be accounted for separately, by reference to speci▢c local, contingent determinants. Finitism denies that inherent properties or meanings attach to concepts and determine their future correct applications; and consequently it denies that truth and falsity are inherent properties of statements. "True" and "false" are terms which are interesting only as they are used by a community itself, as it develops and maintains its own accepted pattern of concept application. (Barnes 1982, pp. 30–31).

2. Brief explanation

Finitism in this sense is a theory about the relations between linguistic meaning, language proficiency and language use. It consists of five claims (cf. Barnes, Bloor and Henry 1966, pp. 55-59; my presentation of the basic tenets of finitism is of course more condensed than theirs, due to limited space in this article):

1. Concepts have no inherent, fixed, stable meanings.
2. The knowledge underlying a decision, whether or not a concept is used correctly in a factual situation, can consist only of knowledge of how this particular concept has been used in a limited or finite number of former situations (hence the name *finitism*, from "*finite*").
3. This knowledge, which is the only and best available, *underdetermines* correct use. Such knowledge does not suffice to determine in an unequivocal way the correct use of a concept in any situation of use. In addition, no other factors of a similar kind, for instance rules, can determine correct use.
4. Therefore, the question of what is the correct use of a concept basically depends on judgment and decisions by the users themselves in the actual situation ("on the spot"). Such decisions are subject to causal influence from many types of factors which can, in such situations of use, influence the individuals or groups concerned: ideology, interests, preference structure, illusions, rationalizations, power and authority relations and the like.
5. This applies to every instance of concept use, in new and unknown situations as well as in old and known, and in all kinds of contexts.

Finitism is therefore also a theory which claims that knowledge about proper concept use can be acquired only in situations of use. The theory entails that it is impossible to generalize about – or to predict – concept use, since conditions of use are always local and unique. It follows from finitism that all concept use is "open-ended", and that there are no incontrovertible classifications (i.e. any classification can be revised) (Barnes, Bloor and Henry 1996, pp 56-57).

3. Background

Barry Barnes, who formulated the thesis in this way, belongs to the so-called *Edinburgh School* in modern theory of science. Its members are a group of sociologists of knowledge and science attached to the Science Studies Unit at The University of Edinburgh. The school has two central names, Barry Barnes (born 1943) and David Bloor (born 1942). Their major works are the books *Scientific Knowledge and Sociological Theory* (Barnes 1973), *Knowledge and Social Imagery* (Bloor, 1976) and *Scientific Knowledge – A Sociological Analysis* (Barnes, Bloor and Henry 1996). The group regards as its most important precursors Thomas Kuhn (1922-94), Ludwig Wittgenstein (1889-1951), Thorstein Veblen (1857-1929), Robert Merton (born 1910), Robin Horton (born 1931), Mary Douglas (born 1931) and Mary Hesse (born 1924).

The members of this group define themselves as sociologists of knowledge with the study of scientific knowledge as their speciality. In several of their works, discussions about the scope and status of the sociology of knowledge occupy a central place. They are anti-rationalists and they aim at the creation of a theoretical basis for the study of scientific knowledge as a cultural phenomenon, on a level with other cultural phenomena (an exposition of "the myth of rationalism" is to be found in Barnes 1984, pp. 85-86). They consider as knowledge all collectively accepted systems of belief: "We refer to any collectively accepted system of belief as 'knowledge'" (Bloor and Barnes 1982, p. 22 fn. 1). The sociology of knowledge can be defined as:

> the branch of sociology which investigates the relations between thought and society, and thus it deals with the social and existential conditions for knowledge. The sociology of knowledge endeavors to relate ideas to the socio-historical environments in which they are produced and accepted. (Coser 1968, p. 428, cf. also Mannhcim 1936, p. 237).

The sociology of knowledge endeavors to find the general and specific *causes* of why social actors have the ideas, beliefs and thought categories which they actually have. Attempts have been made to localize such causes for instance in social class and economy (Marx) and in forms of social organization (Durkheim). An important problem discussed from the very beginning of the sociology of knowledge is related to the question of whether *all* ideas and beliefs can be made objects of sociological research, i.e. if social or psychological causes *can* and *must* be found to explain all types of beliefs that an individual or a group may have (Stehr and Meja 1984, pp. 6-8).

A common rationalist assumption in the history and philosophy of science has been that this is not the case, and that quite particularly scientific knowledge cannot be made an object of sociological studies. The reason given for this is that there is a difference between believing in something which is true or something for which rational arguments can be given, and believing in something which is false or something for which rational arguments cannot be found, if one knows it to be false or impossible to justify by rational arguments.

This assumption has played an important part in research in the history of science. A fairly common view has been that when an individual believes in something true or something for which rational arguments can be put forward, there is no need to find special causes for these beliefs. Truth and good reasons are in themselves sufficiently convincing. There is therefore no need for special explanations of why people are convinced by what is true or by that which can be supported by good reasons. As Barnes puts it, "correct belief" is thus sheltered from "a deterministic account" (Barnes, 1982, p. 4). In short, if NN believes that *p*, and *p* is true, and NN knows *p* to be true, this is a sufficient explanation of why NN believes that *p*. According to the rationalist assumption, nothing more is needed to explain why NN believes in something which is true. To believe in what is true and to do what is rational are self-explaining.

This view contains an implicit assumption about universal, culturally independent standards of truth and rationality, and it presupposes that to be rational means to think and act in accordance with such standards.

Martin Hollis (1982, p 75) formulates this clearly: "true and rational beliefs need one sort of explanation, false and irrational beliefs another". If NN believes that the earth is round, we will, on the basis of such premises, consider his belief as sufficiently explained by the reference to the fact that the earth is actually round, and the assumption that NN knows this. One has then, so to say, assumed the existence of "natural classes" of rational beliefs (and actions), and if an individual acts in a way falling under such a "natural class" (i.e. in accordance with universal standards of rationality), his action or belief need not be given a psychological or sociological explanation. Beliefs which satisfy the standards of rationality are in no need of such explanations. The fact that they satisfy such standards is considered to be a sufficient explanation of why somebody has them.

If, on the other hand, an individual deviates in his beliefs from what is true or rational, special psychological or sociological explanations will be needed, e.g. explanations which refer to ideological bias, power, interests, rationalizations and the like. This implies the formulation of theories about the causes of irrational behavior or irrational beliefs. On the other hand, there is no need for theories concerning the causes of rational behavior or rational beliefs, because the standards of rationality are universally accepted and convincing.

Rationalist theory of science (e.g. the Popper/Lakatos tradition, cf. Lakatos 1971, pp. 106 ff.) and history of science (e.g. the Merton tradition) are therefore based on an *asymmetry condition*: all actions or beliefs cannot be treated in the same way. Rational belief and rational actions need no special explanations, other than that we point to the fact that they are true or rational. On the other hand, false beliefs and irrational actions need "a deterministic account". Consequently, the fact that a person believes in something which is false or acts irrationally must be explained by referring to social or psychological causes. This asymmetry condition confines the legitimate fields of the psychology and sociology of knowledge to what is irrational, abnormal, pathological or, roughly speaking, to what deviates from "the canons of rationality and truth".

In order to see how it is possible to defend the view that scientific knowledge cannot be made the object of sociological studies, we must add one crucial premise: scientific activity and scientific knowledge are the preeminent examples of rational actions and true beliefs. They can be subjected to so-called *rational reconstruction*, that is, they can be reconstructed as chains of arguments which will show a cumulative growth towards increasing rationality and truth. If true beliefs and rational actions are self-explaining, and if scientific beliefs and actions are the preeminent examples of true beliefs and rational actions, then consequently scientific knowledge cannot be the object of sociological explanations. To subject what is self-explaining to further explanation is pointless. The most ardent defender of rational reconstruction in the history of science was Imre Lakatos. According to Lakatos, the core element in the history of science is rational reconstruction. Sociological studies are, however, highly relevant when it comes to errors, persistent mistakes or persistent false theories. But such studies belong, according to Lakatos, in the footnotes of historical investigations, the basic aim of which is rational reconstruction.

Finitism is an attempt to break with this asymmetry condition and prepare the foundations of a *general* sociology of knowledge including sociological studies of scientific knowledge: "all beliefs are on a par with one another with respect to the causes of their credibility. [...] regardless of truth and falsity the fact or their credibility is to be seen as equally problematic." (Barnes and Bloor 1982, p. 154). "(Beliefs) do not fall into two different natural kinds which make different sorts of appeal to the human mind, or stand in different relationship to reality, or depend for their credibility on different patterns of social organization. Hence the relativist conclusion that they are to be explained in the same way" (Barnes and Bloor, 1982, p. 28). Basically, what they say is this: for the sociologist of knowledge true and false beliefs are equally problematic, and the credibility of both kinds of beliefs must be explained by referring to specific local determinants.

The Edinburgh School fits into the traditions in the sociology of knowledge established by Durkheim, Marx and Mannheim, but differs from Marx and Durkheim, for instance, by not assigning priority among different types of causal explanations to classes and forms of organization. They differ from Mannheim through their much more radical view concerning the field of the sociology of knowledge. While Mannheim excluded physics and mathematics from such studies, the Edinburgh School includes them (Mannheim 1936, p. 38, Bloor 1973, pp. 173-91; Bloor 1984 discusses the relation to Durkheim, Coser 1968, pp. 428-35, reviews classical theories).

4. Formalization – precise definition

Finitism is about the kind of factors that determine the actual use of concepts. Its main consequence is a radical sociologization of all knowledge. Such a sociologization is a precondition for the development of a general sociology of knowledge including a sociology of science. In order to develop a general sociology of knowledge, one must justify that all knowledge has social roots. Finitism attacks the idea of rational reconstruction where it is most vulnerable: in its (implicit) presuppositions about concept use.

Let us assume that an essential part of the knowledge which a human being possesses will find its expression in his theories and opinions about the world (for the sake of simplification I shall here disregard knowledge of a practical, craftsman-like kind). To form theories and opinions, concepts of different kinds are, of course, needed. Nobody would deny that.

A classical view of concepts (this classical view is accounted for in Elster, Føllesdal and Walløe 1986, pp. 178 ff.), such as 'swan', 'duck', 'man', 'woman', 'atom', 'reference group', 'alienation, 'surplus value', 'conscience collective', 'anomie' etc. is that they have an *intension* (sense) and an *extension* (scope, range). The intension consists of a set of definitional characteristics. If a phenomenon A (chosen at random) has these characteristics of a concept, A is included in the extension of this concept. If another (randomly chosen) phenomenon – does not meet these same criteria, then – falls beyond the extension of the concept. The extension (scope, range) is a set consisting of all of the phenomena (present, past and future) which fall within the limits of the intension, i.e. which possess the conceptual characteristics.

This view has some important consequences, which are more or less solidly connected with it. The first implication is that it is the sense (intension) as expressed in the definition which determines the scope or range (extension) of the concept. It thus determines which phenomena fall within and which fall outside the concept. This is, in practice, tantamount to saying that if doubt arises in use situations as to whether or not a phenomenon can be subsumed under a concept, a decision can be made by appealing to the definitional characteristics. The definitional characteristics become standards by reference to which one can settle such questions in cases of doubt. The second implication of this view is that knowledge of the intension of the concept is sufficient to be able to use it correctly, as the concept's intension in practice determines what is correct use, by picking out the members of the extension set. All that is needed to use a concept correctly is knowledge about its intension. The intension picks out the set of phenomena about which the concept is correctly used. Thirdly, the view implies that when the concept's intension has been definitely established, an ex ante ruling per definitionem – *before* the concept has at all been used or put to work – has been given as to which phenomena fall within or beyond it, and this applies to all phenomena. When the concept 'horse' has been defined as "four-legged hoofed animal", it is clear from the concept's definitional characteristics that featherless bipeds do not belong to the concept's extension. This will be understood by anyone who understands the definitional characteristics.

To facilitate the understanding of the differences between finitism and traditional theories of meaning we can take a look at some of the criticisms set forth against traditional theories. One type of criticism emphasizes the point that even though the core cases are clear, there will always be many borderline cases of a nature that will render judgment necessary and also often demand "negotiation" in order to establish whether they belong to the extension of a concept or not. Court proceedings are frequently negotiations carried out to investigate whether crimes that have been committed belong to this or that category of violations of the laws, or whether they belong to the category of a crime at all ("subsumption"). It is not always clear in practice which actions qualify for membership in the extension of the concept of 'first-degree murder'. This is often also the case with regard to the use of concepts in the social sciences. Durkheim defined 'anomie' as "a state of normlessness". But where does the borderline run between anomic and non-anomic societies? Is the USA anomic? Was the Republic of Weimar anomic? Social scientists must arrive at a mutual agreement on the classification of different phenomena. This classification does not unambiguously spring from the meaning of the concept of 'anomie', nor from characteristics inherent in the things themselves. Concepts have, as Waismann (1984) said, "open texture". Outside the core cases, it is in practice not clear how to draw the limit for membership in the extension of any concept.

The criticism set forth through finitism is related to this type of criticism, but it is far more radical. An implication of finitism is that what we normally consider valid for borderline cases is valid for *all* cases of concept use. Concept use in the core cases is not less dependent on judgment, decisions and negotiations than is concept use in the borderline cases. This makes finitism into an attempt to present concept use in a way that is radically different from the classical view. Finitism is intended to be strictly universal, that is, to apply to all cases of concept use. Consequently, decisions which define correct and incorrect use are governed by "local, contingent, determinants", i.e. all kinds of social and other factors which can causally influence the individuals or groups in question to opt for the one or other decision.

Finitism has several implications worth mentioning. First, it implies that it is impossible to appeal to the intension of a concept, or to rules for correct use, when a decision concerning the correct use of a concept is to be made. This may be interpreted in two ways: either that there are no such things as meanings or intensions connected to concepts, or that there are no rules for correct use. Each instance of concept use is then "new", because each situation in which it is used is unique. Or it can mean that even if phenomena like meanings or intensions do exist, they are not sufficiently helpful to make decisions about the correct use of a concept. The Edinburgh School advocates the first and most radical version, for example when Barnes says that finitism denies that inherent properties or meanings attach to concepts (Barnes, 1978, pp. 30-31).

The second implication of finitism is that former use of a concept – or the knowledge "in store" in an individual or in a society – cannot unequivocally or quite exactly determine the proper use of the concept in new cases. The decision as to what is correct or incorrect use of a concept is, in the last resort, always based on particular judgments in the situations of use, or, in Barnes' terms, "processes involving successions of on-the-spot judgements". Such processes do not easily admit of generalizations.

Thirdly, on the basis of this view it is impossible to justify the claim that one can decide which phenomena fall within or beyond the extension of a concept before this same concept has been used at all. It is in the use situation ("on the spot") that a decision must be made with regard to whether a phenomenon is included or not in the extension of a concept. Finitism cannot build on the precondition that the phenomena in the world can be grouped in "natural classes". Instead, a precondition of finitism is that any phenomenon chosen at random is at the same time like and unlike all other phenomena along an infinite number of dimensions. Each and every grouping of phenomena in classes is thus a conventional and unique product based on a given society's evaluations of what are relevant and irrelevant similarities or differences. The implication is that there is no classification system based on "naturally" given classes of phenomena. Classes are on the whole conventional, i.e. based on "unique" judgments and decisions made between individuals (Barnes 1984, pp. 195 and 197). The difference between finitism and traditional theories of meaning can be schematically outlined as follows:

Traditional theories of meaning:
Use as a function of meaning

"Independent variable"   "Dependent variable"

Explains/determines

Concept intension/meaning $\Longrightarrow$ Concept use in concrete
+ the actor's knowledge of this   use situations

Finitist theory of meaning:
Meaning as a function of use and use as a
function of social and psychological factors.

"Independent variable"   "Dependent variable"

Former use + social and   Social actors'   Concept use in
psychological causes, $\Longrightarrow$ decisions, evalu- $\Longrightarrow$ concrete use
such as ideologies,   ations and assess-   situations
power, preferences,   ments
interests etc.

Influences   Explains/determines

We can use the concept of 'anomie' as an example. An implication of the traditional view is that the meaning (intension) of the concept determines which societies someone will classify as anomic, and thus also which societies will not be classified as such. The classifier will be bound by the concept's meaning, and he makes a mistake if he does not respect its meaning. But according to finitism there are no stable meanings determining classification. Instead, general social and psychological features of the persons in question, their judgments and decisions, as well as accidental characteristics of the use situations will be the sole determining factors. The concept of "anomie" therefore bears different meanings at different times and in different contexts, and no one can be accused of making a mistake, since there are no trans-situational meanings by reference to which one could delimit what is a mistake and what is not. Decisions about what is a mistake and what is not are also local and unique and subject to causal influence from local determinants.

Finitism tends towards a kind of situational relativism where concept use in new situations cannot be explained or predicted on the basis of use registered in preceding situations. This situational relativism is related to the relativism which we find for instance in Herbert Blumer's version of symbolic interactionism where:

> people do not, out of hand, find premade roles and institutions. All the time they create and recreate their roles from one situation to the next. So-called social institutions – state, family, economy – exist only when people really interact in different situations. (Collins 1985, p. 200).

Finitism is also related to the type of sociological individualism (found in certain Weberian traditions) which endeavors to explain social structure as a result of individual actions. But symbolic interactionism or sociological individualism are hardly deducible from finitism, or vice versa. It is rather a question of different sociological perspectives showing some *family resemblance*. The family in question consists of perspectives stressing the particular and individual, be it persons, individual actions or individual language use situations.

It remains for us to show the connection of finitism to the guiding project of the Edinburgh School: to create a basis for a general sociology of knowledge. If we stick to the view that knowledge is expressed in theories and opinions, and that these must contain concepts, then finitism renders a general sociology of knowledge possible by conventionalizing the dividing line between correct and incorrect use. The dividing line is made dependent on the evaluations and judgments made by social groups "on the spot" and on the factors which influence such judgments. Out of context no concept use is reasonable or peculiar. It is peculiar or reasonable only in relation to the practices in specific groups. Each case of use must, in principle, be "accounted for separately, by reference to specific local determinants", as Barnes puts it. In other words, finitism refers to unique "on the spot" factors as well as to more general, but "arbitrary" conventions existing within social groups.

5. Generality and testability. Critique

It is difficult to know how finitism can be criticized, as it is not clear how to interpret its basic claims. The theory is intended to be strictly universal and to apply to all cases of concept use, thus covering all knowledge which involves the use of concepts. But we face two possible interpretations of it: either it is an empirical hypothesis about the structure of what we might term the social micro-foundations of all knowledge, or it expresses an epistemic, philosophical point concerning the status of human knowledge.

Testable consequences of finitism are conceivable if it is interpreted as an empirical hypothesis about the micro-foundations of knowledge. The consequences will, primarily, apply to two fields: *concept learning* and *classification*.

With regard to learning, two possible consequences should be mentioned:

1. Finitism and more traditional theories of meaning imply different *ideal-typical models of learning*. The ideal-typical model of learning that emerges from traditional theories emphasizes the logical priority of the learning of definitional characteristics. The concept 'man', for example, is acquired by learning, first, its definitional characteristics, and then through attempts to apply these to individual phenomena. One is taught to distinguish men from other phenomena on the basis of already acquired concept characteristics. The use of concepts becomes approximately equal to using algorithms. In order to determine whether a concept is correctly used, appeal is made to the established concept characteristics.

Contrary to this, the ideal-typical learning model of finitism stresses guided instruction and the social sanctioning of behavior. Finitism excludes the possibility that a child initially learns how to use a concept through the acquisition of definitional characteristics (intensions) or anything similar to definitional characteristics. Instead, learning must start with the child's grouping of specific phenomena according to socially relevant and sanctioned similarities and differences between them. A child becomes acquainted with the relations of similarity and difference between the phenomena regarded by society as relevant, through the presentation of society's decisions in concrete situations and the ways in which the use is sanctioned. If it can be proved that concept learning starts with the learning of definitional characteristics, then this will be an argument for refuting finitism.

2. Another consequence concerns the question of which learning methods are the most efficient. An implication of finitism is that learning methods based on instruction and social sanctioning are more efficient than methods based on "autolearning" (meaning that the child is allowed considerable liberty to "discover" for itself how concepts are to be used).

With regard to classification, three consequences should be mentioned:

a) Finitism implies that unclassified phenomena (phenomena not yet encountered by individuals/groups, these individuals/groups thus not knowing whether they fall within the scope or range of any of their concepts), cannot be classified by reference to concept meaning.

b) From the traditional point of view one would expect the same classification regardless of social and psychological characteristics of the individuals, provided they have identical/equivalent verbal definitions of a concept. Finitism relies on the opposite assumption, that even though the members of two groups have an identical definition of, for instance, 'anomie', they may disagree as to which societies are anomic. Classification depends, in practice, on their decisions, and these are influenced by social and psychological factors that will always vary. Classification is not governed by definitional characteristics.

c) More disagreement about classification is to be expected in socially heterogeneous than in socially homogeneous groups, also with regard to the most basic concepts and concepts of which the individuals hold fully identical definitions.

If finitism proves tenable, then also semantics, i.e. the study of the meanings of words and expressions, will become an entirely sociological discipline. In that case finitism must first be given concrete expression by making hypotheses about what social determinants cause what kinds of knowledge/meanings. As formulated on page 74–5, the thesis of finitism goes no further than to contend *that* there is a causal connection between social relations and knowledge/meaning. An important test would be to ascertain whether *different* social groups have the *same* knowledge/meaning. If that proved to be true, it would weaken the proposed causal link between social conditions and meaning.

The problem is, however, whether finitism can reasonably be interpreted as an empirical hypothesis. As explained in Barnes (1982), Bloor (1983), and Barnes, Bloor and Henry (1996), it seems to be more reasonable to interpret it as a *logical* point about the status of human knowledge. Finitism is an attempt to present philosophical reasons for the belief that all knowledge is, in principle, open to sociological (i.e. empirical) studies. If this interpretation is chosen, empirical testing becomes irrelevant. The question is then whether or not the position is logically consistent.

For my own part I should add three logical arguments against finitism. *Firstly*, finitism can be criticized with a simple self-reference argument. The pretension of finitism is to be a general theory about concept use, but at the same time it rejects the possibility of substantiating general theories about concept use.

Secondly, finitism implies a situational relativism which makes it difficult to understand how enduring practices and stable institutions can be established across the endless variety of different situations in which concepts are used. Consequently, finitism seems unable to explain how the use of concepts can gradually be *stabilized*. This argument may be generalized along the following lines: compared to concrete situations of use – "microphenomena" – a stable mode of use is a "macrophenomenon" extending over time and across a series of different situations. But finitism is, logically, too poor to grasp even such small "macrophenomena". It may end in the same problem as Blumer's symbolic interactionism, which in practice solves the micro/macro problem by ignoring macro-phenomena of any importance.

Thirdly, finitism creates logical problems with regard to *concept identity*. If a concept has neither a stable intension nor a stable extension, but is subject to constant change in the situations of use, how can a claim that the same concept can be used in different situations be justified? And how could we claim that the concept refers to the same phenomenon in different situations?

I would nevertheless say that finitism has in a fertile way made us aware that concept use and concept forming might be more closely related to the contingent features of use situations than to formal definitional criteria. And finitism may prove fertile for the creation of theories which cut across different domains of knowledge. But I think the question of whether it has really been proved that a general sociology of knowledge is possible, still remains open.

6. Empirical assessment – conclusion

As far as I know, nobody has ever attempted to shape finitism into a testable theory, and nobody has consequently tried to test it. But it is a fair assumption that studies undertaken in the Piaget tradition, focusing on children's acquisition of central thought categories like 'space', 'time' and 'causality', would be of considerable relevance for assessing the theory's merits.

At least one consequence of finitism is opposed to Piaget's view of learning. Piaget claimed that autolearning is more efficient than instruction and social sanctioning (Braided 1978). This view does not, however, seem to be justified in the light of attempts to test the consequences of Piaget's theory for learning and for the development of intelligence. If an overall assessment can be made on the basis of the known experiments, the conclusion is that instruction and social sanctioning are more efficient than autolearning (Braided 1978).

It is also a reasonable assumption that studies made by the ethnomethodologist Harold Garfinkel and his students relating to the way in which references are established in the social world, would be relevant for the testing of finitism (Collins 1985, pp. 212 ff.). Studies in the history of science of the creation of concepts and classification systems in the research process could also provide highly relevant data.

7. Literature

Barnes, B. 1982: *T.S. Kuhn and Social Science*, The Macmillan Press.

Barnes, B. 1973: *Sociological Theory and Scientific Knowledge*, Routledge and Kegan Paul.

Barnes, B.1977: *Interests and the Growth of Knowledge*, Routledge and Kegan Paul.

Barnes, B. 1984: "On the Conventional Component in Knowledge and Cognition", in Stehr and Meja (eds.): *Society and Knowledge*, pp. 158-206.

Barnes, B. 1985: "Thomas Kuhn", in Skinner (ed.): *The Return of the Grand Theories in the Human Sciences*, pp. 83-100.

Barnes, B. 1985: *About Science*, Blackwell, Oxford.

Barnes, B. and S. Shapin (eds.) 1979: *Natural Order*, Sage Publications.

Barnes, B. and D. Edge (eds.) 1982: *Science in Context*, Open University Press.

Barnes, B. and D. Bloor 1982: "Relativism, Rationalism and the Sociology of Knowledge", in M. Hollis and S. Lukes (eds.): *Rationality and Relativism*, Blackwell, pp. 21-47.

Barnes, B., D. Bloor and J. Henry 1996: *Scientific Knowledge – A Sociological Analysis*, The Athlone Press.

Bloor, D. 1976: *Knowledge and Social Imagery*, Routledge and Kegan Paul.

Bloor, D. 1983: *Wittgenstein. A Social Theory of Knowledge*, The Macmillan Press.

Bloor, D. "Wittgenstein and Mannheim on the Sociology of Knowledge", in *Studies in History and Philosophy of Science* 4, pp. 173-91.

Bloor, D. 1984: "Durkheim and Mauss Revisited", in Stehr and Meja (eds.): *Society and Knowledge*, pp. 51-75.

Braided, C. 1987: *Piaget's Theory of Intelligence*, University of Chicago Press, Chicago.

Collins, R. 1985: *Three Sociological Traditions*, Oxford University Press.

Coser, L. 1968: "Sociology of Knowledge" in *The International Encyclopaedia of Social Sciences*, vol. 8, pp. 428-35.

Føllesdal, D., J. Elster, L. Walløe 1986: *Argumentasjonsteori, språk og vitenskapsfilosofi*, (Theory of arguments, language and philosophy of science) Universitetsforlaget, Oslo.

Hesse, M. 1974: *The Structure of Scientific Inference*, The Macmillan Press.

Hollis, M. 1982: "The Social Destruction of Reality", in M. Hollis and S. Lukes (eds.) *Rationality and Relativism*, Blackwell, Oxford pp. 67-86.

Lakatos, I. 1971: "History of Science and its Rational Reconstructions", in R. Buck and R. Cohen (eds.): *Boston Studies in Philosophy of Science*, vol. 8, Reidl Dordrecht.

Mannheim, K. 1936: *Ideology and Utopia*, Routledge and Kegan Paul, London.

Skinner, Q. 1985: *The Return to Grand Theories in the Human Sciences*, Cambridge University Press, Cambridge.

Stehr, N. and V. Meja 1984: *Society and Knowledge*, Transaction Books, New York.

Waismann, F. 1984: "Verifiability", in G.H.R. Parkinson (ed.): *The Theory of Meaning*, Oxford University Press, Oxford.

5
The Hysteresis Thesis
Path Dependence in Economic and Social Systems

GAUTE TORSVIK

1. Original quotation

I have found it convenient and even necessary to employ a new term, which merely designates this peculiar action without implying any theory as to its cause. *Hysteresis* occurs when there are two qualities *M* and *N* such that a cyclic variation in *N* causes a cyclic variation in *M* [and] the changes in *M* lag behind those of *N*. The value of *M* at any point of time is not only dependent on the actual value of *N*, but on all the preceding changes in *N*. (Ewing 1885, quoted after Cross 1993 pp. 54-55).

2. Brief explanation

The word "hysteresis" is of Greek origin. It means "what comes afterwards". In economic theory we use hysteresis to say that something "still remains". Hysteresis in an economic system signifies that the effect of an impulse remains in the system, even though the impulse disappears. How the system responds to new impulses depends on earlier impulses: the evolution of the system depends on the history of the phenomenon, the evolution is path dependent.

3. Background

It was the physicist James Alfred Ewing (1855-1935) who introduced the concept in an 1885 article on electromagnetism. If a wire is wound around an iron bar and an electric current is sent through the wire, the iron becomes magnetic. Ewing noted that even if the current is interrupted, some of the magnetism remains in the iron. The iron is stimulated by magnetizing cycles (electricity) and brought into a certain state (becomes magnetic), and this state is preserved even though the factor responsible for the state (electricity) is cut off. Ewing dubbed this phenomenon hysteresis.

For some time Ewing was engaged at the University of Tokyo. Later he obtained a professorship in mechanics at Cambridge. He wrote extensively on the magnetic properties of various metals. In addition to his discovery, or formulation, of the hysteresis thesis he is renowned for his construction of instruments for gauging the changes in properties of metals (elasticity, magnetism) brought about by different factors.

4. Formalization – precise definition

When studying physical and social systems, we are often interested in the interaction of different variables. Knowing the value of a set of variables, X, we want to characterize or predict the value of a set of variables, Y. In social or economic systems, Y will typically represent individual actions (or some aggregate measure of individual actions), and X the outer framework conditions – such as prices, technological conditions, etc. – i.e. all the relevant variables that influence these actions. If we study electromagnetism, the impulses (X) are electric power and magnetism is the response (Y).

A good characterization of Y renders necessary the inclusion of as many as possible of the relevant impulses X, and a precise specification of the connection between X an Y. We can represent this link as a function F, and write[1] $Y = F(X)$

If, to characterize $Y(t)$ or predict $Y(t+1)$, it is necessary to refer to what happened in earlier periods, then the system is marked by hysteresis. Hysteresis implies that it is not sufficient to know today's circumstances to predict the evolution of the system, we must in addition know the history of the system.

If a sequence $X(1)$, $X(2)$, $X(3)$ of variables, where $X(1) = X(3) \neq$

---

1   This connection between X and Y will not necessarily be a "one to one" relation. It is possible that the most precise statement we are able to make regarding y (knowing the x value), is that y is located within an interval defined by a lower and an upper limit. In that case F is a correspondence. In most situations there will be "noise" in the system. It is then unreasonable to expect an unambiguous connection between X and Y.

$X(2)$, produce a reaction $Y(1)$, $Y(2)$, $Y(3)$, where $Y(1) \neq Y(3)$, this indicates that hysteresis is involved in the phenomenon. The impulses, which are identical at times 1 and 3, give rise to different reactions because the system has a different history at the two points in time ($X(2)$ is located between them). The system has "memory", i.e. values located at earlier times influence the way in which the system develops. This is how professor Ewing described the magnetization of iron.

5. Generality and testability. Critique.

i) Hysteresis is ontologically impossible

i) Hysteresis is ontologically impossibleIs it *necessary* to refer to the past to be able to say anything about the future development of a system? Note the way I have formulated this question: I am not asking whether or not it is useful to study history. It goes without saying that it is, if we wish to understand the past. The question is whether we must refer to what has happened before, in order to characterize what is happening now, or to predict what will happen tomorrow. Viewed from a sufficiently abstract point of view the answer is no.

A person who claims than he/she *must* refer to what has happened before to characterize what is happening now, implies that history works through something that is not present today. If history had left traces in variables that are present today, then these variables could represent history. In other words, it is only when history has not left traces in any variables that are present today, that we *must* refer to the past in order to explain and predict what is happening now.[2] But such traceless influence is impossible. It is magic. A historic event h cannot influence the evolution of anything today without h having left traces in variables that are present today. Therefore, hysteresis is ontologically impossible. Leibniz saw this and made the following statement:

> For insofar as the impulses of the past no longer exist in the present, they cannot achieve anything without having left behind some or other effect which endures and operates in the present. As far as I can see, anyone who claims anything to the contrary renounces all explanations of specific phenomena, for if what is remote in time and space can operate here and now without any link, we would be equally justified in explaining anything in terms of anything else. (Leibniz 1875-90, quotation in Elster 1976, p. 372).

---

2   Variables that absorb historical impulses are called *state variables*.

Let us go back to Ewing. Imagine that two pieces of iron are subjected to equally strong impulses, but when we measure the degree of magnetism, there is a difference between the two pieces. How can we explain this difference? There are two alternatives. We could explain the fact in the following way. "The two pieces of iron reacted differently to the same impulse, because the pieces of iron were exposed to different electric impulses at an earlier stage". This alternative is a *hysteresis* explanation. It is an explanation that emphasizes the fact that the two pieces have different histories of subjection to electric current. But, of course, since hysteresis is ontologically impossible, there must be an alternative way to explain the phenomenon. If it is differences in the history of subjection to electric current that explains why the pieces of iron react differently to new impulses, then these impulses must have left traces in the iron. The second explanation takes the condition of the iron as its point of departure. We measure the amount of magnetism absorbed by the iron, and incorporate this variable into our explanation. We would then say: "the two pieces of iron reacted differently to the same impulse, because the magnetic condition of the two pieces was not equal when our experiment started."

Now then, suppose we want to predict how a system will evolve in the near future. We are at time point t and want to predict the value of $Y(t+1)$. To make an informed prediction we assess the value of all relevant impulses $X(t)$, and we specify how, to the best of our knowledge, these variables are linked together. Our prediction is then given by $Y(t+1) = F(X(t))$. Suppose our forecast turns out to be bad and that we can improve it by including events that happened in the past. If this is the case, it must be because the preceding history has left traces in variables that are not incorporated in the impulses vector (X). This, then, implies that we left crucial variables out of our original formulation. Y is not a function of the impulses X alone, but is also influenced by a state defined by a set of variables Z. The state variables are marked by the preceding history (i.e. by earlier values of X an Y). Hence, when we wish to represent a system that is influenced by its history, we can do so in two ways: (i) we can give a hysteresis explanation which attaches importance directly to the past (variables dated in the past are included in the model), or (ii) we can extend the spatial dimension of the model. By including more state variables we are able to "dispose of history".

ii) But hysteresis can be epistemologically useful

What formulation should we choose? The scientific ideal is minimalism; only necessary factors should be included, what is superfluous is superfluous and is to be left out. And as history cannot influence a system in any other way than by operating through state variables, it is always, at least in principle, possible to omit historical events from the explanation. If our object is to characterize and predict the evolution of a system, a formulation with state variables will do. But often we want to do something more. We often want to understand, explain and attach a meaning to what we are observing. If we have this kind of epistemological and hermeneutic ambition, it may be of greater use to point to historical events than to state variables.

First, it can be difficult or even practically impossible to measure the traces left by historical events in the conditions that exist today. In other words, it is difficult to gauge the value of different condition variables. And even with "good microscopes" at our disposal, we may find it difficult to understand the connection between impulses, condition and response. Let $Y(t)$ represent the measure of the aggression level in the behavior of a person at time t. The behavior is a function of different impulses (frustration, pain etc.) represented by $X(t)$ and of chemical and genetic condition variables, $Z(t)$. We know, e.g. that a low level of serotonin (a chemical substance) in the hypothalamus (a part of the brain) will lead to more aggressive behavior. Today's serotonin level depends on the history of the person in question. Individuals are born with different serotonin levels. Moreover, diet and other circumstances in the past, e.g. the use of medicines, may influence the quantity of serotonin released in the hypothalamus. I mention this to show that even though it is in principle possible to construct a model that explains aggressive behavior in terms of impulses and chemical (and perhaps genetic) state variables, it does not make much sense to do so.[3]

Whether or not it is possible for social scientists to reduce a social system to a set of state variables and impulses, raises a more fundamental philosophical question. As human beings we interpret our environment as well as ourselves, we search for meaning in what we see and do. One could argue that it is impossible to give a good representation of a social system without referring to variables and mechanisms

---

3   Methodical "behaviorism" (in its most orthodox form) does not admit the use in psychological theories of inner physical or biological (and at any rate not mental) conditions as explication variables. If the preceding history has left "chemical traces", behavior today is to be explained in the light of the events that left the traces.

to which individuals themselves attach importance when interpreting what is going on around them. Taylor (1989) calls this the best account principle.

The main reason for referring to historical events rather than to condition variables is, in my view, that an account of this kind makes evident the need for planning. Hysteresis renders possible the understanding of how our options today influence what we can and will do in the future. To be able to make a meaningful statement concerning future effects on a system in which we stimulate or impede an impulse today, we have to understand the underlying mechanisms operating between the variables. An explanation that focuses on state variables may conceal the connection between what we are doing now and what we shall be able to do in future. To illustrate the point I have drawn the electromagnetic loop Erwin referred to in his article:

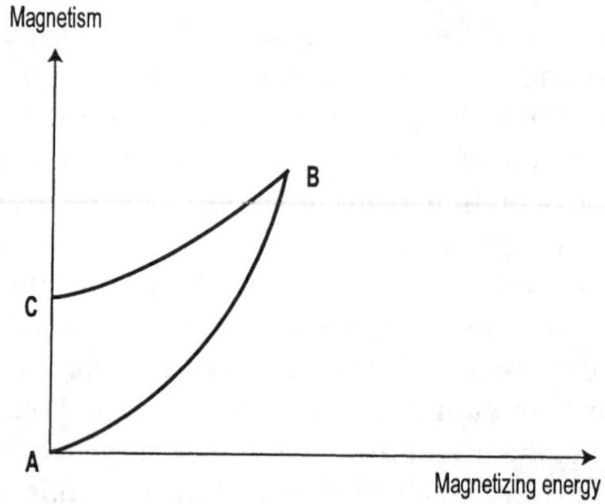

Figure 1. We start at point A. If positive and magnetizing energy is being induced into the iron, the iron becomes magnetic, as shown in point B. The magnetism does not disappear through removal of the magnetizing energy, the iron retains its magnetism equal to point C. This shows that magnetism is a function of the magnetizing energy presently influencing the iron, as well as of the preceding history of the iron.

6. Empirical assessment – conclusion

The basic idea that the outcome of economic interaction is "path dependent" is old in economics. But the hysteresis concept is relative new. The first to talk about hysteresis in economic analysis was Georgescu-Roegen in the 1960s. Recently, analysts have pointed out that this phenomenon is relevant in many economic markets.

i) Hysteresis in capital markets:
the absorbing effect of irreversible investments

To be able to produce goods and services we have to invest in machines and other production equipment. These investments will, to a greater or lesser extent, be irreversible. It is for example difficult to sell the machines (at a good price) if production is shut down. Irreversible investments cause today's production to be a function not only of today's prices, but also of prices and decisions in the past. If the production equipment has already been set up, it is reasonable to expect that a slight rise in the price of an article will result in increased production. But if investments have not already been made, it is wholly possible that investments would not be profitable, even after the price increase. Thus, the reaction (in the form of production) to an impulse (price increase) is dependent on the price of the article in question in the past (if production is already running).

It is possible to be a little more precise (it is in fact possible be much more precise, but that would require considerably more space). Let us assume that all other prices (including that of the production equipment) are constant, while $p(t)$ is the price of the goods produced. The price has two interesting critical values. A lower limit is fixed at a price level $\underline{p}$, which is so low that it does not cover the variable costs. An upper limit is fixed at $\bar{p}$, a price level high enough to cover both variable and fixed costs. For $\underline{p} < p(t) < \bar{p}$ production in period t will depend on the former price level (whether production equipment has been installed or not). If all $p(1)$, $p(2)$ Y $p(t\text{-}1)$ are lower than p, $p(t)$ will result in production. If $p(1)$, $p(2)$ Y $p(t\text{-}1)$ are lower than p, no production will result from $p(t)$. This account is rather imprecise, but I think the point is clear.

Alfred Marshall was the first to argue that irreversible investments could produce hysteresis effects (though he didn't use that term). Since then the theory has been further developed, and at present we know a good deal about the behavior of rational investors when their projects are irreversible and profits (price developments) are uncertain (see e.g. Dixit 1992).

ii) Hysteresis in the labor market: the absorbing effect of unemployment

The number of workers wanted by an enterprise at a certain point in time depends on several factors. Needless to say, the demand for the goods produced by the enterprise is a factor of central importance, as is the wage level. But in addition the number of personnel employed in the past can be decisive for the number a firm wants to employ now. Imagine an enterprise with 20 permanent employees at the beginning of the period t. Considering demand and the foreseen wage level during the period, the firm's board of directors opts to continue with the same number of personnel, i.e. it employs 20 people in period t. Let us then suppose an alternative situation: wage level and demand remain as above, with the sole difference that up until period t the enterprise has had a smaller number of employees, e.g. 18 or 19 workers. Would it then take on new workers, bringing the number of personnel employed up to 20 in period t? This is by no means sure. For various reasons the number of persons employed before entering a period will influence the number of persons employed in that same period. It follows that we cannot explain employment in a period solely by reference to frame conditions (wage level, demand) as they are at present. The consequences is that brief cyclical fluctuations in the market can lead to permanent unemployment. Those laid off when demand is low are not taken on again even though demand returns to normal levels. This shows that the labor market is affected by hysteresis.

There are several reasons to explain how the labor market is affected by hysteresis. One hypothesis (known as the insider-outsider theory) claims that trade unions are concerned exclusively with those employed. Therefore, after a slump those who have been laid off will no longer be of interest to the trade unions. When demand swings back to normal levels, trade unions will push up salary demands and make it difficult for the unemployed to get new jobs.

Another argument is that a person's work knowledge deteriorates if not used. Those who lose their jobs due to cyclical swings in the economy remain outside the labor market due to a decline in their productivity. (If this is true, it is important that public authorities should use economic policy to smooth out economic cycles so as to avoid the hysteresis loss).

A third reason for hysteresis is the quality difference of manpower (people's productivity levels are different), but that each enterprise has private information regarding the productivity of a worker. Thus, those laid off in bad times have been labeled as "low quality" and will face difficulties attempting to reintegrate themselves into the labor market.

iii) Hysteresis in consumption behavior:
the absorbing effect of earlier consumption

This is the idea that present consumption is influenced by consumption in the past. Narcotics which cause physical drug withdrawal symptoms whenever an attempt is made to reduce consumption, offer perhaps the most obvious instance of how present consumption can influence future consumption. A high consumption of such "goods" will change future preferences. But physical abstinence syndromes are not the only cause of endogenous preferences. Other psychological and social factors can produce similar abstinence effects. There is a great deal of economic literature on this subject (see e.g. Elster 1976).

iv) Hysteresis and co-ordination problems:
the absorbing effect of the mass

The notion *glia* is a derivative from a Greek word meaning glue. Researchers originally fancied glia to be some kind of glue or putty keeping the neurons together. Although this idea is now obsolete, the notion is still employed. (Kalat 1995, p. 267).

The quotation is illustrative of an interesting phenomenon. It highlights a situation where an alternative which was once functional is also chosen later, even though there are now good reasons to opt for another solution. The reason why the "status quo" has acquired such weight is that so many have adapted to it. A well-known instance of this phenomenon is the arrangement of the typewriter keys. The arrangement on my typewriter was introduced so as to minimize the risk that the arms of the old mechanical typewriters would jam. My typewriter is electric, as are almost all typewriters today. There is therefore no risk of mechanical jamming. Nevertheless, the letters are arranged as before, even though there exist better alternatives now that the mechanical limitations can be disregarded. The reason why the old system is preserved is probably that it "costs much" to alter the keyboard system. Many are accustomed to it, and producers find it difficult to co-ordinate the introduction of a new alternative. (The phenomenon is known as "the economics of QWERTY", referring to the first five letters on the typewriter. See e.g. David 1985).

Many economic systems are marked by history because at some time or other a critical mass of individuals co-ordinated their activities in some particular way. Such systems have four central distinguishing features: (a) there were, originally, several possible stable situations (equilibria), (b) the question of which solution is realized (which equilibrium is chosen) is frequently decided by casual and time-dependent factors, (c) the original equilibrium persists, even though the external environment changes, rendering another alternative better (if the system were not marked by history, another alternative would have been chosen), (d) it shows that economic systems may succumb to routines, and that the system, after some time, will be unsatisfactorily adapted to the external environment.

v) Hysteresis in other disicplines of the social sciences

The examples given above show that modern economic theory is not ahistorical.[4] But the theory thoroughly disregards a potential source of hysteresis stressed in most other branches of social science. Economic theory pays no attention to the fact that history may change the forces which moderate between the variables of a system. In principle, former X an Y values may disturb the form of the function in which the variables are combined; thus F is dependent on history.

Elemental forces are time homogenous, independent of time and place. The impact of the force of gravity on a stone remains the same, regardless of what has happened to the stone in the past or where it has previously been. Newton's laws concerning movement and thermodynamic forces are equally universal. Economic theory "copies" physics by basing itself on the assumption that there exists an ordered relationship between impulses and reactions in economic (or social) systems. The ordered structure is the result of peoples' acting instrumentally to promote their own interests, at all times, and in all situations.

Many others who study human behavior and social phenomena stress the fact that the forces that moderate between the "variables" can change in the course of time. Here is an example. Suppose someone asks: "Why did he react so aggressively to such a minor impulse?" A possible answer could be: "Because he recently had a traumatic experience. Therefore, he is not able to handle the situation rationally". This answer emphasizes the fact that the forces that link $X(3)$ and $Y(3)$ depend on $X(2)$. Freud liked this kind of explanation. He held the view that "the algorithm (rules) we use when we act, depends on our childhood history".

Another instance: Anne has invited Kari to dinner. Kari watches Anne cut the leg of lamb in two before putting it into the oven. She

---

4　In addition to the hysteresis phenomena dealt with above (there are many more), there exist important institutional theories emphasizing how long-standing structures leave their mark on economic systems (North 1990).

asks why she cuts it into two pieces. After a moment of reflection Anne says: "Because it's the way my mother did it". Her mother lives on the next floor, and Kari goes up and asks her. After some reflection, Anne's mother answers: "Because my mother did it like that". On the next floor grandma's answer is: "Because I have an old oven which is too small for a whole leg of lamb". Now, what does the example show us? At one time the connection between X (kitchen oven) and Y (the preparation of the leg of lamb for the oven) was a result of instrumental problem solving (how can I roast the leg of lamb under the limitations imposed by the oven?). At a later stage the X-Y connection is governed by imitation (how do "the others" roast legs of lamb?).

We have dealt with three alternative "forces" that can be effective between impulses and reactions: we have dealt with three Fs:

F_1: Y is instrumentally chosen to maximize the interests (preferences) of the person making the choice. The connection between X and Y results from a process where existing possibilities are ascertained, of which the most advantageous is then chosen.

F_2: Y is chosen on the basis of routine. Action conforming to rules as governed by what is deemed normal and decent in the situation of the person who makes the choice.

F_3: Y is chosen in a state of excitement, in virtue of a kind of stimulus-response connection which by-passes the field of consciousness.

These examples indicate that it might be useful to refer to history since circumstances in the past can alter the forces that link the dependent and the independent variables. Traumatic events can trigger off affective action (the algorithm shifts from F_1 to F_3). An institutionalization of interaction with clearly defined roles and positions can result in routine action (the algorithm shifts from F_1 to F_2). As I understand it, there is an institutional perspective in the field of organization theory which claims that behavior governed by routine and rules is the central distinguishing mark of organized interaction.

7. Literature

Cross, R 1993: "On the foundation of hysteresis in economic systems", *Economics and Philosophy*, pp. 53-74.

David, P. 1985: "Clio and the economics of QWERTY", *American Economic Review*, PAP, 75, pp. 333-37.

Dixit, A. 1992: "Investment and hysteresis", *Journal of Economic Perspectives*, pp. 107-37.

Elster, J. 19076: "A note on Hysteresis in Social Sciences", *Synthese*, pp. 371-91.

Ewing, J. A. 1985: "Experimental researches in magnetism", *Philosophical Transactions of the Royal Society in London*, pp. 399-402.

Georgescu-Roegen, 1967: *Analytical Economics*, Cambridge, Massachusetts.

Kalat, J. 1995: *Biological Psychology*, Brooks & Cole (5th ed.).

Leibniz, G. W. L. 1875-1890: *Die philosophischen Schriften* (ed. Gerhardt), Berlin.

Marshall, A. 1918: *Principles of Economics*, Macmillan.

North, D. 1990: *Institutions, Institutional Change and Economic Performance*, Cambridge University Press.

Taylor, C. 1989: *The Sources of the Self*, Harvard University Press.

6
The Self-Fulfilling Prophecy

JAN ERIK KARLSEN

1. Original quotation

If men define situations as real, they are real in their consequences (Merton 1948, p. 193; Thomas and Swaine 1928, p. 572).

2. Brief explanation

In fact, this law has two names: *the self-fulfilling prophecy* and the *Thomas theorem*. The first is related to Robert King Merton's description of how social structures trigger patterns of thought and action which subsequently reinforce themselves. The second is related to the grand old man of American sociology, William Isaac Thomas (1863-1947) who wrote (1923):

> 'Facts' do not have a uniform existence apart from the persons who observe and interpret them. Rather, the 'real' facts are the ways in which different people come into and define situations.

In sociology it was Merton who introduced this idea as the Thomas theorem, whereas Merton himself formulated it as the self-fulfilling prophecy law. This is in effect a creative extension of Thomas' work on "situation definition", which in turn provided the basis for Merton's theory concerning reference group behavior. (Coser 1977, p. 546). Even so, I prefer to regard Merton as the sociological originator of the self-fulfilling prophecy concept, and of the more widespread understanding of the logic it describes.

3. Background

Robert King Merton (born 1920) is one of America's most prominent sociologists. He studied at Harvard University under the outstanding theoreticians Talcott Parsons (1902-1979) and Pitrim Sorokin (1889-1969). Merton is regarded as Parson's most prominent successor. After taking his doctorate in 1936 he pursued his academic career at Tulane and later at Columbia University. As an adherent of Durkheim's functionalism Merton strongly stressed the importance of empirical research in sociology.

Merton's strength was research on social institutions during their developmental phase, bureaucratic structures and personality traits. He popularized the sociology of deviance by developing concepts of logical categories such as conformism, innovation and ritualism, and non-logical categories like the thirst for rebellion. He refuted the view that man is unpredictable, and that a new social order creates social robots. Thus, in a time when analyses focusing on the individual became more comprehensive and popular, he introduced a conservative element into sociological research.

Merton himself in no way claims to have "invented" or discovered the self-fulfilling prophecy. On the contrary, he maintains that this theorem has been presented numerous times, also before W.I. Thomas. Among others, he points to Bishop Bossuet's defense of Catholic orthodoxy in the 18th century, Mandeville's 19th century allegories which focused on the contradictions of human society, Marx's 19th century revisions of the Hegelian theory of historic change, Freud and his theories of wishful thinking, and W.I. Sumner as a kind of middle-class Marx for modern times. In Merton's view they were all concerned with the crux of the Thomas theorem. Moreover, Georg H. Mead (1936, p. 29), who moved in sociology circles at the University of Chicago at the same time as Thomas (and was born in the same year), has formulated a more restrictive version of the same theorem: "If a thing is not recognized as true, then it does not function as true in the community" (see Merton, 1967, p. 19). Merton's own contribution is a presentation of this theorem in clearer sociological language, the provision of a catchy name and the popularization of the description.

Merton has an extensive production behind him, which includes the important works *Social Theory and Social Structure* (1949) and *On the Shoulders of the Giants* (1965), as well as several other works such as *Mass Persuasion* (1946), *Continuities in Social Research* (1950), *The Student Physician* (1957), *Sociology Today: Problems and Prospects*

(1959) and *Contemporary Social Problems* (1961) in collaboration with Robert Nisbet.

4. Formalization – precise definition

It is possible to present the logical structure of the self-fulfilling prophecy in a way similar to that found in functional explanation models (Stinchcombe 1968). The general pattern expressed in this model is this: some social structures create action and thought patterns which reinforce themselves and their social structures. If these patterns are opposed to reality, they can give rise to antagonisms among the members of a society. A vicious circle of this kind may be broken via the introduction of measures suited to change the structure of society itself (Østerberg 1978, p. 152).

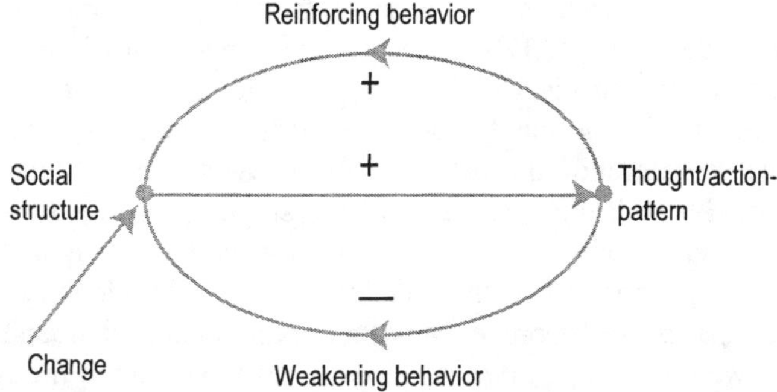

Fig. 1 The sociological circle: the self-fulfilling prophecy

Merton's term "self-fulfilling-prophecy" has just such a logical, functional form. Here, change is directly linked to social structure and not, as it usually is, to the homeostasis variable, i.e. the thought and action pattern. A prediction calls forth behavior which in turn results in the fulfilment of the prediction, which would not have occurred, had the prediction not been made. The self-fulfilling prophecy is therefore an active and necessary cause for the fulfilment of the prediction. It is at the same time "false", being based on an erroneous (i.e. subjective) assessment of the original situation.

The model demonstrates that the way of thinking ought to include reinforcing as well as weakening behavior. Merton's own empirical illustrations include e.g. the behavior of bank customers at the height of the 1932 crisis. The bank customers hear a rumor (*the thought pattern*) that their bank is insolvent (*assumed social structure*), thereupon hurrying to the bank to withdraw their deposits (*behavior*), and very soon the bank has no more cash available (*real social structure*). By means of this self-*reinforcing* behavior the bank becomes insolvent, even though it was not so initially. This behavior was also observed among Norwegian bank customers in October 1991, when the rumor spread that Kredittkassen had gone bankrupt. In the course of one single day depositors withdrew 1400 million kroner, which, although far too little to make the bank insolvent, was sufficient to send the worried directors running to the media to assure depositors that their money was safe. The same reaction occurred in several Asian countries after the financial crash in the autumn of 1997, where depositors stormed the banks to secure their savings. Another example from our domestic context can be found in connection with the debates on EU entry of 1972 and 1994. On both occasions solid arguments were put forward by the employers' federation (NAF/NHO) to show the need for EU membership to guarantee the survival of Norwegian trade and industry. If Norwegian industry had adopted a policy of crisis-maximization following the negative referendum result, this could have become a self-fulfilling prophecy. Instead, the perception of the situation changed and consequently behavior as well, so that the result was if anything a self-*denying* prophecy: economic activity is flourishing, and trade with the EU is increasing as never before, even without Norwegian membership.

Thus we could depict two developmental trends, as in the four-field table below:

		The situation as experienced	
		(correct) +	— (incorrect)
Correct knowledge	(right) +	Self-reinforcing (increasingly correct experience)	
of circumstances	(wrong) —		Self-weakening (distorted picture of the situation)

The self-reinforcing behavior implies the assumption of an increasingly "correct" perception of the circumstances. The self-weakening behavior, on the other hand, creates an increasingly distorted image of the actual situation, i.e. it widens the gap between the original assertion and expectations. We could illustrate this as follows:

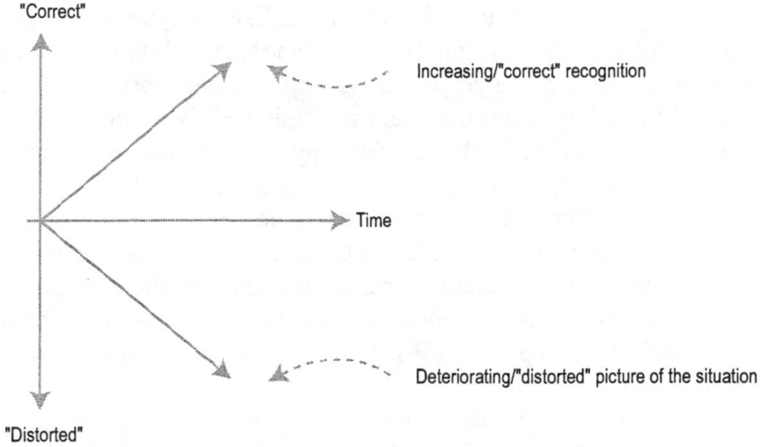

Correct information and the correct perception of circumstances will lead to self-reinforcing cognition. The more correct information is available, the more the situation is confirmed. And inversely: the faultier the information, the faultier the perception of the situation, which in time results in a distorted picture of reality.

The *definition of the situation* is thus a key factor in initiating the self-fulfilling process which results from the prophecy. The point is that most people construct their own social reality and act on the basis of what the situation means for them, rather than base their behavior on genuinely objective features. If a student is convinced that the most important thing in the world is to pass an examination, then this conviction will define his situation and constitute his description of reality. He therefore goes to extreme lengths to achieve his aims. A self-fulfilling prophecy occurs when this student misjudges the situation: he can be worried at the thought of failing, which again makes him so nervous that he cannot cope with his syllabus. Hence he fails, and the prophecy is fulfilled. Likewise, people may define certain groups of people or races as inferior, or certain cultural attitudes and behavior as anomalous, quite independently of the objective situation.

In Merton's words (1957, pp. 421-436) "confident error generates its own spurious confirmation", which is in fact a description of the logic of many everyday episodes, our reality being subjective and socially structured. People create their own reality through common interaction and communication, the consequences becoming real if the situation is believed to be real (Landis 1974, p. 19).

Jon Elster (1978, p. 111) discusses a group of phenomena which he terms "counterfinality", and which are not unlike the type of prophecy we have called self-denying. These include the unintended consequences that arise when a person in a group acts in accordance with a relationship to other group members which is merely assumed. When this assumption is generalized, the opposite of the intention is achieved. Merton uses Herbert Simon's description of "bandwagon" and "underdog" effects. These reveal that in certain circumstances it is possible for a person predicting the result of an election to take into account the effect of the prediction, the result being that the opinion poll is confirmed by the actual result. However, in his formalization of Simon's model (1978, pp. 165-166), Elster regards these conditions as rather implausible.

From the preceding figures it is evident that, strictly speaking, the self-fulfilling prophecy should not be regarded as a "law", but rather as a structure. In fact, the definition of the situation determines whether the behavior initiated is reinforcing or weakening, and consequently whether the prophecy will be maintained *or undermined*. Thus the model is not determined, but dependent on external factors, including social attitudes such as personal resolution, fatalism, the abundance or scarcity of information, and so on.

5. Generality and testability. Critique

It may seem as if the self-fulfilling prophecy gets stuck in the total subjectivism of the situation description. The individual's actions are governed by his/her interpretation of the situation. But social situations are also associated with objective facts. In his vigorous style Stinchcombe (1975, pp. 15-16) links the definition of the subjective situation with the objective basis that was emphasized by Marx:

> People define situations, but do not define them precisely as they want.

Merton suggests a critical revision of the Thomas theorem along the same lines:

> And if people do *not* define real situations as real, they are nevertheless real in their consequences. (Merton, 1976, p. 22).

It is the things you don't know about, or don't notice that are really damaging to you, since you are unable to guard against them. Before HIV/AIDS had been socially defined, nobody knew how to protect themselves against infection. The population explosion in Africa has obvious objective consequences for nutrition and employment, even though the reasons for this do not appear to have been socially understood in the Africans' everyday life.

Scarce attention has been paid to the role of the "prophet", i.e. the rumormonger. Like the original religious prophets who proclaimed the will of the gods to mankind, the modern version must be some sort of authorized spokesman, a visionary, an author of opinions, a forecaster or fortuneteller, who conveys a message which is considered significant. The prophet's message must be taken seriously. More generally, we can therefore pose the question of how strong the prediction or rumor has to be for it to trigger some kind of collective behavior which results in a new social structure. Evidently, the prophecy cannot be a statement about the future which merely presents a scenario or similar. The message must contain something unexpected and at the same time create a conviction that it is possible to influence the impending crisis by means of action in the present. The advantage of immediate action must be obvious and individual, as must also the disadvantage of being the last to react. These individual thought and behavior patterns have consequences on the collective level, all of which could in fact have been avoided by all concerned, had their definition of the situation been correct. It is perhaps somewhat doubtful whether or not such outcomes are reversible (Karlsen 1990, p. 270).

What interested Merton was that the self-fulfilling prophecy which "transforms fear into reality is effective only in the absence of conscious institutional control" (Østerberg 1978, p.171). The sociological vicious circle exemplified by the bank collapse can therefore be broken by means of a new definition of the situation. Well-considered institutional changes, e.g. guarantee arrangements which secure banks against collapse, can change the basis for behavior, thus mitigating the withdrawal panic which was so threatening. In the functional model presented above this is illustrated by means of a variable that influences the real social structure, i.e. the bank's solvency.

In organization theory Pondy and Mitroff (1979, p.28) have formulated an interesting pendant to the self-fulfilling prophecy: "What we teach leaders today brings forth the phenomena which we shall be able to study in the future". Sociological explanatory models focus on what is artificial and created (as opposed to what is natural and undeveloped), i.e. the social structures and processes resulting from human behavior. In explaining the artificial, it is assumed that the phenomenon is the cause and the theory is the effect. In this perspective, the social sciences presuppose an objective reality independent of the theories: truth exists and is waiting to be discovered. However, symbolic perspectives suggest the opposite: reality is a result of our theories and truth a product of our thinking. As pointed out by Stinchcombe (1975), neither man nor social systems permit limitless modification. But leaders can of course be schooled to believe in theories of leadership and organization, such that they can form social circumstances accordingly. In which case the essential distinction between valid forecasts and self-fulfilling prophecies will also vanish. Our environment is influenced by the theories and methods available for understanding it, such that any perspective can in fact become self-fulfilling (Bolman and Deal 1991, p. 277).

Karl Popper (1902-95) has introduced a similar theorem, which he called the "Oedipus effect" (1945, p. 22, 1957, pp.13 and 15-16). This describes the influence of a theory, expectation or prediction on the event it describes or predicts: "It will be remembered that the causal strain leading to Oedipus' patricide was started by the oracle's prediction of this event" (Popper 1963, p. 38). More generally this is termed the "auto-reference" problem: people who answer questionnaires try to guess at the researchers' expectations, which they endeavor either to fulfil or disappoint. This does not imply the impossibility of sociological predictions, but the assumption that they cannot independently serve to confirm or falsify a theory, since the results of the prediction are not independent of the theory. The possibility for independent testing and control of the theory's validity, as required by scientific method, is lacking (Skagestad 1980). It is this that Popper refers to as the Oedipus effect.

6. Empirical assessment – conclusion

The self-fulfilling prophecy is hardly suitable for testing by means of large-scale surveys. It is rather a matter for sociological case studies. An example of such a sociological situation might be people who believe in astrology and who modify their behavior to ensure that the predictions come true. Examples from the sociology of deviance are perhaps of greater interest. Some researchers assume that a person does not become a deviant before being labeled as such by people with social authority. Labeling theory appears to have incorporated the concept of the self-fulfilling prophecy. The main point is that this concept describes what happens when widespread opinion concerning certain people – even if these opinions are mistaken – creates a social environment which limits behavioral options, such that the actual behavior confirms these opinions. A self-fulfilling prophecy is created when people are generally treated as deviants, even if it is known that their behavior is deviant in only one respect. This phenomenon has been well described by, among others, Becker (1963, p. 34), Erikson (1966, p. 17) and Payne (1973, pp. 39-40). According to Merton, this applies to a wide group of sociological phenomena, which he describes as "the reflected self-image adopted by a deviant ensuing in deviant behavior" (1967, p. 20). Call a man a thief and he will steal, as the saying goes.

Likewise, the behavior of pupils can reflect the expectations of their teachers, which in turn produces school losers. If it is assumed that a pupil has a negative attitude to learning or that intellectual capacity and motivation are lacking, the teacher adjusts his attitude to expect only modest achievements and ambitions. In many experimental studies there is a tendency to regard theories as "proven", even where different theories make conflicting predictions. This is known as "experimenter bias", a conscious or unconscious attitude which unintentionally influences the outcome of the research in such a way as to confirm the prediction made by the researcher.

In the 1990s economic life offered many practical examples of how collective behavioral mechanisms function, e.g. in the increasingly heated financial markets. Now, it is by no means an unknown phenomenon that fluctuations in financial markets can be triggered by rumors, vague expectations and sheer speculation. But it appears to be increasingly usual for a person or group to spread a rumor with the aim of increasing or reducing the value of some particular stock or bond. If such rumor spreading works, the market becomes uneasy when it notices that the rate and volume of trade does not match what would otherwise be expected. This enables the manipulative person or group to buy and sell at times favorable to themselves.

Similar patterns of behavior are reported also in the marketing of modern "management" literature, where the aim is to create a self-reinforcing sales effect. An editor or a consultant bureau launches a new idea, a so-called "management fad", desiring to sell it to as many as possible. Leaders of different activities often quickly become aware of such ideas, but sales are greatly helped if the book is presented as a bestseller. The impression of this being the case can be achieved if the editor himself buys up most of the books from the bookshops. Since it is then out of stock, new books have to be ordered, and this apparent increase in sales is used for marketing purposes. Many managers fear the disapproval of their professional environment, and buy the book, thus also increasing real sales. This logic is inspired by Hollander's description (1979, pp. 13-17) of the socio-psychological mechanisms implied in the self-fulfilling prophecy.

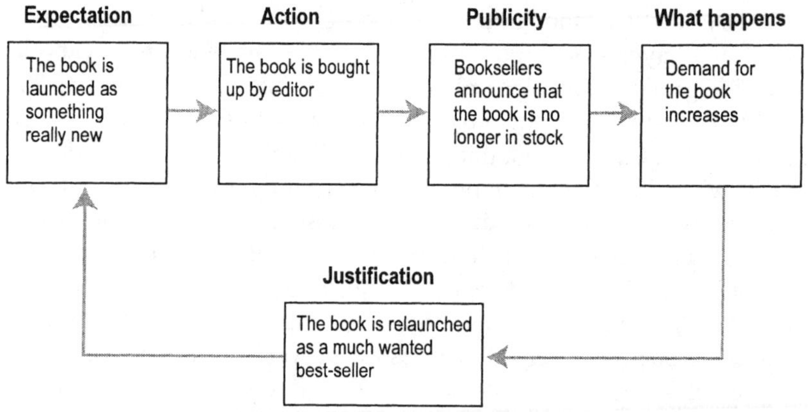

In itself this is a trivial example of processes that can have far wider effects. International relations can be influenced by ascribing to other nations motives which they don't actually have, thus leading to armed conflict (Richardson 1960). Tuchman (1962) seems inclined to explain the prelude to the First World War as a self-fulfilling prophecy. The parties involved were stockpiling arms on the reciprocal assumption of hostile intentions, each regarding their own preparations as purely defensive. The intense arms race encouraged both sides to feel they had the advantage. Sooner or later the expected event, namely the outbreak of war, was sure to happen.

In retrospect, it is also possible to see the communist prophecy, that both the economy and culture can be governed, from this perspective. Lenin exploited Marx's theory of the dialectical progress of history to enforce the dictatorship of the Communist party as "self-fulfilling" and necessary for the validity of the prophecy. The State would "fade away", although when and how this would happen was a matter for Lenin and, later, Stalin to decide.

A self-fulfilling prophecy does not necessarily imply undesirable consequences. In most of the examples given, the change in behavior is motivated by fear: fear of losing one's bank deposit, of failing an exam, of deviants coming too close, of not selling one's book. But hope and confidence can inspire their own prophecies, which lead to the result desired. In election campaigns almost all politicians avail themselves of the argument that their support is increasing even though, objectively speaking, this is impossible for all of them at the same time. The aim of such assertions is to create confidence among the voters, thus encouraging them to vote for the winning side. Opinion polls made for the various parties are selectively interpreted to emphasize only the most encouraging results. The effect may be that a candidate who started as a marginal contender is seen as a safe bet, rather than as someone who is doomed to lose and hence as a waster of good votes.

Attempts to create expectations of election success can also backfire. Merton (1948) formulated the so-called *suicide prophecy* as an illustration of this kind of social phenomenon. It was an effect of this kind which defeated the former Prime Minister Torbjørn Jagland in the Norwegian election of 1997. With the obvious aim of increasing support for himself and his party, Jagland declared that his party would not be able to continue in government if it polled less than 36.9% of the vote. He got 36.5% and consequently had to accept the resignation he had declared in advance. In his description of this type of socio-psychological boomerang effect Hollander (1979, p. 17) claims that few experienced politicians take such chances out of thoughtlessness. Thus the self-fulfilling prophecy can strengthen the one who initiates a change in collective behavior, but it can also crush him.

7. Literature

Bolman, L.G. and T.E. Deal 1991: *Nytt perspektiv på organisasjon og ledelse. Strukturer, sosiale relasjoner, politikk og symboler* (New Perspective on Organization and Management. Structures, Social Relations, Politics and Symbols), Ad Notam, Oslo.

Bråthen, S. 1982: "Kognitiv kartlegging og gyldiggjøring" (Cognitive Survey and Validation) in H. Holter and R. Kalleberg (eds.): *Kvalitative metoder i samfunnsforskningen (Qualitative Methods in Social Science)*, Universitetsforlaget, Oslo.

Coser, L.A. 1977: *Masters of Sociological Thought*, Harcourt Brace Jovanovich, New York.

Elster, J. 1978: *Logic and Society*, John Wiley & Sons, New York.

Hollander 1979: *Social Psychology. Principles and Methods*, Cappelen, Oslo.

Karlsen, J.E. 1990: *Pegasus og sigarkassen. Myter og symbolsk ledelse* (Pegasus and the Cigar-box. Myths and Symbolic Management), Universitetsforlaget, Oslo.

Martinussen, W. 1991: *Sosiologisk analyse* (Sociological Analysis), Universitetsforlaget, Oslo.

Mead, G.H. 1936: *Movements of Thought in the Nineteenth Century*, University of Chicago Press, Chicago.

Merton, R.K. 1948: "The Self-Fulfilling Prophecy", in *The Antioch Review*, Summer 1948, pp. 193-210. Reprinted as chapter 13 in Merton: *Social Theory and Social Structure*, Free Press, Glencoe, 1957.

Merton, R.K. 1967: *On Theoretical Sociology*, Collier-Macmillan Ltd., London.

Merton, R.K. 1976 "The Sociology of Social Problems", in R.K. Merton & R. Nisbet 1976: *Contemporary Social Problems*, Harcourt, Brace, Jovanovich, Inc., New York.

Pondy, L. R. and I. Mitroff 1979 "Beyond Open Systems Models of Organization" in B.M. Staw (ed.): *Research in Organizational Behavior*, JAI Press, Greenwich Connecticut.

Popper, K.R.: 1945: *The Open Society and Its Enemies*, Routledge & Kegan Paul, London.

Popper, K.R. 1957: *The Poverty of Historicism*, Ark, London.

Popper, K.R. 1963: *Conjectures and Refutations. The Growth of Scientific Knowledge*, Harper Torchbooks, London.

Richardson, L.F. 1960: *Statistics of Deadly Quarrels*, Boxwood Press, Pittsburgh.

Simon, H. 1954: "Bandwagon and underdog effects in election predictions", *Public Opinion Quarterly* 18, pp. 245-253.

Skagestad, P. 1980: *Fornuft og feilbarlighet. Karl Poppers kritiske rasjonalisme* (Reason and Fallibility. Karl Popper's Critical Rationalism), Universitetsforlaget, Oslo.

Thomas, W.I. and D. Swaine 1928: *The Child in America*, Knopf, New York.

Stinchcombe, A.L. 1968: *Constructing Social Theories*, Harcourt, Brace & World Inc., New York.

Stinchcombe, A.L. 1975: "Merton's Theory of Social Structure", in L.A. Coser (ed.): *The Idea of Social Structure: Papers in Honor of Robert K. Merton*, Harcourt Brace Jovanovich, New York.

Thomas, W.I. 1923: *The Unadjusted Girl*, Little & Brown, Boston.

Tuchman, B. 1962: *The Gins of August*, Macmillan, New York.

Østerberg, D. 1978: *Handling og samfunn* (Action and Society), Pax, Oslo.

7
The Placebo Effect
On Imaginary, Real and
Measurable Effects

OLE JACOB BROCH

1. Original quotation

A placebo is:

1. A form of medical therapy, or an intervention designed to stimulate medical therapy, that at the time of use is believed not to
be a specific therapy for the condition for which it is offered and
that the use is for its psychological effect or to eliminate
observer bias in an experimental setting.

2. (by extension from 1) – A form of medical therapy now believed
to be inefficacious, though believed efficacious at the time of
use. Clause 2 is added to make sense of a sentence such as:
"Most of the medications used by physicians one hundred
years ago were actually placebos." (Brody 1977: p. 43)

2. Brief explanation

Placebo is the first person singular, future tense, of the Latin verb plac-
ere, the same word as French "plaire" or English "please", i.e. "I shall
please".

In modern language we might call placebo treatment a "dummy
treatment". Gaddum (1953) distinguishes this ("dummy tablets") from
placebo, but there is little reason to note a difference. "Dummy treatment" is the original sense of the word. The enlarged definition in point
2 is due to the later, more imprecise use of the notion to indicate that

treatments given in earlier times had no effect, i.e. "it was a mere placebo treatment". "Dummy treatment" is not a correct description when the doctor himself believes in the treatment. As we shall see later, the placebo effect can be stronger when the therapist also believes in the treatment and is able to persuade the patient to register the effect by means of suggestion. In what follows, we shall deal with the effect and not with the purpose motivating the treatment.

Placebo tablets are used in therapeutic experiments because they may have an effect of their own which disturbs the interpretation of the experiment. This placebo effect can be studied separately, and we can begin by formulating this rule:

By influencing the patient in some direction or other by means of sympathetic or arrogant attitudes or by means of some remedy or other, one may also influence the complaint either favorably or unfavorably.

3. Background

We do not know who invented the placebo notion. According to several editions of the *Oxford Shorter Dictionary* it has been used in this sense since 1811. The word in itself is well-known from the Catholic requiem mass, so it is quite possible that it has made its way into medical terminology more or less on its own, as have many new notions in modern language. Certainly, the problem of inefficacious treatment has been known since ancient times. One of Hippocrates' aphorisms claims that "the doctor can often comfort, sometimes alleviate and rarely heal", and in my opinion this is sufficient to indicate that the author was aware that most medicines administered were at best inefficacious, because it was at least quite as normal in those times as it is now, that "one had to give them something". Moreover, in stating elsewhere that a treatment should "at least not injure the patient", Hippocrates probably realized that the effect was at best doubtful.

Since the time of Hippocrates and up to the beginning of the 20th century, many doctors certainly forgot his advice, at the very least not to injure the patient. The belief in the progress of science was too strong. Even so, it should be emphasized that the placebo notion is a child of the rational way of thinking of the 19th century. Strictly speaking, Brody's definition no. 2, as given above is an incorrect use of the word. The treatments of earlier times were not ineffective, although it may be doubted whether the effects were to the benefit of the patient. It would suffice to mention the mercury treatment of syphilis and the widespread use of antimony in 17th century France. The doses were large enough to cause evident poisoning symptoms in the patients, and these very symptoms were supposed to produce a healing effect. For instance, a great many plants contain substances which for various reasons provoke nausea and vomiting. These were popular, because the emptying of the body (blood-letting, the use of enema etc.) was regarded as a cleansing out of poisonous substances. Thus theoretically the drugs had an effect. In the scientific theory of the 16th and 17th centuries it was not usual to investigate systematically the effect of the treatment on the illness as such.

Today we do not regard it as advantageous that a seriously ill patient should, in addition to his/her other ailments, also be made to suffer from nausea or anemia. Many doctors and laymen opposed established treatment routines, on the assumption that they were directly dangerous to the patient. Molière is known as a biting critic of clergymen, lawyers and doctors. This is very clear in the following exchange between Scagnarelle and Don Juan, from his Don Juan:

- There was a man lying in convulsions for five days. They did not know what to do, because none of the remedies had any effect. Finally, they made up their minds to try antimony.
- Did he recover?
- No, he died.
- A fantastic effect, indeed.
- Oh yes, wasn't it? To think that he lies five days in convulsions without dying, and then it could be done in the twinkling of an eye!

It has been contended that homeopathic therapists were already highly popular at the beginning of the 18th century, because with their ineffective remedies they did not provoke any disagreeable side effects. Hence at that time there was no reason to point to possible placebo effects. The study of the placebo effect belongs to the new scientific era which started in the middle of the 19th century, when systematic, empirical studies of the effects of therapy were undertaken.

Some few remedies had a documented effect which is recognized also today, but in special cases only. However, these were frequently administered also in the treatment of other complaints with similar symptoms. Neither in this case could we talk of a placebo effect. Quinine has been a popular anti-fever remedy ever since the first Western patient, Duchess Cinchón of Peru, was treated with it around 1660. Undoubtedly, the remedy has an effect, but as a matter of fact only when the fever is due to malaria. This fact was recognized at the end of the last century. Even so, in Norway the preparation could be bought free of prescription together with acetyl-salicylic acid under the name of "acetyl-quinine" for use against fever right up until the 1970s. Likewise, digitalis was introduced by Withering in 1785 against dropsy (edema), but Withering did not fully realize why the remedy was efficacious only in some patients. The explanation was some 15 years after: The remedy is efficacious when the edemas are caused by cardiac insufficiency, not if they are due to a kidney disease.

4. Formalization – precise definition

In scientific experiments the ideal is to vary just one single factor (the "independent" variable) at a time, while keeping all other factors constant ("controlling for these"). It can then be claimed that the changes observed are due exclusively to changes in the independent variable. All other influences are checked by means of "controls". In practice, it is impossible to isolate the person or group used for experimental purposes in a scientific experiment from the many possible factors apt to influence them. Instead, a control group is used, which is not subjected to the stimuli or the influence directed at the experiment group. The purpose is that "no effect" should be observed in the control group, while some kind of influence/change should be seen to occur in the experiment group. The comparison undertaken between control group and experiment group then provides the "effect" of the experiment: the effect of the "independent" variable on the "dependent".

The placebo effect is an example of the "control" problem in such idealized experiments. In many cases there will be two experiment groups, both of which receive stimuli, but where the control group does not receive the same stimulus as the experiment group. The control group gets the "dummy pill" while the experiment group gets the "real" pill. The result of the experiment will then be gauged as the difference between the effects of the pills in the two groups. The difference between the "idealized" scientific experiment and the situation where a dummy pill is provided, is that the persons in the latter case are actively "involved" in the experimental situation by "getting a pill" (i.e. treatment). This triggers off certain processes which are not easy to "control for".

An implication of the first of Brody's two definitions is that an inefficacious remedy is deliberately administered (i.e. inefficacy known to doctor, but not to patient). In the second case the doctor also believes in the effect. Though this does not fall under the definition, it is of course of no importance for the proper placebo effect. Today we could hardly imagine a medicinal treatment being tested without a patient group getting "dummy pills". Such tests are called "double-blind" investigations, meaning that neither the doctor nor the patient knows what is administered. Sometimes "cross-over" is used, i.e. administering the drug to be investigated during one period, and the placebo during the next. In case of serious diseases, where an efficacious treatment is already known, the new treatment is often given in addition to the old one.

Research on a pill type assumed to be a prophylactic for angina pectoris was carried out by registering consumption of nitroglycerine – the standard treatment for acute cardio-spasm attacks – in alternating periods of placebo and the efficacious substance. In conducting such experiments today it is required that the patients should always be informed beforehand as to how the investigation is to be made.

It is not certain that a "double-blind" investigation is the best method for researching new remedies. An investigation of this type must necessarily be so organized that everybody involved receives a standard dose. For many types of remedy the efficacious dose can vary considerably from one individual to another, as can the dose that produces side effects. This makes it impossible to change the dose when no effect is observed, or in order to handle side effects. In many cases the genuine pill might betray itself in terms of some specific taste or certain side effects. It would suffice to mention nitroglycerine in the treatment of angina pectoris. Those who have tried nitroglycerine know that a pressure is felt in the head due to dilation of the blood vessels, and it is impossible to conceal this effect. Even though these problems have been known for a long time and control groups who receive placebos have been used regularly, far less research has been done concerning the placebo effect as such. It has been said (Skoglund 1991, Wolf 1959) that interest in the phenomenon came to the fore in 1946, when Cornell University held a symposium on the subject (Wolff et al. 1946) and we have Jellinek's 1946 research on the effect of placebo on headaches as compared to various analgesics. He discovered for example, that some 40% of the persons involved in the experiment never felt any placebo effect. This figure crops up frequently in relevant literature. We often call such experiment subjects "non-responders", but it is not possible to indicate a number. It lies in the very nature of the placebo phenomenon that its effects are scarcely reproducible. The number of non-responders varies considerably depending on the way the experiment is organized, for the simple reason that the circumstances of the experiment might well constitute the principal factor.

In psychiatric institutions several efforts have been made to identify those who react to placebos. In one place (Wilcox et al. 1992) men were found to react slightly more than women, married patients most of all, while the patients' education and duration of the disease were of no decisive importance (this referred to depressive patients). There is good reason to be wary of reading too much into such information. The results show enormous variations, depending on the circumstances. There are, however, some recurrent points which allow us to formulate a more detailed *law* of the *placebo effect*. This we shall do by presenting a list of the problems that occur in trying to delimit the placebo effect in relation to other aspects of a treatment, by formulating the main preconditions for the occurrence of a placebo effect, and by assessing questions related to the way in which it can, in practice, be taken into account:

a) Due to its nature, the placebo effect is difficult to reproduce.
The circumstances during the experiment are of a great importance for the result, and these are difficult to reproduce accurately. The conditions that prevail in various clinics are of enormous importance. If, during the testing of a new medicine, the doctor leaves it to a nurse to inform the patient that he/she is receiving a remedy for test purposes, and that nothing is known as to whether or not it will have any effect, the effect is much feebler than when the doctor personally and enthusiastically informs the patient that a new and very good remedy is about to be administered. The doctors easily disclose the secret, even when doing their best to avoid it.

b) The experiment subject must have a motive, if a placebo preparation is to have an effect.
In 1938 Bahnsen, Jacobsen and Thesleff found that dummy amphetamine pills did not induce any stimulating effect in normal, informally chosen experiment subjects, whereas in 1959 Joyce obtained good effects among students. The explanation is presumed to be that the students were more interested in providing the professor with a good result. In a study of anti-anxiety (POS) drugs it was registered that a placebo preparation reduced anxiety symptoms in 50% of the patients of a medical ward, but in only 33% in a psychiatric ward. The patients in the psychiatric ward had other preconceptions of therapy, such as psychotherapy etc. If the dose was stepped up from 1 to 4 pills per day,

the figures were 87% and 50% respectively. This corroborates the two preceding laws and allows us to formulate one more:

c) The placebo effect is dose-dependent, and tolerance develops with time.
Four pills a day is always better than just one. After some time the effect decreases. It will be possible to reactivate it by changing the pills, e.g. by shifting from red to yellow pills or by varying their shape.

d) The placebo effect is additional to other effects.
For example, it can increase the effect of analgesic remedies.

e) The effect varies depending on the kind of symptoms.
Generally, placebo preparations are most effective against pain, but also against symptoms related to the autonomous nervous system: anxiety, blood pressure and gastric juice secretion. Psychological symptoms like insomnia (hot milk in the evening) are also influenced. On the other hand, psychoses and hysterical symptoms are not influenced. Typically, the symptoms are most susceptible to influence when more than one psychological mechanism is involved. In the course of studies on experimentally induced pain, placebos could raise the pain threshold by 3% (Beecher 1960), while in clinical situations an effect on pain is observable among nearly 50% of patients. This supports what has already been said: one condition for an effect is that the patient has an interest in it.

f) Placebos can have adverse side effects, sometimes considerable.
Many side effects are rather uncharacteristic: dizziness, dry mouth, nausea, metal taste in mouth, fatigue, restlessness and palpitations. In many cases such adverse effects may be placebo effects, and it might perhaps help to shift to a preparation with a different name and appearance, although with an identical content. Research into the effects of reserpine on blood pressure showed that those who received the placebo developed blocked noses as often as those who received the medicine. This is a conspicuous, well known side effect of this preparation. In an investigation of hydralazine, a substance that lowers blood pressure, a typical hydralazine headache was reported in a patient who received the placebo (Wolf 1959).

g) In many cases placebo effects can be objectively registered.
They are not "imaginary". Serious side effects have been reported, such as medicine rash. In connection with research on an emetic it was

possible to measure directly that stomach contractions ceased when the emetic was administered. After some time vomiting began. A test subject received a placebo preparation through a tube after the contractions had ceased, and was told that it was a remedy against nausea. Shortly afterwards stomach activity started again, and the patient felt better (Wolf 1943).

Among these seven properties I would point out two, which should always be kept in mind, namely, points a and c: the placebo effect is not easily reproduced, and it is limited in time. And then there is point b, concerning the motivation required to achieve an effect. It is well known that any kind of treatment has a poor effect until a decision has been reached in an insurance case!

5. Generality and testability. Critique

Many attempts have been made to understand the placebo effect. It is related to the mechanisms underlying the effects of acupuncture and Pavlov's conditioned reflexes (Kaada 1986). These effects have been related to the so-called endorphin system. Endorphins are substances (polypeptides) found in the central nervous system which influence the receptivity of nerve cells (neurons) at their synaptic receptors. This means that endorphins can regulate the activity of the neurons. Encephalin is liberated from the endorphin molecule and transmits impulses from one nerve cell to another, a so-called transmitter (signal substance). The endorphins owe their name to their morphine-like effect – endorphin could be translated as "the inner morphine". It is commonly held that most effects of morphine-like substances are explicable in terms of their effects on the endorphin and encephaline receptors.

Many of the placebo effects on pain can be neutralized by means of naloxone, a preparation counteracting the effect of morphine (Skoglund 1991). Direct measurements of endorphins in the spinal fluid have also been made under varying conditions, and at one time much attention was given to the fact that increased quantities were registered during the activity of jogging. Joggers felt exhilarated and could develop a feeling of euphoria. They could also feel abstinence symptoms if for some days they didn't jog. Such results are of course entertaining when reported in popular science reviews, but we should keep in mind that such analyzes are not easy to carry out. It is a question of small quantities and the methods entail the risk of various errors. There is no satisfactory explanation for what actually takes place. In my view the mechanisms are so complex that neither acupuncture, the exhilaration associated with jogging, nor the placebo effect can be ascribed to the agency of endorphins alone.

There are several factors in the central nervous system that can also be of importance. It remains to be explained how psychological mechanisms are "translated" into neurophysiological reactions. But if it is true that naloxone can neutralize the placebo effects, the assumption would seem justified that the endorphin mechanisms are of essential importance, since no effect of naloxone is known other than that it counteracts the effect of endorphin and morphine.

Several types of afferent nerves go into the spinal medulla. Thick fibers convey impulses from touch, vibration and deep pressure. Thin fibers convey pain and temperature impulses. These form connections at various points within the medulla, and transmit the impulses to higher centers in the central nervous system and the brain via separate pathways. Encephaline neurons can hamper the transmission of impulses in the pain fibers. Stimulation of the thick fibers (massage) can also reduce activity in the paths that register pain, probably via an influence on the encephaline neurons.

Hence it is possible to influence the impulses to the medulla 1) by stimulating other neurons and 2) by stimulating downward paths from higher centers, these in turn being governed, among other things, by psychological factors. This demonstrates that there is an anatomic basis for the explanation of effects of certain psychological circumstances on chemical (and hence also physical) reactions in the body. The placebo effect can thus be empirically described by reference to the anatomic processes and systems in the body which are susceptible to influence by – or which are most sensitive to – "mental" changes or changes in the consumption of medicines or other kinds of treatment.

Regression towards the mean
This is a statistical phenomenon that can be confused with the placebo effect. During the selection of patients to be treated for a disease or for symptoms which show a highly unstable development, the patients are chosen during their worst period. On conducting a control later on, they are already better. This is not a placebo effect, but simply a retrograde swing in one of the parameters. This applies particularly to symptoms that are not obvious and directly perceptible.

Suppose that we want to investigate the effect of some special diet on cholesterol levels (a good example from experience is rolled oats). We have already established an inclusion limit, i.e. the cholesterol level required for an individual to be included in the investigation. If the cholesterol level fluctuates, we will have a number of patients just above the limit, but who are not normally above it. On the other hand, we will not have included some with a cholesterol level just beneath the limit but who might later swing upwards, since these have been rejected in the first investigation. Thus at the first control we will already have a number of patients who show an improvement in their condition due to their having swung back to a lower level. If we have started the treatment, this might be credited to the improvement.

Another obvious instance is high blood pressure (hypertension). It has been argued that the effect of treatment on light hypertension is due exclusively to such a regression towards a mean value. Several studies (e.g. MRC 1977) which compare the effect of treatment with that of a placebo, and also with a group receiving no treatment at all, have been unable to confirm any difference between placebo treatment and no treatment. However, we should not disregard the fact that admission to a large-scale health study where everything is thoroughly controlled can in itself be of enormous importance to physical well-being and may perhaps result in a considerable placebo effect. The results of alternative treatment like homeopathy may often involve a regression towards the mean which is equal or even greater in effect to that of a placebo. It is particularly in cases of chronic but not life-endangering diseases, the course of which involves fluctuations and pain, that homeopathic and similar treatments are most successful.

6. Empirical assessment – conclusion

What is the importance of placebos for the treatment effects of modern medicine? We like to believe that today's medicine is rational natural science. In earlier times it was different; we need only think of bloodletting, leeches and Mesmer's galvanic therapy at the turn of the century. As a matter of fact, many contemporary methods of treatment also go back to a time when the demands for documented effects were not particularly high. Up until the 1970s it was common to treat pains in or around joints by irradiating the area with X-rays. It was commonly held that in some cases this might help, and the patients were often content. The treatment was not without risk, since lasting injury to the joint could result from too much treatment. Gradually a certain scepticism arose towards this treatment, and eventually a radiologist prepared his patients as he would for treatment, but switched on the current in only half the cases. He could find no difference between the two groups. This was prior to problems with ethical committees and the requirement that those participating in clinical experiments should be informed, although the consequences of omitting to send X-rays through a fairly healthy person are presumably not too serious.

Today we do not use this treatment, but we have more physiotherapists. They use a far greater variety of procedures, but much of the physical treatment given might rightly be termed placebo treatment. Instead of X-rays we use short-wave and laser rays, connective tissue massage (for some time very popular, but actually not so much used) and psycho-motoric massage, all of which are undoubtedly effective in many cases, although the reasons for their use are not always equally strong. In many cases it is rather a kind of placebo treatment or regression towards mean value. Non-authorized therapists often have an even greater range of treatments like foot massage, aroma-therapy, nasal rinsing and meditation with incense.

What about psychotherapy for psychological disorders? It is a well known fact that comprehension of, and interest in, the troubles of the patient are of help, but is the conversation theme really of any importance? Or, in other words: is a special education needed to help human beings in difficulties? The therapist in most cases has a scheme for the arrangement of the treatment, but few have examined the effect of reversing the scheme. In such cases there can be a considerable placebo component, and nobody has systematically investigated the question whether one trend in psychotherapy is better than another. As regards alcoholics, we know that lay people can in many cases achieve results equaling those of psychologists or psychiatrists.

There is a fairly common belief that a cold can be checked by means of large doses of vitamin C. After the disappearance of the bitter tasting acetyl-quinine there was a demand for a substitute. Everybody knows that a cold is a rather diffuse illness with different symptoms in different individuals. The symptoms are also very susceptible to influence by placebos. Brænden's nose drops were claimed to be effective against colds and initially sales were huge. Many people felt a curative effect on incipient colds. But gradually people felt the effect was so minimal that they saw no reason to be bothered with these drops. The same happened to ash tree decoctions which were reputed to be good for almost everything. Many of those who used them probably experienced stomach troubles. Both remedies disappeared after a year or two. Many so-called alternative treatments are quite clearly fads, and can be seen to support the law which states that placebo effects decrease over time.

The "happiness pill" has fared much better. Drugs with documented effects on depression have proved effective in the treatment of a great many other, more or less well-defined, psychological complaints. There is always good reason to be skeptical about miracle cures, which are claimed to have an effect on numerous conditions. Anti-depressants have been around for a long time, but they never gained any great popularity, even though they were not significantly different from newer ones. But they had several unpleasant side effects, and their use against trifling complaints was therefore not very tempting. When new remedies with considerably fewer side effects become available, one can fully enjoy the placebo effect. Typical for placebo effects is that they will prove effective for a couple of months.

Another well-known placebo treatment was the operations undertaken by American surgeons against angina pectoris in the late 1950s. This consisted in redirecting an arteriole from the inside of the thoracic cavity to the heart, and sewing the end into the outermost strata in order to increase the supply of blood to the heart. Research proved that the treatment had quite a good effect on the frequency and strength of the fits of cardio-spasms. In this case it was difficult to defend a real placebo treatment which would involve anaesthetizing the patient and making a major incision in the chest and then doing nothing more. But angina pectoris is one of the diseases most susceptible to environmental influence and psychical factors.

In many cases the impressive, costly surroundings may be assumed to be of rather greater importance than the instruments in themselves. Muscle development in connection with body-building is based on a very simple principle, viz the straining of certain muscle groups by means of resistance. This can be done with small weights on the bathroom floor at home, but everybody is convinced that the result is better when achieved with complicated, costly devices in a training studio.

Acupuncture is another field where placebo might partly account for the effect. But the importance of the needles and the procedure is not clear. The impression of comprehensive knowledge is of great importance for the result. It is not easy to investigate the placebo effects of acupuncture by means of not applying the needles, but there are schools which do just this with good results.

Lewith and Vincent (1995) have looked into three fields where research on the effect of acupuncture has been undertaken. These are addiction (mainly tobacco), states of pain (migraine) and nausea. Many of the attempts to separate the acupuncture effect from that of placebo are faulty. The patient groups are often too small, a fact which carries the risk of "losing" real differences due to a lack of statistical significance.

The conclusion of their research was that acupuncture could be effective in the treatment of certain pain conditions such as back pains, but was considerably less so in cases of chronic pain conditions. The effect on migraine, in terms of a more lasting, preventive effect, was uncertain. Naloxone, which reduces the effect of morphine-like remedies, in most cases neutralized the effect of acupuncture, regardless of where the needless were applied. On the other hand, the place where the needles were applied was of importance in the treatment of nausea, a fact that might suggest that here the mechanism is not governed through the encephaline neurons, as is the case regarding pains, but through the nervous system governing the stomach and the upper part of the intestine (autonomous nervous system). The effect of acupuncture on inveterate smokers who sought help in kicking the habit was also uncertain. Most of the research which showed no effect other than placebo had in fact not been conducted thoroughly enough.

Conclusion

Knowledge of the placebo effect affords us a better insight into the effect of acupuncture and various other alternative methods of treatment. It is, however, of equal importance to gain insight into additional components in treatments, which we believe in and which have, in certain cases, potentially documentable effects. It is a fair assumption that most doctors are willing to admit that several so-called alternative treatments may have positive effects, even though there may be disagreement as to how these effects are brought about.

7. Literature

Archer, T. P. and C. V. Leier 1992: "Placebo treatment in congestive heart failure", *Cardiology* 81, pp. 125-133.

Bahnsen, P., E. Jacobsen and H. Thesleff 1938: "The subjective effect of beta-phenylisopropylaminosulphate on normal adults", *Acta Med. Scand.* 97, pp. 89-131.

Beecher, H. K. 1955: "The powerful placebo", JAMA 159, pp. 1602-1606.

Beecher, H. K. 1960: "Increased stress and effectiveness of placebos and 'active' drugs", *Science* 132, pp. 91-92.

Brody, H. 1977: *Placebos and the Philosophy of Medicine*, Chicago University Press, Chicago.

Gaddum, J. 1953: "Walter Ernest Dixon memorial lecture: Clinical pharmacology", *Proc. Roy. Soc. Med.* 47, pp. 195-204.

Grünbam, Adolf 1984: "Explication and implications of the placebo concept", in Gunnar Anderson (ed.): Rationality in Science and Politics, pp. 131-158 (vol. 79 in the series *Boston Studies in the Philosophy of Science*).

Jacobsen, E. 1971: "Placebovirkningen ved udprøvning af lægemidler", (Placebo-effect in the tests of medicaments) in Hallberg, Johnsson and Sövell (eds.): *Klinisk värdering av läkemedel. Nordiskt symposium*, Göteborg, pp. 87-92.

Jellinek 1946: "Clinical tests on comparative effectiveness of analgesic drugs", *Biometrics* Bull 2, pp. 87-91.

Joyce, C. R. B. 1959: "Consistent differences in individual reactions to drugs and dummies", *Br. J. Pharmacol.* 14, pp. 521-521.

Kaada, B. 1986: "Placebo-gåten mot sin løsning?" (Is the placebo-puzzle approaching it's solution?) *Tidsskrift for Den norske Lægeforening* 106, pp. 635-641.

Lewith, G. and C. Vincent 1995: "Evaluation of the clinical effects of acupuncture", *Pain Forum* 4, pp. 29-39.

Medical Research Council Working Party 1977: "Randomized trial of treatment for mild hypertension. Design of a pilot trial", *BMJ* 1, pp. 1437-1440.

Shapiro, A. K. 1960: "A contribution to a history of the placebo effect", *Behavioral Science* 5, pp. 109-135.

Shapiro, A. K. 1968: "Semantics of the placebo", *Psychiatric Quarterly*, pp. 1-43.

Skoglund, E. 1991: "Placeboeffecter og kontrollerte kliniske forsøk". (Placebo effects and controlled clinical experiments) *Tidsskrift for Den norske lægeforening* 111, pp. 2728-2731.

Wilcox, C. S., J. B. Cohn, R. D. Linden, J. F. Heiser, P. B. Lucas, D. L. Morgan og R. N. DeFrancisco 1992: "Predictors of placebo response: a retrospective analysis", *Psychopharmacol. Bull.* 28, pp. 157-162.

Wolf, S. 1943: "The relation of gastric function to nausea in man", *J. Clin. Invest.* 22, pp. 877-882.

Wolf, S. 1959: "The pharmacology of placebos". *Pharmacol. Rev.* 11, pp. 689-704.

Wolff, H. G., E. F. Dubois og H. Gold 1946: "Cornell Conferences on Therapy: Use of placebos in therapy", *NY State J. Med* 46, pp. 1718-1727.

8

The Hawthorne Effect or the Human Relations Theory On Experiment Situation and Influence

Tom Colbjørnsen

1. Original quotation

[...] whatever the problem (in connection with the workers productivity), it was partly, and sometimes wholly, determined by the attitude of the individual worker. (Mayo 1949, from Pugh 1971, p. 223).

2. Brief explanation

This, in a highly condensed form, is the main element in what is known in organization sociology as the *human relations theory*. The point of departure of the theory was provided by the findings registered in the so-called *Hawthorne experiments*. These field experiments were made at the Hawthorne Department of the big American concern Western Electrics in the period 1927-32 (Roetlishberger and Dickson 1939).

The object of the experiments was to ascertain *what would be needed to maximize the productivity of the personnel employed*. The basic assumption was the existence of an unambiguous relation between physical and material work conditions and productivity. At the start of the experiments this was a universally accepted hypothesis. The researchers wanted, e.g. to study what kind of light conditions were required to obtain maximum efficiency in the workers' production. The hypothesis was: the better the light, the higher the work productivity.

The conditions for the experiment were drawn up in compliance with the very best standards of the time. The researchers set up experiment rooms and control rooms, and changes were introduced one at a time, while at the same time controls were made for all other conditions. This is what the researchers experienced when they started varying the light conditions of the experiment group:

> ... the results were perplexing : [...] lighting improved in the experimental room, production went up; but it rose also in the control room. The opposite of this: lighting diminished from 10 to 3 foot - candles in the experimental room and production again went up; simultaneously in the control room, with illumination constant, production also rose (Mayo, p.215).

Thus, the unambiguous connection that was expected between physical work conditions and productivity was not confirmed. The control effect did not materialize. To explain this seemingly paradoxical result, the attitude of the workers to the enterprise and the experiments was integrated as an explanatory factor. Since then, the effect on the research project of the attitude of the experiment persons has been termed the *Hawthorne effect*.

The results registered were at variance with the conventional wisdom of the time to a degree that stimulated fresh thinking in the field of social science. Drastic changes in the view of individuals in a work situation followed in the wake of the Hawthorne experiments. We even find instances of the word "revolution" being used to describe the way of thinking in this field (Björvik 1973, p. 270). As already mentioned, what was focused on as a precondition of productivity was the staff's *attitude to the enterprise*. The researchers found that this attitude was determined by the extent to which the individual worker *felt* him/herself appreciated and taken into account, that their own needs were satisfied etc. This resulted in changes in views on *communication* and *conflict* in organizations, thus diverting attention towards *group building* and *informal organization* among the workers. The paradigm that presented itself to explain behavior in *work organizations*, such as it was revealed during the Hawthorne experiments, was called the human relations theory.

The inspiration for the theories that were put forward during the Hawthorne experiments was the observation already described, which showed that there was no clear connection between light conditions and work productivity. It was even possible to observe a reverse connection: productivity increased even when the amount of light was reduced. The researchers explained this result – at first sight paradoxical – as resulting from the workers' attitude to the enterprise; to be involved as part of an experiment made them feel more positive, which in turn made them willing to increase their efficiency. In conducting these experiments the management of the enterprise had shown an unusually great interest in the workers. The background to the experiments was presented at a meeting where also the employees were allowed to put forward their views. This made the workers feel that the management cared for them and listened to them – a feeling that the enterprise took an interest in their needs and opinions. This subsequently resulted in *the attitude of the workers to the enterprise* becoming far more positive. The researchers took the view that this was the explanation of the productivity increase registered in the test room.

If we suppose that there is a connection between attitude and productivity, a natural question is: which factors have the strongest influence on the attitude of the working staff to the task in hand? And how should work conditions be arranged in order to raise this attitude to its highest possible level of positivity, thus raising productivity to its maximum? The dominant view is that the attitude is a result of the social relations in the work place. Throughout the rest of the Hawthorne experiments research therefore concentrated on *communication, informal organization* and *group building*.

An interview program carried out by the researchers among the workers clearly illustrated the importance of communication. Not fearing sanctions the workers were allowed to state their views on conditions in their work place. They were allowed to vent their frustrations and got a feeling of being cared for, a feeling of being important. This caused their attitude towards their employer to become more positive, which in turn resulted in the anticipated productivity increase. In human relations theory communication is an important factor concerning conflicts within the organization. The basic hypothesis is that the various groups within the enterprise have concurrent interests. When conflicts occasionally arise, they are due to emotional reactions among the staff, which may be explained as the result of uncertainty, rumors, frustrations and so on. Such conflicts can be eliminated by means of good communication, i.e. the management should provide information about the "real circumstances" and the staff should be allowed to bring forward their views. For the management the consequence is the extensive use of notice boards, enterprise newsletters, depth interviews etc. (Björvik 1973, p. 274).

In particular, the importance of work groups and informal organization was highlighted during the last phase of the experiments. It was observed that the workers controlled the volume of production by means of group standards, for instance by establishing a ceiling to daily production. These group standards were governed by such things as informal status relationships within the group, and the emergence of informal leaders. Against this background the view developed that work had to be considered a group activity, and from the point of view of productivity: "The existence and influence of the group - those in active daily relationship with one another - became the important fact". (Mayo, p. 225).

The Hawthorne effect, such as it was observed, provided new insights on the *methodological* level. In specialist literature the term Hawthorne effect has since been employed to denote the effect of the experiment situation itself on the dependent variable, regardless of the value ascribed to the independent variable. Traditionally, any variance observed in a dependent variable during an experiment was explained as resulting from changes in the values of one or more independent variables. The Hawthorne experiments made it clear that the experiment situation has an effect in itself. When individuals become the objects of systematic observation and/or influence, a change is brought about in their social environment and attitudes. This change can be more or less drastic:

> Almost any change, any specific attention or particular manipulation – or even the absence of manipulation, but the knowledge that a study is being made – is sufficient to produce changes in the behavior of the research objects. (Kerlinger 1975, p. 345).

3. Background

The human relations theory acquired significant renown as a *theory for work organization* as well as a *guide for practical works management*. To understand how this could come about, we must return to the general economic situation of the 1920s and 30s.

At that time, scientific management, a line of thought in organization theory associated with the name of the American F. Taylor, had begun seriously to assert itself in practice. It implied that every single worker should be as highly specialized for his job as possible, that there should be a direct and continual control system and a communications system that channeled all contact between the employed via their superiors. At the same time the wage system was linked exclusively to the production volume of each worker, in practice amounting to a time study based piecework system. Taylor's theory is based on an "economic man" model, one of the basic postulates of which is that man's primary need is to maximize the economic profit of his work (Taylor 1911).

In many cases these principles for the structuring of jobs and organization proved effective in increasing company profits. But from the same point of view these principles also had some obvious drawbacks. To many workers detailed time studies and merciless piecework systems represented increased exploitation, to which they responded with protest actions. Moreover, in many cases the number of days of sick leave increased, which had a negative effect on productivity. Furthermore, the very power structure of the enterprise came under pressure. The rights of the owners and management were challenged by a trade union movement that was quick to develop. A way of responding to this development was to arrange work conditions in a way that would encourage the workers to identify more strongly with the aims of the enterprise – aims as defined by owners/management. There was also a control problem in the enterprise: informal social structures existed among the personnel which extended beyond, and often across, the formal organizational structures of the enterprise. Therefore, within the established power structure an important need would be satisfied by a theory which offered more insight into the social system of the enterprise – a theory which would furnish better *insight into production conditions* and *make conflicts easier to handle.*

The organization-sociology of the time could not easily satisfy such a need. The scientific management theory was unable to explain how conflicts could arise in an enterprise that followed the principles for job design which that same theory recommended. Since, according to the theory, human beings were governed by economic needs, and since the economic remuneration was provided in accordance with "scientific" time studies, workers got exactly what they had a claim to and a need for. Cause for conflict therefore did not exist. Another central theory in this field is Weber's bureaucracy theory (Weber 1971). But since Weber's theory focused exclusively on formal organization structure, it was unable to grasp the informal social relations that could be observed among the personnel. The same applied also to the so-called administration doctrine associated with the name of Henry Fayol (Gustavsen 1972). As Björn Gustavsen has said in referring to these theories: "They present the organization as a well-oiled machinery, built up according to sound, technical principles" (Gustavsen 1972, p. 30).

This map obviously did not accord with the real terrain. Marxist theory, with work-capital antagonism as its basic element, was presumably no alternative to enterprise management as a guide in the practical task of structuring jobs and organization. Moreover, Marxism was at the time a rather isolated theory in Western scientific circles. Human relations theory, on the other hand, preserved the established power structures and objectives of the enterprises as guidelines for practical enterprise management, while at the same time apparently bringing organization theory more up to date with regard to matters among the labor force. Human relations theory thus performed an important function. Against this background it is easy to understand why it acquired such authority.

4. Formalization – precise definition

The aim of human relations theory is to increase our understanding of the conditions an enterprise must satisfy in order to achieve maximum carnings on the capital invested, i.e. *the highest possible profit*. Mayo (p. 215) contends that whether or not an enterprise attains this aim depends on three factors: 1) the ability of the enterprise to avail itself of modern technology, 2) systematic organization of jobs, and 3) a good organization of the social system of the enterprise, i.e. the relations of workers to one another and to the management. Mayo's objections to earlier organization theory and management practice are that only the first two factors have been duly taken into account. If organization of the social system is neglected, the enterprise will not achieve its objectives (Mayo, p. 216). To avoid this, human relations theory poses the following question: what *social conditions* are required for the work force to do its utmost to achieve the objectives of the enterprise, i.e. under what conditions will they be willing to make their maximum contribution towards fulfilling these objectives?

It is a fairly widespread idea that the purpose of human relations theory is to secure maximum well-being and welfare for the work force. If this is seen in connection with the postulates of the theory as expressed by authors such as Mayo, this will turn out to be a misunderstanding. Well-being and welfare are of interest primarily because these factors influence worker productivity, they are not objects in themselves.

In more simplified versions, human relations theory is often represented as implying that material and physical working conditions are uninteresting in a productivity perspective. This is not correct. The main point of the theory here is that a *direct* relation between such work conditions and productivity is refuted so that all circumstances and all events in the place of work are made objects of a system of sentiments. From such a point of view material goods, physical work conditions, wages, working hours etc. cannot be assessed as isolated factors. They must, on the contrary, be interpreted as implying social values. (Roetlishberger and Dickson, p. 56). Thus, physical and material circumstances influence productivity via an intermediate variable: the attitude of the workers towards the enterprise.

Viewing the theory as part of a more general theory on productivity conditions in an enterprise, we could illustrate the various links as follows:

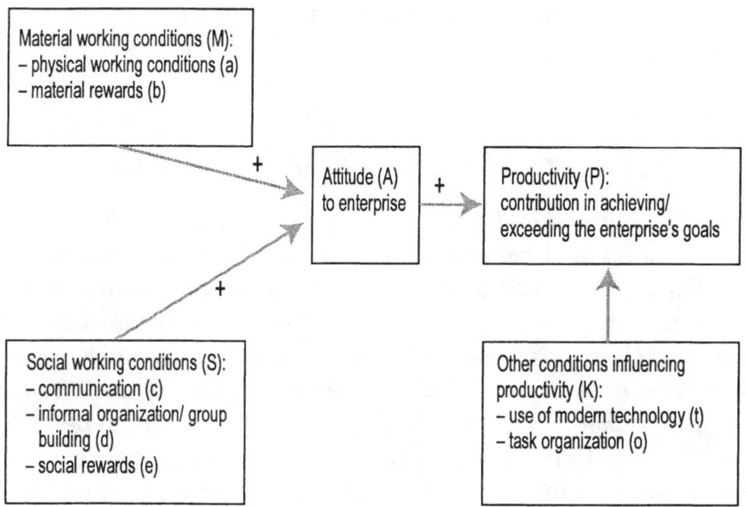

We can also represent this in the form of functions (the symbols are defined in the figure; the letters f, g, h, j and i are functions). Generally, productivity of an enterprise can be represented thus:

$$P = f\,(K, A)$$
where $K = g\,(o, t)$, and $A = h\,(S, M)$

Human relations theory specifies the conditions that actively influence productivity through the attitude of the working staff towards the enterprise. In its formalized form the theory can be represented thus:

$$A = h\ (S, M)$$
$$\text{where } S = j\ (c, d, e) \text{ and } M = i\ (a, b)$$

At this point the question naturally presents itself: *to what extent must attitude (A) to the enterprise be changed to increase productivity (P), other productivity conditions (K) being kept constant?* Further, it would seem natural to ask about the extent to which changes can be made in the values of the different links in the material and social conditions that influence productivity (M and S), before they result in important attitude (A) changes. This leads us into problems of gauging and operationalization hitherto not clarified in the discussion of the theory. Thus, the theory has the nature of a qualitative hypothesis. It is postulated that the various elements of the theory are interdependent, without anything being said as to how the *size* of the different elements, and changes in these, would directly influence a percentage change in productivity (P).

5. Generality and testability. Critique

It goes without saying that a theory that so radically challenged established views would become the object of debate and criticism. One type of critique has focused on the question *whether the Hawthorne experiments and the conclusions drawn from them satisfied scientific standards* (Carey 1967, Björvik 1968). It has been contended that the experiments do not comply with the methodological standards required of an experiment if scientifically tenable conclusions are to be inferred from it (Carey 1967, p. 403). The groups involved in the experiments were not selected in a way that satisfied the requirement of representativity. Also, the experiment group was too small to allow statistical generalizations. In addition, two of the workers in the group were replaced after some time since their attitude to the experiment was deemed inappropriate – they were not sufficiently co-operative. After pointing out that no comparison was made between productivity in the experiment group and the rest of the enterprise, Carey draws the following conclusion: "The weak points of the Hawthorne experiments render them obviously unsuitable to seriously support whatever kind of generalization" (p. 416). Carey's conclusion is that the experiments can be seen as corroborating the traditional view, which stresses wages incentives, firm leadership and discipline as important productivity conditions, just as much as they support human relations theory.

An objection to the latter aspect of Carey's critique is that human relations theory in no way excludes such circumstances. Rather, it goes no further than to claim that their influence is conveyed through the attitude of the workers and not directly, as was earlier believed. Though Carey's critique fully justifies doubts as to the results of the Hawthorne experiments, later research has confirmed the importance of workers' attitude and social relations for productivity (Schein 1968, p. 80 ff.).

The Human relations theory has been criticized as *too general*. This critique has been aimed particularly at the *human model* employed in the theory – what we might call a "*social man*" *model*. Its main element is the assumption that man's basic needs are of a social character, i.e. the need for encouragement, respect and consideration etc. However, later research appears to arrive at the conclusion that the structure of human needs is *complex and situation-dependent* (Schein 1968, p. 96), which implies that in addition to their social needs human beings also have material needs, the need for self-realization, learning, sharing of authority etc. These needs are not static, but arise in an interaction between man and environment. Others go even further, claiming that it is not sufficient to regard workers' participation in production on the sole basis of subjectively felt needs. Attention must be paid also to the fact that different groups have different *interests*. These interests are objective in the sense that they are not related to a person as such, but to the *position held in the social organization of the production*. This is particularly important in connection with the view of conflicts implied by human relations theory. We shall return to this point.

The theory has, however, also been criticized for being too *specific*, in that it doesn't take into account all the circumstances that influence the productivity of the work force. First, the theory is said to concentrate too one-sidedly on the internal conditions of an enterprise, without taking into account that circumstances outside the enterprise will also influence the attitude of the workers to the enterprise. Here, reference is made, e.g. to family relationships, housing conditions, and to social relations within the local community (Gustavsen 1972, p. 45). Others have pointed to the fact that in its original form the theory does not consider the role of trade unions in the enterprise. These critics consider it inevitable that trade unions will influence attitudes among the staff. It is important, therefore, to take trade unions into account, i.e. it is important to provide them with information and allow them to present their views etc., thereby involving the trade unions in the creation of a positive attitude towards the enterprise among the staff (after Mouzelis 1967, pp. 104-05). The common point in these two theories is that they do not question the basic feature of human relations theory. The critique is that the original theory represents a far too simplistic view of the circumstances involved in the creation of a positive attitude.

One critique that goes further is the so-called *structuralist* critique (Etzioni 1964, p. 41 ff.). Here, the essential point is that the social system must not be seen in isolation from the rest of the enterprise. The social system does not consist exclusively of the staff's need for safety and respect. Great importance must be attached, e.g. to *technology*. Technology allows for the *division of labor* and the establishment of a *task pattern*, factors that create a particular interaction between the individuals employed, and it is in this interaction that the social system is created. Therefore, from a productivity standpoint both technology and the social system must be taken into account: if attention is paid exclusively to the attitude of the workers and the factors that give rise to it, optimum results for the enterprise as a whole will not be achieved. This type of critique is among the factors that provided the basis for the *socio-technical* organization theory (Herbst 1969), which has found strong support in Norway.

The most fundamental critique of human relations theory comes from *Marxist* quarters. Marxists criticize the theory for not acknowledging the problem of power relations in the organization, in other words, it does not tackle the question of *who owns the results of the production*. To the extent that human relations theory is at all concerned with power relations, it focuses so exclusively on group and personality factors that it is blind to many of the power relations within the enterprise (Mouzelis 1967). If the organization is viewed as a whole and an analysis is made on the basis of the positions held by the different groups in the social organization of production, groups with different interests become visible within the organization. Conflicts cannot then be regarded as caused by deficient communication or personal antagonisms, but as the results of different objective interests in relation to the enterprise. This point becomes clearer if we consider the enterprise in relation to its environment, e.g. in connection with the economic system that constitutes the framework in which it functions. The Marxist critique is aimed at enterprises operating within a capitalist production system. The internal power structure of the enterprise cannot be viewed as independent of the distinguishing characteristics of the economic system within which it exists.

The capitalist production system constitutes and reproduces an antagonism between work and capital, and this antagonism cannot be abolished within the framework of that system. The reason is that an irremediable antagonism arises between the workers' interest in keeping at their disposal the values created by their own work, and the market's demand for the accumulation of capital and profit. This brings to light what Mouzelis has called *the paradox of human relations theory*: its attempt to revolutionize organization without revolution, i.e. without changing the social basis underlying organization.

From such a perspective human relations theory can become a guide for *a technique of domination.* By manipulating the social organization on of the enterprise the management can make the personnel *feel* that they are taken into account, are being listened to and esteemed etc. One way of achieving this is to allow the work force to participate in decisions regarding strictly limited areas of the enterprise's activities, such as choice of tools, establishment of the order of tasks and the like. By establishing such frame conditions – premises – the management to some extent controls these decisions. Thus it is possible to bring about a stronger identification with the enterprise among the working staff, while creating an impression of common interests on the subjective level. In this way conflicts of interests can be kept out of sight. This may additionally be a method for increasing productivity, which has prompted some (Christiansson et al. 1971, Bårtveit 1973) to call human relations theory a strategy for rationalization on the management's premises.

6. Empirical assessment – conclusion

Let us finally take a look at the position of human relations theory today, asking particularly how great its influence has been in Norway. Considering the criticisms to which it has been exposed, it is hardly surprising that, at present, it hardly exists in its original form, as presented above. Nonetheless, it still plays an important role in more modern schools of thought, both in organization theory and in practical enterprise management.

As already mentioned, of particular interest in Norway is the school of thought that originated in the structuralist critique of the theory. In Norway this trend is called *socio-technical theory,* and it was this that provided the theoretical framework for the Cooperation Project LO/NAF (Norwegian Trade Unions Association and Norwegian Employers' Association respectively) (Gulowsen 1975). The purpose of this project was to ascertain conditions for giving employees a greater say in the reorganization of work and in the organization of conditions for the individual worker "at ground level". One of the dominant ideas was the autonomous group. Workers who depended on each other in the production process were to be given, on a group basis, greater influence in decisions concerning daily work operations. This was expected to start a growth process which would give staff the right of codetermination on increasingly higher levels.

Although the basis for this project involved a far more complex organization outline than that of human relations theory, common features are clearly recognizable. *Firstly*, a higher degree of influence on the individual worker's own job situation was expected to increase productivity through the increase of contentment and the reduction of "alienation". Social relations were thus regarded as a condition that influenced production (though only one of several). *Secondly*, it was deemed possible to grant the workers codetermination in the enterprise regardless of the conflicts of interests relating to the enterprise's fundamental power structure. There was no question of altering the purpose of the enterprise. The socio-technical strategy can therefore be regarded as a method of increasing productivity within the existing power structure, as is the case also in traditional human relations theory. Against this background it has been argued (Bårtveit 1973) that the strategy must be regarded as a form of rationalization. *Thirdly*, also here the work group is conceived as the fundamental organizational element, with regard both to productivity and to codetermination.

Another field in which human relations theory holds a strong position is that of certain so-called *organization development programs*. The background is the increasing demand for enterprises to adapt in response to continuous environmental changes. Internal flexibility is becoming a key word, and thousands of managers are sent on courses to learn how to "handle" the resistance which is often put up by the work force. Because it so strongly stresses the importance of *communication, information* and *group processes*, human relations theory makes itself strongly felt. Leaders must learn how to inform the staff and listen to their views. Conflicts are often explained as responses to *aspects of the leader's personality*, e.g. he provokes resistance through an authoritarian management style. The personnel are often included in so-called project groups where, together with the representatives of the management, they are allowed to participate in decisions concerning ways to implement certain changes. There is a tendency to regard conflicts as results of deficient communication within the group, and leaders are therefore often sent on sensitivity courses to learn better methods for handling group processes.

In several areas there are therefore obvious parallels to human relations theory, also with regard to the criticisms that can be brought against some of the measures in question. First, fundamental power relations may be obscured when conflicts are analyzed exclusively in terms of group dynamics and personality. This is reflected also in the fact that working staff and management participate in cooperative groups with different strategic backgrounds, e.g. with regard to relevant knowledge. The personnel can thus be persuaded to accept solutions that might in the long run have consequences that are detrimental to their basic interests.

7. Literature

Bjørvik, Kjell Inge 1968: "En myte i arbeidspsykologisk forskning" (A Myth of Labor Psychology Research), *Bedriftsøkonomen* nr. 5, 1968.

Bjørvik, Kjell Inge 1973: *Arbeids- og lederpsykologi* (*Labor and Leadership Psychology*), Oslo.

Bårtveit, Harald 1973: *Sosio-teknisk forskning som rasjonalisering* (*Socio-Technical Research as Rationalization*), Bergen.

Carey, Alex 1967: "The Hawthorne Studies: A Radical Criticism", *American Sociological Review* vol. 32 no. 3, June 1967.

Christiansson, Lennart et al. 1971: *Kunsten å dressere mennesker* (*The Art of Training People*), Oslo.

Etzioni, Amitai 1964: *Modern Organizations*, New Jersey.

Gulowsen, Jon 1975: *Arbeidsvilkår* (*Working Conditions*), Oslo.

Gustavsen, Bjørn 1972: *Bedriftsorganisasjon – alternative modeller* (*Business Organization – Alternative Models*), Oslo.

Herbst, P.G. 1969: "Utviklingen av sosio-teknisk analyse" ("The Development of Socio-Technical Analysis"), *Tidsskrift for samfunnsforskning* nr. 3-4, 1969.

Kerlinger, Fred N. 1975: *Foundations of Behavioral Research*, 2nd ed., New York.

Mayo, E. 1949: *The Social Problems of an Industrial Civilization*, Routledge (page references are to Pugh, D.S. (ed.): *Organization Theory*, London 1971).

Mouzelis, Nicos P. 1967: *Organization and Bureaucracy*, London.

Roetlishberger, F.J. and W.J. Dickson 1939: *Management and the Worker*, Cambridge, Mass. (page references concern excerpts from O. Grusky and G.A. Miller: *The Sociology of Organizations*, Basic Studies, New York, 1970).

Scheim, Edgar H. 1970: *Organisations-psykologi* (*Organizational Psychology*), Stockholm.
Taylor, F.W. 1911: *The Principles of Scientific Management*, New York.
Weber, Max 1971: *Makt og byråkrati* (*Power and Bureaucracy*), Oslo.

PART II

Theories from different Social Science Disciplines

9
Adam Smith and 'The Invisible Hand' The Market Mechanism

JAN ERIK ASKILDSEN

1. Original quotation

As every individual [...] by directing that industry in such a manner as its produce may be of the greatest value, he intends only his own gain, and he is in this, as in many other cases, led by *an invisible hand* to promote an end which was no part of his intention [...] By pursuing his own interest he frequently promotes that of the society more effectually than when he really intends to promote it. (Adam Smith, *Wealth of Nations*, Book IV, II, 1776/1981, p. 400).

2. Brief explanation

This statement is interpreted as praise of the good – or even optimal – qualities of the perfectly competitive economy. In promoting his/her own interests through productive activity, every individual will also, under certain conditions, work to the benefit of society as a whole. Society's production is maximized by every individual doing what is individually optimal. This is brought about in that every consumer will always seek to purchase goods where they can be obtained at the lowest price. Similarly, those producing the goods will use their time and abilities in a way which will secure them the highest possible profit.

We can use one of Smith's own examples to illustrate the point: it is not profitable for a tailor to use his time making shoes. Consequently, he will buy them at the shoemaker's. Likewise, it is not profitable for the shoemaker to use his time making clothes, which he will therefore buy from the tailor. The farmer is best advised to buy both his clothes and his shoes in the market, using his time for food production, the activity for which he is best equipped. In their own interests people will buy from others those goods that would cost more if they had to produce them themselves. The greatest profit is achieved when everyone specializes in doing what he or she is best qualified to do. Thus, if every individual profits from using his/her capacity for work and capital where these will yield the highest return, this must also be the most profitable for society as a whole.

Smith mentions that these consequences of the pursuit of self-interest also apply to the exchange of goods and services among nations. The theory of the *invisible hand* is therefore also a theory that explains the merits of free trade at a global level.

The implication of Smith's theory of *the invisible hand* is that the productive value of society is maximized, provided that free trade and perfect competition prevail. The conditions that have to be satisfied to achieve this outcome are, however, not trivial. On the other hand, the conditions are not so problematic that the theory has low predictive value. A basic condition is full freedom to enter into contracts. In reality it is often the case that perfect contractibility does not exist. Both governments and market operators might impose limits on the type of contracts which private individuals and enterprises may enter into. Thus, the reality might be very different from the theoretical ideal. But in such cases the theory provides guidance as to the kind of policy that ought to be implemented so as to approach the best possible situation. Smith devotes a large part of *The Wealth of Nations* to point out how monopolies, protection of producers, and trade restrictions between countries hinder the objective of maximization of production – or the prosperity – of a nation. Much of this is presented in the form of arguments against what was the prevailing school of economic thought at Smith's time. In contrast to Smith's ideas, the mercantilism of the time favored government protection of existing industry, in particular against foreign producers.

3. Background

Adam Smith (1723-1790) is often, and with good reason, referred to as the founder of modern economics. As a true-born child of the Enlightenment he was anxious to understand and explain the underlying mechanisms that drove the economic interactions within a nation, as well as among nations. He was looking for a logical explanation for the behavior of enterprises and individuals, with a desire to ascertain the connections that existed, regardless of whether he personally considered them commendable. Even so we should add that Adam Smith himself, as it also comes to expression in the law, undoubtedly considered the results of market competition and complete freedom of choice better for society than public intervention in economic activity.

The Scotchman Adam Smith graduated at Oxford University and was a professor of moral philosophy at the University of Glasgow (see also Stolz 1990 and Blaug 1980). At that time, at the end of the 18th century, Glasgow and Scotland were an intellectually flourishing region. Moreover, Adam Smith was sufficiently open-minded to undertake extensive travels in Europe in search of intellectual stimuli, particularly among French intellectuals. Smith's academic career did not last very long. He started work on his main project (with the full title *An Inquiry into the Nature and Causes of the Wealth of Nations*), after giving up his professorship in 1764. The book was published in 1776. He was subsequently appointed one of Scotland's customs commissioners, a fact that may appear somewhat paradoxical considering the content of *The Wealth of Nations*. In Smith's view, national prosperity is maximized through the removal or reduction of customs barriers and other kinds of formal and technical trade obstacles.

There are two main reasons why *The Wealth of Nations* has played a central role in recent history. Firstly, the work marks the starting-point of what is called the classical school of economic theory. In the following century the classical school was further developed by David Ricardo and John Stuart Mill, who made it a precursor to the science of economics as we know it today. But the contribution made by Smith is far more than a precursor. Several of the mechanisms and properties of the economic system discussed by Smith are today central elements of economic science. Of greatest importance are of course the theory of the price mechanism and *the invisible hand*. The second essential contribution of *The Wealth of Nations* is the author's methodical approach. Smith was presumably the first to analyze the economic system as a process of equilibrium in which interaction takes place among a large number of participants. Assuming a set of behavioral conditions he formally demonstrated how a market will function when left to itself. Smith himself did not make use of the mathematical tools that have been so extensively employed by later economists. Nonetheless, the purely verbal argumentation is of a strictly logical nature, comparable to that of the natural sciences. It should also be mentioned that, in his day, Smith was not the only one to formalize the economic system. The French Physiocrats, for example, with whom Smith maintained contacts, formulated similar logical systems to describe national economies. In contrast to Smith's contribution these attempts have not, however, survived the verdict of history.

Adam Smith was unquestionably a supporter of what we term economic liberalism, yet his opposition to all kinds of official intervention hardly made him a fanatic champion of free markets. His standpoint has to be seen in the light of his own time. As briefly mentioned above, the dominant line of economic thought at the time when Smith was doing his most significant work, was the system which he referred to as "the mercantile system" – mercantilism. This idea was based on the assumption that society would prosper through the accumulation of wealth. More precisely this meant the accumulation of precious metals, which nations acquired through trade with other nations. A current account surplus from trade resulted in claims on other nations, which could be converted into precious metals. To some extent this can be understood in terms of what nations needed for national defense, insofar as their resources allowed them to procure at short notice arms and mercenaries in an international market. But it also resulted in conspicuous opulence, as expressed in the palaces built by the autocrats of the time. A consequence of the need to accumulate claims on other nations was the desire of each and every nation to protect their own productive activities by all possible means. There were several ways of doing this, the most favored being high customs tariffs and import duties. As far as possible, there should be no export of raw materials, since it was preferable to process these in the country itself. In some countries craftsmen were not allowed to emigrate, since they were competent manpower. Of significance, at least in Adam Smith's view, was the extensive establishment of monopolies and the privileges bestowed upon established producers. The granting of exclusive rights to produce and sell specific goods constituted an efficient means of protecting national producers from cheaper or better imports. *The Wealth of Nations* represented an attack on this system. Smith argued that national wealth would increase if every worker were allowed to specialize in what he did best, and if every nation produced the goods that could most favorably be produced in that country.[1]

---

1   Adam Smith was wrong in assuming that *absolute* differences in production costs between the respective countries were necessary for them to benefit from trade. David Ricardo later showed that the important feature is *relative* differences, i.e. the comparative advantages of each country. See Norman 1986.

Adam Smith's ideas represented a considerable break with the established and dominant system. Yet he was not alone in the criticisms he made. Similar objections to mercantilism were raised by the Physiocrats, although they committed the error of focusing on agriculture as the central economic sector. Smith regarded all economic activity as equally productive. Therefore everybody had important contributions to make, even philosophers, whose profession was, in Smith's view, "not to produce anything, but to observe everything and who often can, therefore, combine the forces of the most separated and dissimilar objects".[2] Smith's own contribution also gained importance in his own time, and his book became a bestseller. On the other hand, considering its voluminous content, it is rarely read in its entirety. But what is most important is that his ideas gained popularity and in due course became crucial in the shaping of practical policy. The book and the political economy it represented were enthusiastically greeted by the growing class of new industrialists. This group clearly realized the advantage of breaking up established monopolies, which were obstructing their own growth and development. As an economic system Liberalism developed on the basis of Smith's ideas, and probably found its clearest expression in the so-called Manchester Liberalism of the 19th century. These thoughts were to form the foundation of the general principle that the economy functions best under "laissez-faire". The role of the State should be restricted to intervention only when markets do not function properly, or to protect private interests and shield the economy when vital national interests are at stake.

4. Formalization – precise definition

The Wealth of Nations contains no systematic representation of the basic conditions that have to be met to achieve optimal allocation of resources, i.e. the situation where the value of societal production is maximized. Several of these conditions, always referred to in modern textbooks, are nonetheless mentioned in the work.

The conditions which are indispensable if free competition is to maximize the value of society's production are as follows (see e.g. Munthe 1986):

---

2   Quotation: *Aschehougs Verdenshistorie (Aschehoug World History)* vol. 10, p. 136.

1. There must be *many market participators*, on both the supply and the demand sides. All market participators should be small, and therefore incapable of influencing prices individually. They have to accept market prices for what they are.
2. Producers and consumers must be *free to enter and leave* the supply and demand sides. This implies the right to freely establish oneself freely or dissolve a firm, and that no advantages are bestowed upon established market participators to the detriment of newcomers.
3. The goods and services available in the market must be *homogeneous*, in the sense that, if a given product is offered by many producers, all these products will be identical. On neither the supply nor the demand side should there exist conditions giving one agent an advantage to the detriment of others.
4. Perfect information should be available concerning all goods and services offered. This requirement is in fact more stringent than it need be. It would suffice for information to be symmetrical, ensuring that nobody has any advantage or disadvantage with regard to information.

As mentioned, Smith did not specify all these assumptions clearly. In the discussion of prices he mentions the importance of many sellers and perfect information, plus the necessity of perfect resource mobility. Strictly speaking, it is only product homogeneity condition that is omitted from his list of the conditions required to optimize the competitive economy. It is also worth mentioning that Smith makes a clear distinction between long- and short-term economic equilibrium.

Although it does not influence the market's ability to establish a price equilibrium, from the point of view of welfare we should include one more requirement: the activities of consumption and production must have no *external effects*. To the best of my knowledge, Smith neither discusses nor mentions this subject. This might be considered a serious omission, since Smith claims that the solution sketched above is the best possible insofar as it maximizes society's production. In order to be optimal, production and consumption of goods must not have indirect effects on persons or enterprises other than those involved in the market transaction in question. If the actions of an agent operating in the market have such extra effects which are not "passed on by the market", these will not be accommodated in prices, which do not then correctly reflect the value of the goods to society. Conversely, when there are no external effects all factors relevant for the evaluation of the price of the goods are reflected in the market price. The classical example of an externality is pollution. A polluting enterprise does not take into account the costs that accrue to others due to its emissions of potentially dangerous particles into the air or water. In the case of such external effects competitive markets and individualistic behavior will not result in society's best possible utilization of resources. On the other hand, Smith is concerned with the framework and the institutional conditions under which an economy will function. He sketches a kind of harmonious model of society where there are no undesirable effects as a result of everybody caring only for his own interests. This might well leave a role for the state, as the body that ensures that any undesirable effects of competition are solved through proper intervention, which should not disturb the agents' behavior beyond its intended effect. In modern variants of the perfectly competitive model we would say that this involves correcting market imperfections and missing markets, which results in incorrect pricing.

Smith's methodical approach

The discussion of market equilibrium and pricing is one of Smith's most important achievements. In several ways he demonstrates how prices are determined by the actions of consumers and producers. The main interpretation of Smith's price and wage theory, and of *the invisible hand*, is the famous market cross. The established market price will be such that supply and demand are balanced, and buyers and sellers agree as to how many units will be traded. At this established price, in a perfectly equilibrated competitive market there can be no unsatisfied demand. At the same time, each individual agent on his own, whether buyer or seller, is too small to be able to influence the price. Nonetheless prices are such that all desirable trade is realized. In leaving all these separate traders to themselves one should expect chaos. Instead an equilibrium is established where noone wants to alter the situation. This is the result of *the invisible hand*.

Let us examine the mechanisms involved by means of the figure below. In the figure, price P is measured along the vertical axis, and quantity Q along the horizontal axis. In accordance with the general pattern, we can assume that the lower the price, the higher will be the quantity demanded by the consumers. Therefore, the demand curve, D_0, is downward sloping. The upward sloping curves S_0, S_1, and S_2, are three different supply curves. If more is produced the supply increases, which generally takes place at increasing marginal costs. This explains why the curves slope upwards.

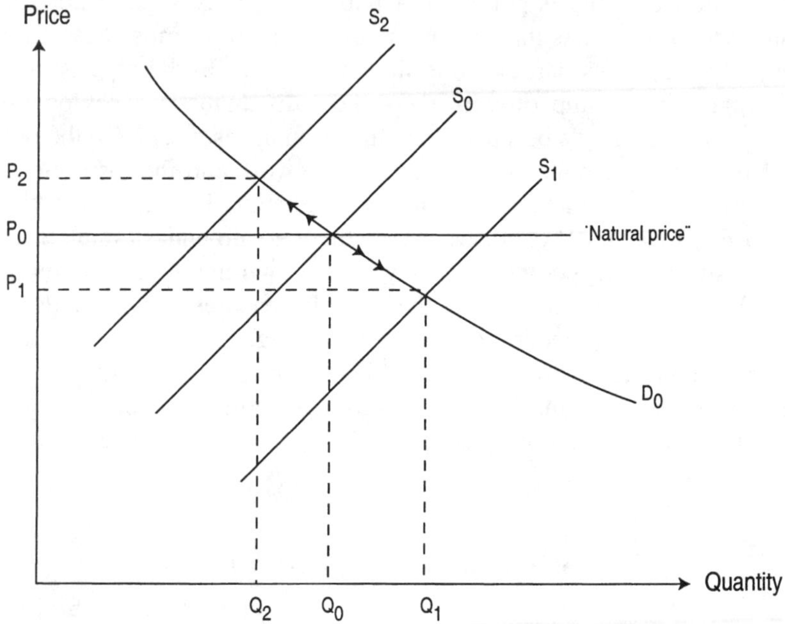

Assume there to be a state of equilibrium where the quantity demanded by the consumers is exactly equal to what is produced and supplied. The goods are traded at the Anatural price",[3] as indicated by the point P_0, which lies where the demand curve D_0 intersects the supply curve S_0. The quantity traded is given as Q_0. Now, suppose that for some reason supply increases. In the figure this is represented by the rightward shift in the supply curve, from S_0 to S_1. At the current price, P_0, more goods are now available than the consumers are willing to buy. The price must fall, to P_1, where demand equals supply, and the quantity traded is Q_1. Next, assume the opposite, i.e. supply decreases as indicated by a shift to the supply curve S_2. At the market price P_0 there is unsatisfied demand. Some consumers will be willing to pay more for the available goods, thus securing these for themselves in competition with other consumers. This results in a price increase, which will con-

---

3   Smith considered "the natural price" to be a long-term equilibrium. According to Smith "the natural price" would cover labor costs and rent. In a perfectly competitive system, price will be equivalent to the costs of producing the goods, but there will be no pro☐ in excess of costs for use of the factors of production. A rent will originate if there is a scarce factor, e.g. land. Smith reasoned on the basis of labor value theory, leaving no room for a price on capital, which is of course different to neo-classical economic theory.

tinue until there is no unsatisfied demand. The new equilibrium is established at price P_2 with quantity Q_2 traded. The same will go on in all markets, for consumer goods as well as investment goods. We will always observe that those producing at too high a cost will not be able to sell their products. This is how a nation's production attains its highest possible level. Under the assumption of perfect competition, we find that demand for all goods equals production, and the consumers pay exactly the marginal costs when buying these goods. Then there is no way that firms can change their production so as to increase total output from the resources available.

Adam Smith's thesis, and the representation in the figure of how this market mechanism works, is based on the assumption that a stable market equilibrium actually exists. Yet the requirements for stability to occur are not always fulfilled. This problem is discussed in standard economics textbooks.[4] It is possible to imagine situations where, instead of converging, the economy will diverge, so that supply and demand are unable to equilibrate. Moreover, we can imagine situations of indefinite circulation around a point of equilibrium. However, there are two reasons why such cases are of merely marginal interest. Firstly, we observe that most economies in reality are rather stable, and after unexpected shocks the systems appear to revert to a kind of normality. Secondly, exploding or perpetually unbalanced systems should be ruled out for methodological reasons. In such situations we are to a large extent unable to present interesting and meaningful predictions of how the economic system will function. It is particularly in analyses of economic growth that the requirements for stability and convergence are of great importance (see e.g. Mork 1993, chapters 18 and 19). In order to study the growth process of a country, and to find explanations why different nations follow different growth paths, we must assume that all nations have a growth process which in some sense converges towards a state of stable equilibrium. Otherwise, the economy will either "disappear" or become infinitely large.

Adam Smith considered demand to play a role only in the short-term. In the long-term all goods would be valued according to the value of the resources needed in the production, i.e. their "the natural price". First and foremost this means the value of the labor, which in the long-run would be paid at subsistence level. Today, this way of dis-

---

tinguishing between short- and long-term perspectives is not considered meaningful. The demand side plays a role regardless of the time scale of the analysis.

It is worth noting another shortcoming of Smith's analysis. He generally considered the production of goods from the supply side. Smith has no adequate utility theory. The concept of utility was introduced a century later by the marginalists. Consequently, Smith is unable to explain the importance of demand in the creation of value.

5. Generality and testability. Critique

The Wealth of Nations, and in particular the theory of *the invisible hand*, has had significant practical consequences. The theory established economics as a scientific, academic discipline, and provided the basis for the development of a method and a way of thinking, the principal content of which remains unchanged today. The theory has also given legitimacy to the belief in free markets and the capitalist system.

From the time of Adam Smith, academic research within the field of economics has taken his contribution as its starting point. A considerable part of the research within economics during the past 200 years has been aimed at further development of the hypotheses attributable to Adam Smith, and at different ways of testing them. The modern version of the theory of *the invisible hand* and the market mechanism, with its consequences for general welfare, has been formulated by Debreu (1959) and can be associated with the concept of "the two main theorems of welfare economics".[5] These theorems state that a competitive economy secures an optimal allocation of resources, and that any equilibrium can be achieved by initially redistributing the available resources accordingly. There is no doubt that the price mechanism works, and that, given the conditions stated above, when markets are left alone an equilibrium will emerge which cannot be improved upon in a Pareto sense.[6] However, we may not approve of the results that arise for reasons of fairness. The market equilibrium is not necessarily fair, and distribution of resources may be far too skewed and unequal to be acceptable, both before and after trade. It is probably fair to say

---

5   Gerard Debreu was awarded the Nobel Prize for Economics for his work.

6   The Pareto requirement states that it is impossible for there to be a change in the distribution of resources that makes one person better off without harming another person's interests. Another way of saying this is that no resources are wasted.

that this did not bother Adam Smith much. A 'justification' for this may be that he had no theory of utility, and was therefore hardly able to consider the problem of distribution. It must also be noted, as was noted above, that his concern was primarily monopolies, which he believed definitely did not work for the welfare of people in general. Moreover, judging by what we know today, many of the forces that lead to unfair distribution of resources constitute market imperfections which Adam Smith was unable to foresee, and therefore did not address. Investigating market imperfections has been a main focus of later research, as we shall see below. When conditions for a perfectly competitive market are not met, free markets may not work in the best interests of society.

While not refuting the price mechanism, there are economists who are skeptical about using it as an important mechanism when analyzing real economies. One of the most prominent critics of this intensive reliance on the market mechanism was the Marxist economist Michael Kalecki. His critique was based on the view that the price mechanism and the neo-classical equilibrium concept are not of particular interest. According to Kalecki, existing economies are rather far removed from the idealized conditions of the perfectly competitive market. He therefore made only limited use of the traditional analytical tools. Instead he concentrated his efforts on the study of monopoly formation, and on how monopolies influence profits and fluctuations in the economy.[7]

Adam Smith also discusses some possible consequences of market imperfections, but primarily in relation to monopolization. Today, the study of market imperfections plays a far more prominent role, and focuses on several relevant and interesting problems. In addition to problems related to imperfect competition in the market for goods, there are the matters of unemployment, pollution and other types of external effects, and informational problems that may give rise to missing markets for insurance, credit rationing and allocational imbalances in the capital markets. Nevertheless, the analytical framework and the role attached to the price mechanism are still essentially the same as in Adam Smith's model. Markets function along precisely the lines sketched out in *The Wealth of Nations*. But where market imperfections exist, the consequence is that *the invisible hand* does not always work for the "good" of society as a whole in the way that might be desirable. In such circumstances regulation of the market may be called for. It may be the case, however, that Adam Smith would not have approved of the

---

7   Sawyer 1985 offers an interesting and thorough discussion of Kalecki's work.

fact that his theory is being used to justify state interventions in free markets.

Nonetheless, it is important to bear in mind that unfavorable effects in some or several instances do not imply that economic analyses based on the price mechanism become irrelevant or uninteresting, rather the contrary. The price mechanism has its virtues and deficiencies: competition in the market place implies that those who are most efficient and thus able to sell their goods at the lowest price will gain. This is also advantageous to society, in the sense that resources are allocated according to their most profitable use. But this might also provide incentives for the most efficient producers to use resources to protect their production, so as to receive potentially higher individual gains. Even where the market mechanism are at work, it is not unlikely that monopolies, so disliked by Adam Smith, will establish themselves. Such tendencies worried Smith, since monopolies implied a less than optimal use of resources. Moreover, today we also worry about the distributional effects of free markets. This particular theme has been analyzed by the Nobel Laureate Amartya Sen, see e.g. Sen 1973. One consequence of free markets which may occur particularly when monopolies are allowed to establish themselves, is that some people may become extremely rich, while others gain little. In non-regulated market systems this distribution of income may prove undesirable.[8] Another problem is that in some instances it might be difficult to establish properly functioning markets as noted in the former paragraph. The prices that are established in such situations are then "wrong"; they give the wrong signals, and the use of resources is either higher or lower than the optimum. Thus, the non-regulated price mechanism, *the invisible hand*, can lead to unacceptable outcomes, and not always to the highest possible wealth of a nation.

It is easy to come up with examples to illustrate that a free market will *not* secure the highest national income possible. It would suffice to draw attention to fisheries: free and non-regulated access to the oceans' fish resources would result in the best and most efficient vessels making, in a short time, large catches and profits. But a probable consequence is then that fish stocks will be over-utilized, such that it may fall below reproduction level (see the chapter "The Tragedy of the Commons"). In the long-run the resource may disappear. It is a reason-

---

8   This line of reasoning is based on a social welfare function for the whole nation, which in particular takes into consideration distributional issues. Samuelson (1947) makes an important modern contribution, and a more recent reference is Stiglitz (1988).

able assumption that it is profitable to preserve fish for coming genera-tions, and to extract gains from fisheries over a long period. This being so, the task should be to calculate how much fish may be caught annu-ally. The annual quota has to be apportioned by regulation. Unregulat-ed competition will not result in a suitable amount being caught. Pollu-tion is a similar problem. As a basic principle, air is a free and common resource. Everybody is entitled to the free use of air. Firms' emissions of gases into the air can result in greenhouse effects, the acidification of watercourses, and infections of the respiratory system. Later costs of eliminating these problems can be considerably higher than the sums saved through not removing the affluents from circulation at the point when they were emitted into the air.

In fact, the price mechanism and the line of reasoning underlying *the invisible hand* theory can also be used to solve these problems. The problem originates from *lack of ownership rights*. Resources are over-utilized since nobody owns them. A solution is therefore to give prop-erty rights to somebody, or to have these property rights vested in the State. As owner the State will have the right to impose a fee for the use of the resources, or to grant temporary property rights. The correct use of incentives or distribution of property rights will give the market agents the right incentive to avoid over-utilization. Thus, the price mechanism may be used for regulation purposes within fisheries, as well as for solving the negative external effects of pollution. A system of fees, imposed on goods that pollute, such as oil products, could be based on the need to pay for the damage inflicted on nature. Since such fees would lead to higher prices, the result would be a reduction in de-mand for the goods produced by industries that pollute. The reduced demand would give an incentive for self-interested producers to reduce their pollution. Likewise, fishing could be efficiently controlled through the allocation of quotas. It is possible that these quotas will, in the course of time, be traded in a free market, and that they will thus pass into the hands of those able to catch the given quota at the lowest cost. However, the total catch is still within the limits given. Yet there may be objections about going that far. Income distribution and region-al issues may restrain society from using the price mechanism to the full, and result in limits to the right to sell and purchase quotas. Never-theless, the most important point is this: if the price mechanism, as an-alyzed by Smith, is ignored or not taken into account, the result for so-ciety as a whole will be bad. It is therefore important to know that the price mechanism is actively at work. Today's prevailing line of thought is this: wherever markets function smoothly and without undesirable effects, they should be given as much freedom and subjected to as little regulation as possible. Undesirable consequences of the price mechanism have to be corrected if and when they occur. The normal way to do this is by using the same medicine, namely by applying the price mechanism, as in the example with environmental pollution.

6. Empirical assessment – conclusion

Testing Adam Smith's hypotheses in *The Wealth of Nations* is not an easy task. They are hard to falsify, and alternatives, with which they may be compared, are not readily available. However, we do observe that monopolization leads to higher prices, and that the liberalization of markets results in lower prices, at least in the short-term. A possible procedure would be to look at the alternatives to 'free markets', i.e. to study systems that claim to disavow the market, e.g. the former Communist command economies of Eastern Europe. These economies, however, are not perfect examples. To a considerable extent even these made use of the market mechanism, or rather were compelled to do so. What could nevertheless be observed, was that when efforts were made to 'beat the market', the outcome was often disappointing. This is not to deny that for periods central planning worked well and the authorities succeeded in achieving high production and in providing food and necessary goods for a large population. However, productivity was probably low. The agricultural sector will serve as an example. Compared to the large collective farms where proceeds had to be shared, productivity was far higher on pieces of land where individual cultivators were allowed to keep the profit for themselves. It was precisely this phenomenon which, at an early stage, persuaded the Chinese authorities to reward individual achievement also on collective farms, and which later led to the total abolishment of the collective farm system.

Adam Smith drew attention to fundamental mechanisms that govern non-regulated market economies. At the outset it is of course easy enough to ascertain that in a market with identical products, all producers charge an identical price. Yet this does not imply that there is perfect competition. Identical prices in a market might also be the result of a small number of producers tacitly colluding in fixing a monopoly price. Much effort within so-called industrial organization theory – as well as within the theory of regulation – has been devoted to defining this kind of competition-hampering agreement, and to establishing the conditions required for competition to function properly. It has also been discussed how desirable perfect competition is for economic growth. The central problem is what market conditions will best further research and innovation: among small enterprises in a competitive system, or among large enterprises which are able to protect their inventions from excessive competition. Incentives for firms to introduce new and efficient modes of production, or new products, depend on them having at least a minimum of protection from competitors who want to use the innovations. Today such protection is provided via the patent system. Thus, the advantages of competition have to be balanced against growth enhancing considerations.

Thus, the discussion about the best way to organize the market is still ongoing. The price mechanism and the theory of *the invisible hand* constitute the academic basis for this discussion. When economists analyze how society's resources are to be put to their best use, and to the benefit for the inhabitants of a nation, they use the tools originally developed by Adam Smith.

7. Literature

Aschehoughs Verdenshistorie, (History of the World, Aschehough publisher) vols10.

Blaug, Mark 1980: *Economic Theory in Retrospect*, Cambridge University press (3 ed.)

Debreu, Gerard 1959: *Theory of Value*, Wiley, New York.

Mork, Knut Anton 1993: Makroøkonomi (Macroeconomics), Bedriftsøkonomenes Forlag.

Munthe, Preben 1986: Markedsøkonomi (Market economy), Universitetsforlaget (4.ed.), Oslo

Normann, Victor D. 1986: *En liten, åpen økonomi* (A small, open economy), Universitetsforlaget (2.ed.), Oslo

Samuelson, Paul A. 1947: *Foundations of Economic Analysis*, Harvard University Press, Cambridge

Samuelson, Paul A. 1955/1967: *Economics: An Introductory Survey*, McGraw –Hill Book Company

Sawyer, Malcolm C. 1985: *The Economics of Michal Kalecki*, Radical Economics, Macmillan.

Sen, Amartya 1973: *On Economic Inequality*, Oxford University Press, Oxford

Smith, Adam 1776/1981: *Wealth of Nations*, J.M. Dent & Sons Ltd. Everyman's Library

Stiglitz, Joseph E. 1988: *Economics of the Public Sector*, W.W. Norton & Company

Stolz, Gerhard 1990: *John Stuart Mill* (manuscript), Norges Handelshøyskole.

10
Von Thünen's Isolated State The Law of Area Utilization in Agricultural Production

PETER SJØHOLT

1. Original quotation

Man denke sich eine sehr große Stadt in der Mitte einer fruchtbaren Ebene gelegen. [...] Die Ebene selbst bestehe aus einem durchaus gleichen Boden, der überall fähig der Kultur ist. [...] Die Ebene enthalte weiter keine Städte, als die eine große Stadt, und diese muss also alle Produkte des Kunstfleisses für das Land liefern, so wie die Stadt einzig von der sie umgebenden Landfläche mit Lebensmitteln versorgt werden kann.

Es ist im allgemeinen klar, dass in der Nähe der Stadt solche Produkte gebaut werden müssen, die im Verhältnis zu ihrem Wert ein grosses Gewicht haben, oder einen grossen Raum einnehmen, und deren Transportkosten nach der Stadt so bedeutend sind, dass sie aus entfernten Gegenden nicht mehr geliefert werden können; so wie auch solche Produkte, die dem Verderben leicht unterworfen sind und frisch verbraucht werden müssen. Mit der grösseren Entfernung von der Stadt wird aber das Land immer mehr und mehr auf die Erzeugung derjenigen Produkte verwiesen, die im Verhältnis zu ihrem Wert mindere Transportkosten erfordern.

Aus diesem Grunde allein werden sich um die Stadt ziemlich scharf geschiedene konzentrische Kreise bilden, in welchen diese oder jene Gewächse das Haupterzeugnis ausmachen. Mit dem Anbau eines anderen Gewächses, als Hauptzweck betrachtet, ändert sich aber die ganze Form der Wirtschaft, und wir werden in den verschiedenen Kreisen ganz verschiedene Wirtschaftssysteme erblicken. (von Thünen 1842, pp. 11-12).

2. Translation and brief explanation

Imagine a great town situated at the center of a fertile plain [...] The plain itself consists throughout of a uniform soil type, and can be cultivated in its entirety. [...] The plain holds only the one large town, and this town must therefore supply the country with all industrial products, just as the town depends entirely on the surrounding countryside for its food supplies.

It would appear self-evident that in the immediate surroundings of the town cultivation would have to be concentrated, on the one hand, on products of considerable weight or volume compared to their value, products that would cost so much to transport to the town that they could not be supplied from far-off regions, and on the other hand, on perishables that must be consumed fresh. The further one moves away from the town, the greater the reliance on cultivation of products with lower transport costs in comparison to their value.

This is sufficient to explain the formation of rather sharply divided concentric rings around the town, each of which is devoted to some particular staple product. But as soon as a different crop is produced, the whole configuration of the economy changes, and we find wholly different economic systems in the different circles. (von Thünen 1842, pp. 11-12).

Here we see a law formulated in the form of a model. Von Thünen is the first virtual model builder in social science. He gives a brief and clear account of the conditions assumed, and on this basis formulates theses of inherent orderliness. His preconditions are rational agents (economic man) and homogeneous production conditions. The most important variable of the law is location in relation to the market. This market, *the site*, is a given. What von Thünen endeavors to show, is how differences in distance to the market influence the way in which land is used.

This approach is fundamentally different from that formulated by another German scholar a hundred years later in the so-called central place theory. This theory describes where the market or site will be located on the basis of population distribution and the costs of overcoming distance (Christaller 1933). Von Thünen's approach, which focuses on the exploitation of an *immobile* resource, in this case land, differs also from that found in classical models for industry location (Weber 1909). These models also focus on the choice of location, because the fundamental production factors are *mobile* (Chisholm 1962).

3. Background

The background to this law is an astute combination of deductive theory and keen empiric observation. Von Thünen was acquainted with the most important economic thinking of his day, as well as with that of the recent past, Adam Smith (1723-1790) undoubtedly being his most important model. One of von Thünen's central notions, explicitly borrowed from Smith, but further elaborated in terms of his discussion of the model, is land rent. Another important teacher was Albrecht Thaer (1752-1828), the foremost agricultural researcher of his day. Von Thünen learnt a great deal from him concerning important principles in English agriculture, and like him he also realized the importance of mathematical precision (Thaer 1798).

Born in 1783 in Eastern Friesland, von Thünen graduated from an agricultural academy near Hamburg. For a short time he studied at Göttingen University. He spent the rest of his life in Northern Germany. From 1810 until his death in 1850 he ran an estate in the area southeast of the old Hansa town of Rostock. His background and experience were certainly of great importance for his scientific work. He had observed the influence of a large city, Hamburg, on the structure of agriculture and land use. His own contact with the market, laid down in scrupulously kept accounts, has contributed to the elaboration of the relationships that he observed.

Already before 1820 von Thünen had finished elaborating an abstract model of an economy based on empirical data. The first edition of his book appeared in 1821, entitled *Der isolierte Staat in Beziehung auf Landwirtschaft und Nationalökonomie*, and was revised several times.

Von Thünen's standing as a theoretician is unchallenged. His work might well have been entitled "The Idealized State", his method being idealization: he isolated one factor and then proceeded to study how a phenomenon varied when different values were given to this factor, while all others were kept constant. Von Thünen realized at an early stage that only simplified thought models can help clarify complex relations. He is thus two generations ahead of his time in formulating an important theoretical principle in social science. Later researchers are indebted to him also in other fields. Marshall (1842-1924) emphasizes his role in the development of the concept of marginal productivity (Marshall 1890), and Schumpeter (1954, p. 466) does not hesitate to characterize his empirical documentation and model testing as good econometrics already 100 years before this notion gained general acceptance.

4. Formalization – precise definition

As we have already mentioned, von Thünen's central concept is that of land rent. To enable production in market-oriented agriculture the land rent of the product in question must be positive. Von Thünen shows that the land rent varies with the yield per unit of land. This yield is dependent on market price, production costs and transport costs per unit produced. In their turn, transport costs are a function of distance to market. Von Thünen disputes Adam Smith's notion which sees land rent merely in terms of a landlord-tenant relationship. Thus, von Thünen points out the nature of the land rent as a result of yield (calculated for the actual site), variable operational costs and fixed capital and financing costs, including value depreciation of real capital.

The general calculation of land rent can be thus defined:

$$LR = Ym - Yc - Ytd = Y(m - c - td)$$

where LR = land rent
Y = yield per land unit
m = market price per unit produced
c = production costs per unit produced
t = transport costs per unit produced per distance unit
d = distance to market

However, von Thünen's original calculation was not quite that simple and general, since he had to consider several special circumstances inherent in the production and marketing system of his time. But in principle the systems are the same. Von Thünen could formulate the equation as follows:

LR = Ym – td – (cl + c2)

In order to calculate, e.g., the grain price at a given site, the first step is to subtract freight costs from market price. Then follows the subtraction of the so-called farm-based costs, fixed as well as variable, these expressed in subsistence products . Finally, there are the town-based expenditures, meaning farm inputs bought in the town, and expressed in money. These are in reality variable costs, but stipulated by von Thünen as a constant 1/4 of total costs, and not varying with distance. Later, the costs related to subsistence products are converted into money. These costs decrease with distance to the market due to the lower product price (higher transport costs). The total costs will decrease at a slower rate than will product price as a consequence of the fixed town costs implied, and a marginal value will be reached where gross product value minus costs will be 0. This is the marginal value for profitable production, or the *marginal location*. At all points at a greater distance from the market production will be carried on with a loss (fig. 1).

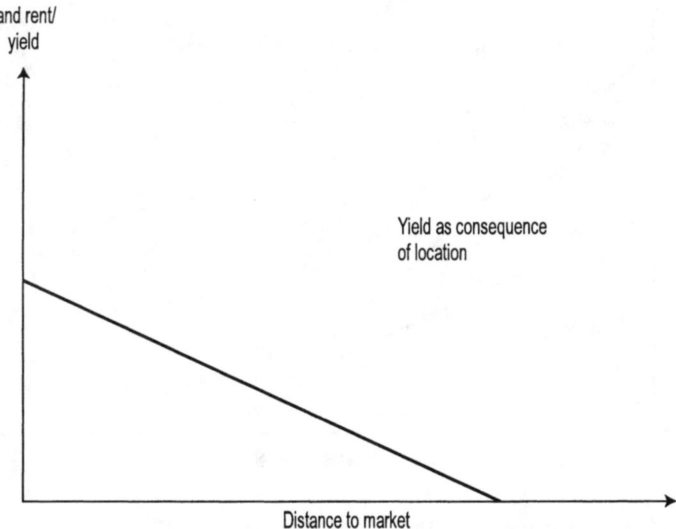

Fig. 1 Yield as consequence of location

Nearer the market there will be a *location-specific profit* ("situation rent" or "location rent"). Von Thünen has thus formulated an economic law which states that the profit, and, consequently, the land rent for a particular production system will decrease with increasing distance from the market. At the same time he has formulated a general localization principle based on *relative location*: the decisive factor is always location in *relation to the market*.

Von Thünen also studied variations resulting from extensive or intensive farming. In the agriculture of his time the systems used were primarily the more traditional, so-called three field rotation system and a more intensive, improved system ("Koppelwirtschaft", i.e. "improved system"). He demonstrates that with increasing net prices (nearer to the market) increased intensification will result in an extra profit which exceeds the profit due to location. This principle can be termed profit resulting from *intensification*, implying increase of profitability with decreasing distance to market. Inversely, intensive farming involves a more rapid decrease in profitability with increasing distance to market, than does extensive farming, due to the rapidly falling profit rate (fig. 2).

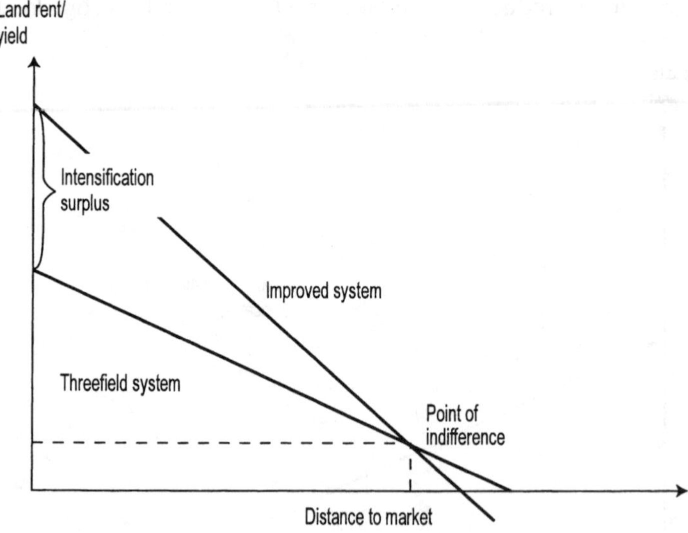

Fig. 2 Profit, intensification and distance to market

As in the first case presented above (profit resulting from location), where von Thünen had discovered the general *marginal location or situation* principle, he here adopts the marginal productivity principle. This obtained a wide general economic application, long before its later formulation by neoclassic economists.

Von Thünen was also preoccupied with the choice of different cultivars. The choice is not determined by the degree of intensivation or extensivation, although cases of concurrence may be observed. On the contrary, what occurs is a complicated interplay between profit and cost factors that have to be calculated for each cultivar. In the end, the decisive variable is the land rent. The most rational choice of cultivar will be the one giving the highest land rent. Of two or more alternative crops the one that is produced nearest the market will be the one that shows the highest degree of cost increase as a result of increased distance to market and the highest cost reduction when that distance approaches zero. This is von Thünen's law of alternative land use. This means that with equal profit from two crops the cultivar with the lowest costs per unit of production will be located nearest to the market, and inversely. In a von Thünen system costs generally decrease with distance.

What this implies is that if *costs* per unit produced are equal for two or more cultivars, the one with the *highest profit* will be produced nearer the markets, due to transport costs.

Von Thünen has thus formulated three basic principles or laws for production when considered in relation to the market:

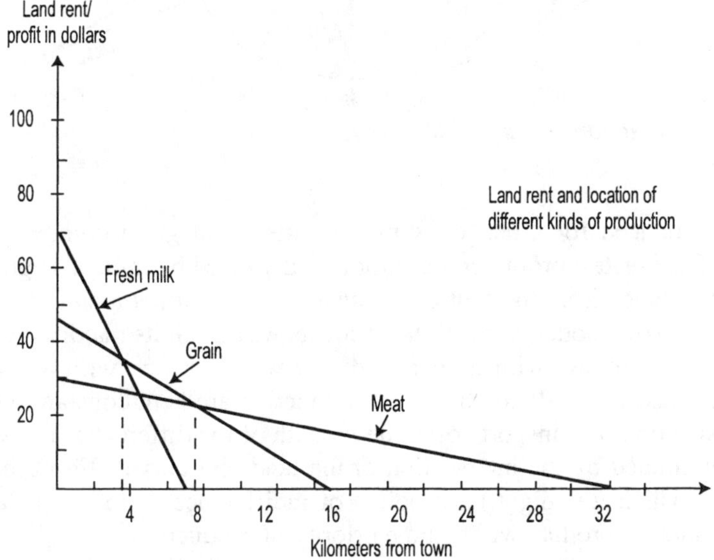

Fig. 3 Land rent and location of different kinds of production

1. How land rent varies in relation to distance from the market
2. How land rent varies as a result of intensification and distance
3. How land rent varies as a result of alternative cultivars and distance

The law presented at the beginning of the chapter refers to the third point, which is illustrated in figure 3, where the theme of the investigation is highest possible yield per area unit, all other factors being kept constant.

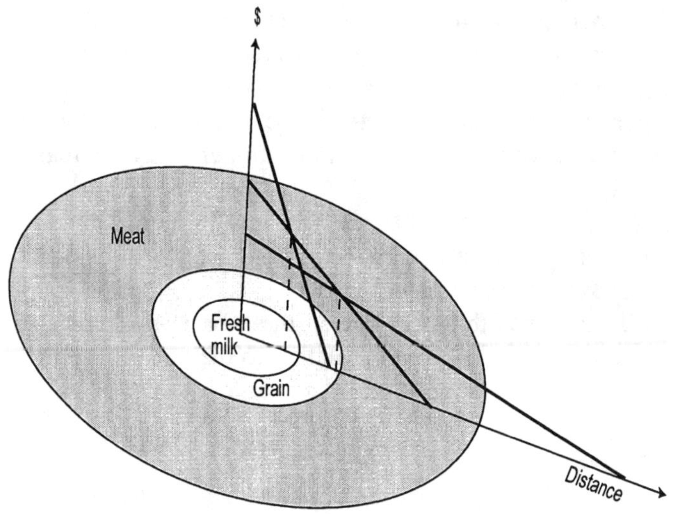

Fig. 4 Production zones and land rent

Milk produced for direct consumption, meat and grain compete for land. The greatest profit per area unit is that yielded by milk. The greater the distance from the center, the smaller the profit per area unit. According to the model, none of the products will reach its maximum extension. A product with higher land rent will oust one with a lower yield. Thus, when all conditions of production are kept constant, with the exception of transport costs, the breadth of the different zones will be determined by the intersection of the land rent curves. From these points, which we might term points of indifference as to yield (land rent), another product will assume priority of production..

In the innermost zones we find the high-yielding, intensively cultivated and transport-sensitive products, such as vegetables and milk for consumption. Between this circle and a grain zone we find the energy

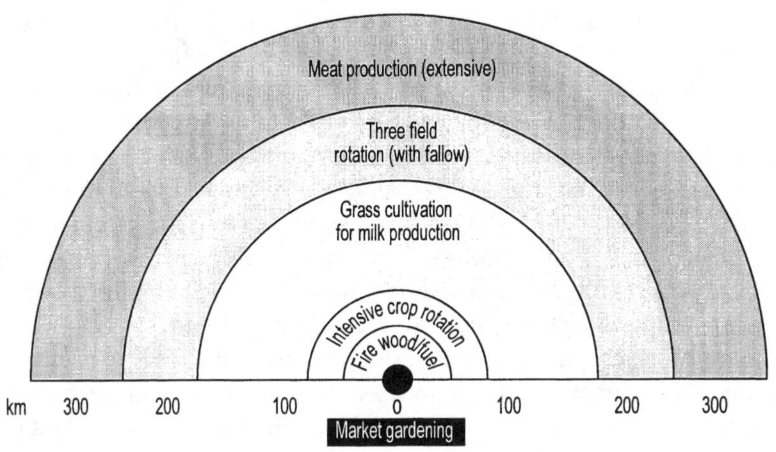

Fig. 5 Production zones in von Thünen's isolated State

zone of the time – firewood. Because of its weight and volume (high transport costs), firewood had to be produced near the market. This is, moreover, in accordance with early industry location theories which stress the importance of energy and raw materials being available near the heavy industry plants (Weber 1909).

The energy zone gives way to a crop rotation belt cultivating grain and other suitable crops. The outermost zone is dominated by pasture and meat production, in von Thünen's times the most extensive of all productions. However, there will not necessarily be a general development of extensive production in this zone. Here too there is space for a number of cultivars, which in fact also amount to industrial raw materials. Some of the crops will yield smaller or equal gross profits, but will entail higher production costs than those of, e.g. grain. This circumstance will push the production of such crops towards this marginal zone, in accordance with the relative reduction in costs which result from distance, when other conditions are kept constant.

5. Generality and testability. Critique

Much of the discussion concerning von Thünen's model has centered on its restricted preconditions and, consequently, the problems facing the theory in the real world. Innumerable doctorate theses have been written on the subject (Hall 1966), several of these bearing the mark of vulgar argumentation. The central point of the debate is whether or not von Thünen's model (figure 4) is valid in relation to empirical studies of more modern agriculture. According to Saey (1997) this "empirical" approach to the theory is an obstacle to really understanding its explanatory power.

In the second edition of his work von Thünen added some finer structure to his model and abandoned some of the rigid preconditions, e.g. that of one single market. The result as far as land use is concerned, is basically the same, but the picture is more complex, thus approximating more closely real world conditions (figure 5).

A more serious critique involves objections to the logic of the calculation. Von Thünen has been accused of focusing too closely on the conditions of his own time in his specification of several important elements of the model.

This is an angle taken by the most meticulous von Thünen researcher, Petersen (1944), in his criticism of the cost curves of the original von Thünen models. As has already been noted, these decrease with distance from the market, since most of the costs can be expressed in terms of subsistence products. Although this was, in von Thünen's times, in harmony with theory as well as with empirical findings, later economic development has reduced the validity of this "inherent orderliness". The increasing element of external investment and other input factors in modern agriculture have caused costs to increase with distance from market, thus making the cost curves steeper.

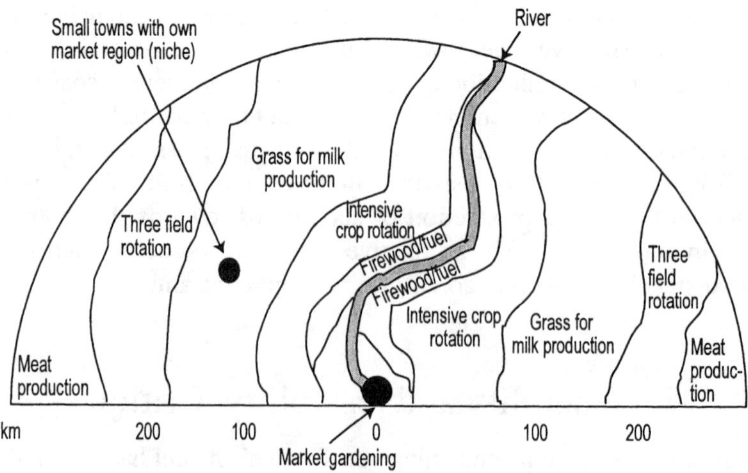

Fig. 6 Modified presentation of land use in von Thünen's isolated State.

Von Thünen's model has also been criticized for varying only one factor – transport costs – independently of the others. Carell (1950) has demonstrated that transport costs influence the variables, such as wages expressed in money, which von Thünen kept constant. In reality there occurs an increase in real income in relation to distance. Carell showed that the model regains consistency if allowance is made for an increased use of cheaper labor near the market, changing the net surplus in relation to "situation rent" into a kind of profit due to intensification. There is, however, good reason to doubt how far a manipulation of this kind is logically tenable in a present-day situation.

Petersen (1944) also maintains that von Thünen's law concerning location of alternative products has no general validity. The claim that high profit cultures will be located nearest to market is true only if costs are lower in the area in question.

Neither is it self-evident which products will be grown nearest to the market. One and the same farm product may involve both higher value of output and higher production costs than another. All income and cost variables will have to be assessed in context before it can be definitely established which product should be grown nearest to the market.

In spite of these objections, von Thünen's principles generally prove valid when we relate them to the preconditions laid down. They may even be claimed to be more widely applicable than von Thünen and his contemporaries were aware of. This applies particularly to his demonstration of marginal productivity. Samuelson (1983) holds the view that this alone should be sufficient to make him famous in the annals of economic theory.

In our century researchers have further generalized the basic principles of von Thünen's model, by applying them to urban geography. In the first place, the model has been applied to the description of urbanization in general terms. Starting with von Thünen's model centered on one single town in the middle of an agricultural area, Wang and Guldmann (1997) analyzed the interaction between the town and its surrounding agricultural area. They demonstrated how the mechanisms of urbanization and town development are dependent on the structure of the surrounding hinterland, on changes in production and transport technologies and on the demand for agricultural and industrial products.

In the second place, von Thünen's hypotheses are even more clearly demonstrated in the attempts to explain land use in urban areas. As already noted, von Thünen's definition of land rent confined itself to the yields of agricultural activity. However, the rent concept may be further generalized to agriculture in general, and finally to price of land. There is a close connection between land rent as expressed by von Thünen and "rent" values as a result of competition for land for agricultural and other purposes (Ricardo 1932). Von Thünen was of the opinion that the farmer, considered as "economic man", will use the land rent as a guide when buying or renting land, thus turning it into a bid rent. For fertile soil he can afford to pay a high price per land unit near the market, while at a great distance from the market there will be a far lower demand for land of the same quality, and this will result in a lower price. In such zones the farmer will be able to substitute high-yield with low-yield cultivars which require a larger area, and still secure for himself a satisfactory income. Here we clearly recognize the similarity to urban competition for land. In many respects theories of land use in urban areas are a logical extension of location theory of agricultural production (Isard 1956).

As early as the second decade of the 20th century a land rent theory was formulated for land use for business purposes and residential areas (Hurd 1924 and Haig 1926). Here as well the principle depends on relative location. Land use will vary according to the distance to the center and transport costs. The keenest competition for land will be found in the very center. In this competition the winners will be those whose activities yield the highest profit per area unit. Provided there is a free market, they will be in a position to outbid those needing land for more extensive purposes. Thus only those able to offer the highest ground rent will be able to establish themselves in the most central area, or, in Hurd's words:

> As value is dependent on land rent, land rent on location and location on utility and nearness, we can eliminate the intermediate links and say that value is dependent on nearness (Hurd 1924, p. 13).

Haig's main concern was the differentiation of activity:

> The center is the point where transport costs can be reduced to a minimum. As there is not sufficient room in the center for all the activities that would profit by being located there, the most central sites are rented by the activities making the best use of the advantages. The other ones will be located in less accessible sites (Haig 1926, p. 421).

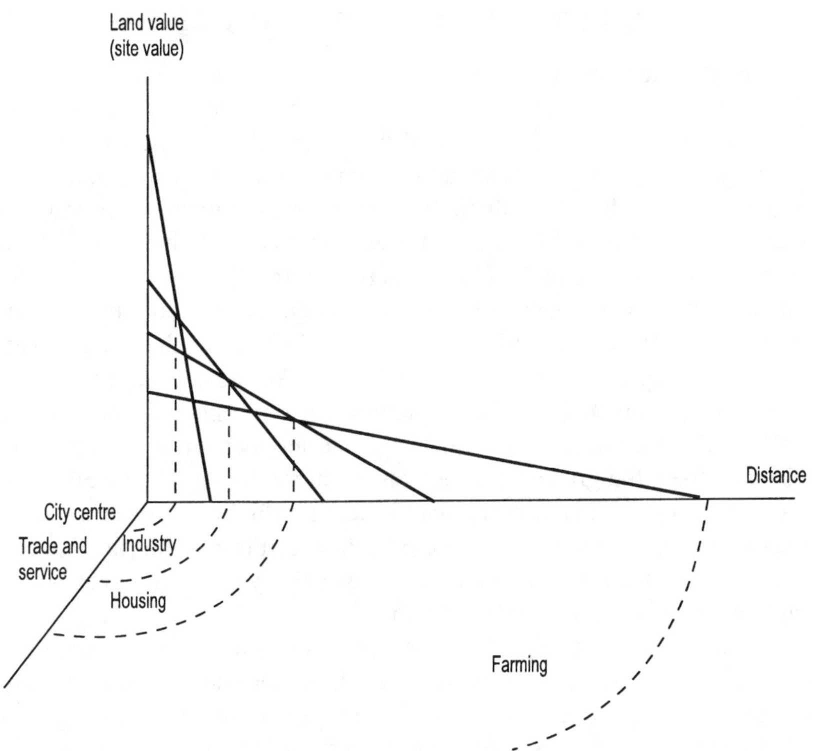

Fig. 7 Relation between land values and land utilization in an urban area.

The innermost zone is that of commercial and service activities, then follow an industrial and a residential zone, and then finally we find, outside the built-up area, an area of intensive agriculture (fig. 7). Thus, one kind of use ousts another, just as von Thünen contended with reference to agricultural production (see fig. 3). At the time of the classical urban land use theorists, this pattern was regarded as so uncontroversial that it was formulated as a general 'law' of city development.

Later development has rendered it necessary to modify this "law". This reorientation is due first and foremost to technological innovations which, in the course of development, have created problems for the old city centers. As we know, the car as a means of transport has rendered access to the center rather difficult, which has resulted in areas of intense industrial activity being located at a greater distance from the center. Incidentally, this is a pattern not wholly unlike that of von Thünen's modified model which allows for more than one market.

6. Empirical assessment – conclusion

When divested of their time-dependent elements, some of von Thünen's "laws" appear to have survived. They refer to processes and relations which are so fundamental that some of the principal features of the geographic model remain valid regardless of time and place.

Thus, horticultural production near markets remains a prominent feature of agricultural land use all over the world. It should suffice to mention New Jersey in the US, or Lierdalen and Frosta in Norway, the latter serving the markets of Oslo and Trondheim respectively. Production of milk for consumption is still located closer to the market than butter and cheese production (cf. Upper New York State and the "milkshed" of Vermont and the cheese factories of Wisconsin, in the US).

We still find many of the world's granaries located at considerable distance from the greater markets, on an intercontinental as well as on a national scale. This also applies to meat production based on ranching. A good example is the increased sheep farming in the rural mountain districts of Eastern Norway, and particularly so in the most outlying areas of Østerdalen and Gudbrandsdalen.

The existence of zones of different intensification in European agriculture is also often used as good evidence of the model's validity (Bradford and Kent 1977). The main features of von Thünen's circles can be verified on the basis of figure 8, in this case on a continental level.

Although several of the main features of the classical model correspond with empirical findings, we can also point to a series of deviations and even different patterns. Vegetables and fruit are grown in special niche areas far from the markets. The classic example is that of specialized Californian lettuce production, which started long before the region itself became a major market. Even if the classical model retains a certain validity also in newly colonized areas of the Third World, with a clear extensivation of production and long fallow periods in market-remote areas and intensive small-scale production near markets, the picture is far from unambiguous (Walker and Homma 1996). Near the great towns of Brazilian Amazonas we find that vast estates are used for pasture, occupying far greater areas than intensively cultivated small farms. This phenomenon is due to far more complex conditions than those expressed in the original models. It seems also to be rooted in socio-political circumstances. Town based cattle farmers, who profit from the advantages of large-scale business, interact with property-protecting authorities.

Today we can witness that milk for consumption is transported over great distances, and that the clear border lines that used to exist between production sites of different milk products are being wiped out. In today's Norway we can even contend that we have an inverse location pattern. The old zone of intensive cultivation near the larger markets (Romerike, Hedemarken) is used for grain production. Milk for consumption by the Oslo region is supplied from far-off valley and mountain districts as well as from Jæren (SW coastal region). Also in continental Europe considerable quantities of grain are produced near the market, even within the innermost circle, as shown in figure 8.

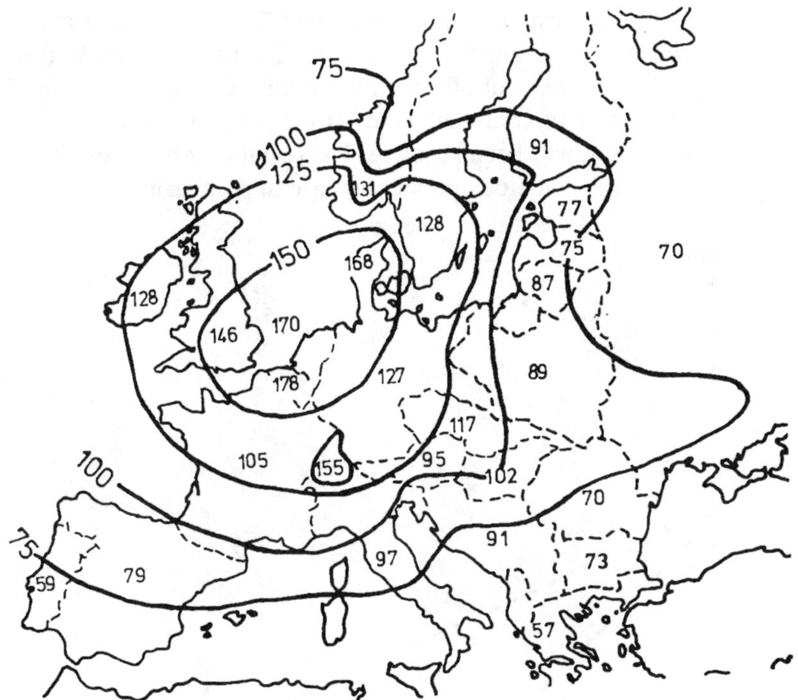

Fig. 8 Zones of different intensification in European agriculture.

It goes without saying that all these departures from the classic model do not imply that von Thünen's model was "wrong". They are rather evidence that the different variables in his model have changed. What we see in the real world is a complex dynamic which results from the interaction between the variables. Peter Hall (1966) points to three such variables: agricultural technology, transport technology and population increase. We might term the latter a dynamic market variable, and, at the same time, add organizational and political variables.

To illustrate our argument let us return to figure 3. Imagine a doubling of production value per area unit, while transport costs remain unchanged. This might quickly result in a considerable enlargement of the zones where cultivation of the product in question is profitable. Another variable likely to change is that of freight costs. This too would result in an extension of the possible range for land use (fig. 9). Both production value per area unit and freight costs have changed since the times of von Thünen, thus increasing the division of labor possible in the agricultural sector in a global perspective. This means that factors other than transport costs have become decisive for location. Without this change the enlargement of agricultural areas on the North American and the Australian continents and on the southern cone of South America would not have been possible. The real motor has been the explosive growth in population and the increase in purchasing power.

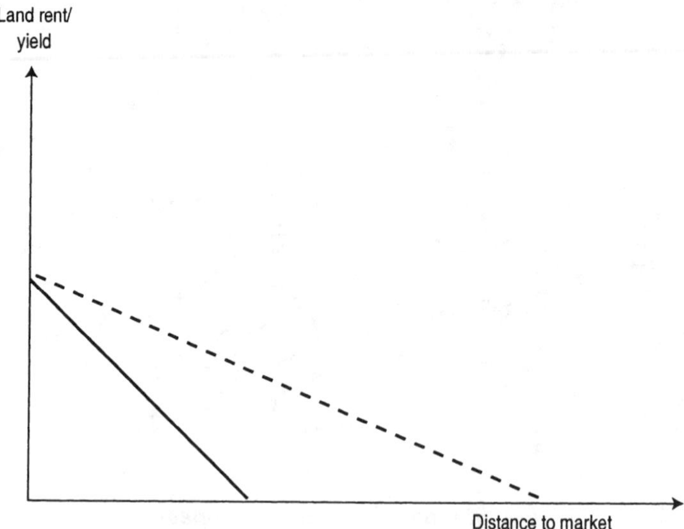

Fig. 9 Changes in transport costs and production areas. The broken line indicates the possible potential of land use by decreasing freight costs.

To some extent this has led to an increased use of organizational and political measures in agricultural production, made possible partly through use of the price mechanism, partly through customs and subventions. The agricultural regulations of the EU have thus contributed to obvious distortions in production. Without these regulations parts of the production would either have been closed down or reduced to the most productive units. This again could have stimulated a considerable increase in world trade, particularly in products like sugar and grain, but also in animal products and fruit. The paradoxes of our own domestic location can also be explained as the result of political decisions which establish price and freight regulations by means of a complex network of agreements based on organized action and not, as assumed by von Thünen, on individual, anonymous participants in the market. This is true of grain production in what was formerly the country's "natural" milksheds, as well as the displacement of this production to more outlying regions with the attendant increase in production and freight costs.

We started with a fairly straightforward location principle. We then endeavored to present a more complete account of the far more complex relations underlying the principle. Even though several of the conditions may today seem dependent on time and space, not least due to recent technological changes, the main point remains valid: the reciprocal constellation of the variables. Consequently von Thünen's work continues to be of considerable relevance, and an exciting subject for further study.

7. Literature

Bradford, N.G. and W.A. Kent 1977: *Human Geography,* Oxford University Press.

Carell, E. 1950: "Die Lagerente", Zeitschrift für die gesamte Staatswissenschaft, p. 106, pp. 473-91.

Chisholm, M. 1962: *Rural Settlement and Land Use: An essay in location,* London.

Christaller, W. 1933: *Die zentralen Orte in Süd-Deutschland,* Jena.

Haig, R.M. 1926: "Toward an Understanding of the Metropolis", *Quarterly Journal of Economics* 40, 421-33.

Hall, P. (red.) 1966: *Von Thünen's Isolated State*, Pergamon Press, London.

Hurd, R.M. 1924: *Principles of City Land Values,* The Record and Guide, New York.

Isard, W. 1956: *Location and Space Economy,* M.I.T. Press, Cambridge, Mass.

Marshall, A. 1890: *Principles of Economics,* London.

Petersen, A. 1944: *Von Thünen's Isolierte Staat: Die Landwirtschaft als Glied der Volkswirtschaft,* Berlin.

Ricardo, D. 1932: *Principle of political economy and taxation,* ECK Gonner (ed.), London.

Saey, P. 1997: "The Theory of von Thünen and the Geographical Structure of Core areas in the World System", paper presented at the 10th European Colloquium on Theoretical and Quantitative Geography, Rostock.

Samuelson, P.A. 1983: "Von Thünen at Two Hundred", *Economic Literature* 21, pp. 1468-88.

Schumpeter, J.A. 1953: *History of Economic Analysis,* Allen and Unwin, London.

Smith, A. 1776: *An Inquiry into the Nature and Causes of the Wealth of Nations,* London.

Thaer, A. 1798: *Einleitung zur Kenntnis der englischen Landwirtschaft,* Hannover.

Thünen, J.H. von- 1826 (1842): *Der isolierte Staat in Beziehung auf Landwirtschaft und Nationalökonomie,* Rostock.

Walker, R. and A. Homma 1996: "Land use and land cover dynamics in the Brazilian Amazon: An overview", *Ecological Economics* vol. 18. No 1, pp. 67-80.

Wang, F. and J.-M. Guldmann 1997: "A spatial equilibrium model for region size, urbanization ratio and rural structure", *Environment and Planning* vol. 29, pp. 929-941.

Weber, A. 1909: *Über den Standort der Industrien,* Tübingen.

11
Hart's Inverse Health Care Law On the Distribution of Health Resources

THOR ØIVIND JENSEN

1. Original quotation.

The availability of good medical care tends to vary inversely with the need for it in the population served (Julian Tudor Hart, The Lancet 27. February 1972).

2. Brief explanation

The claim made in this law is that access to health care becomes easier and its quality improves in inverse proportion to how much it is needed. By inverting the formulation we get the contention that the greater the need of the population, the poorer the quality of these same services, and the less developed will they be. The succinct formulation of the law makes it easier to apply and facilitates its examination by means of statistics on many levels. A simple and general investigation would involve the search for a negative relation between health problems and health service development. By looking at how the law is formulated in the original article, we find that its author takes for granted the validity of such a relation for private, market-governed development of health care services. The challenge is that Hart applies this logic also on the public health services with is "welfare state and social equality" goals.

The content of the law is rather dramatic, implying that the (public) health care system tends to function at complete variance with one of its clearest purposes: the distribution of services according to the needs of the population. It is a serious law and not a subspecies of paradoxical and amusing laws of "the inherent devilry of all things". At the same time, the formulation of the law is sufficiently general and rhetorical to suggest that its primary intention is hardly to be a quantifiable, precise hypothesis, but rather to call attention to a tendency, a statement to provoke discussion and analysis leading to knowledge and reform. To the extent that the law is valid, it points up a fundamental dilemma in the welfare system and the development of health care in our type of society. In this context we shall take a closer look at the nature of this law-like relationship, consider the extent to which the law reflects reality, and examine the consequences of such a relationship.

3. Background

Julian Tudor Hart was a general practitioner in Wales and very much preoccupied with social differences in health matters. It is important to note that the district in which he practiced was severely affected by the law he formulated: the mining districts of Wales (Glamorgan). Both the original article of 1972 and other essays have made Hart known in health service research. His name is associated particularly with the bitter acknowledgment of great social differences in health standards and parallel differences in modern health care, even after the implementation of a public health care system which was committed to the provision of equal treatment and the eradication of health differences. He has published some 50 different essays, all to be found in standard source indexes, most of them rather brief. In these essays he follows up the discussion of the social lopsidedness of distribution, and deals with such themes as the doctor's role as general practitioner, preventive medicine, and the treatment of high blood pressure.

Hart belongs to a solid and strong tradition in English health service research. In the 1970s many were deeply involved in the issue and published reports which, in contrast with general expectations, showed an increase in social differentiation in health matters. It also became clear that these growing differences had developed during the first decades of England's National Health Service (NHS). English research benefitted from fairly fixed definitions of social strata, based on occupational groups. On the basis of well-known differences in death rates and in health complaints in different social classes, such as they had developed from the turn of century, it was found that, in relative terms, these differences had not been mitigated since the establishment of the public health service. Distinct social differences were also noted with regard to accessibility and the use of health care services.

The critical research became known in public debate through *The Black Report*, a report ordered by the British Government. The report was named after the leader of the research group. It showed that the differences in health and in the death rates between different social strata were still considerable and had increased from the 1930s to the 1960s, even though the general health situation had improved considerably. (A brief and precise summary of the most relevant data will be found in Baxter 1976). This was dramatic information for a society which based the development of its extensive public health service on a principle of equality. The government tried to keep the report out of the public debate (it was printed in 260 copies only, with internal distribution to a restricted group). This made it the object of even greater public interest when it was published as a Penguin paperback (Townsend and Davidson 1982), which ran to several editions. The debate among the public and in research circles was correspondingly intense. To some extent, later critical research added nuances to its conclusions, but the main pattern remained, and still remains, valid.

Neither have the health differences between the high and low status social groups been leveled out in the way that many hoped would be possible after the 1960s. Recent documentation shows that if anything the relative differences increased up to 1990, both in England (Townsend, Davidson and Whithead 1990) and the USA (Pappas et al. 1993). We can now assume that for social reasons the frequency of most suffering is disproportionate, for many disease groups the mortality rate is 3-8 times higher among low-status groups than among high-status groups. E.g. such status differences are more significant for life expectancy than smoking (Angell 1993). It is a fair assumption that some 2/3 of the mortality rate differences, in rich as well as in poor countries, are related to income differences. (Hurowitz 1993).

Both the law and its author can thus be connected with a problem in Western health care and a tradition in health care research that can be characterized by the term "social maldistribution". The problem has not been reduced during the 20 years that have passed since the law was formulated.

4. Formalization – precise definition

This is not a simple causality law. E.g. it is not reasonable to believe that the absence of health problems would in itself create a good health care system. Essentially it is a law concerning empirical covariation.

The causes can be numerous and complex. In Hart's opinion the most important causes can be deduced from market-like factors in the health system.

Returning to the original 8 page article of 1972, and considering what we know from health care research, we can assume that the fundamental conditions that give rise to the law are connected with several underlying variables. Presumably it is only of secondary importance to consider the possibility of there being a direct link due to the active concentration of health care services in areas where the tasks are few and simple. However, we should not disregard the possibility that health personnel will sometimes choose their places of work where tasks are few, patients healthy and the work situation simple and well-structured.

The common underlying variables that create the connection are primarily of a social nature: low social status and generally poor living conditions in an area result in health problems in the population. Through many complex mechanisms these same social conditions generally lead to poor health care or at least a health care not so large that it corresponds to the problem load. Health personnel will, for instance, not apply for positions in such regions if they are free to choose. Regional funds might also vary with social status where the budgeting units are local and regional. Further, it could be that socially deprived local communities will be less adept in lobbying to have health institutions located in their areas. Finally, various forms of services based exclusively on private financing will of course follow purchasing power rather than needs.

The simplest way to analyze the background of the law is to point out two parallel mechanisms:

1 Parallel variation of low social status in a region with over-accumulation of health problems.
2 Low social status in a region results in poorer development of health care.

As a direct causal law Hart's inverse health care law is therefore strictly speaking ambiguous.

The original article also strongly cautions against the misunderstanding that the law is due to our expectation of a clear connection between health care and health, such that the lack of health care facilities results in bad health. Unfortunately, health care services, in the way that they are now geared towards curative tasks, are not an important factor for the health standards of greater population groups (McKeown 1976). Hart holds the view that health care should nevertheless be developed according to the population's needs. On the individual level health care services offer prevention, relief, nursing, and important medical assistance, even though they do not in general prove to be of great importance in the amelioration of nationai health problems.

As regards form as well as matter Hart's law has an obvious logical relationship to several other laws concerning social maldistribution.In its form and content Hart's law has an obvious logical relationship to several other laws concerning social maldistribution. "The paradox of the welfare state" was formulated by Eskeland and Finne (1973) after studies of in Oslo low-status areas:

> The welfare state is organized so that it is most efficient for those needing it the least.

The well-known Biblical "Matthew effect" has some of the same structure:

> For unto every one that hath shall be given, and he shall have abundance: But from him that hath not shall be taken away even that which he hath. And cast ye the unprofitable servant into outer darkness: there shall be weeping and gnashing of teeth. (Matthew. Chapter 25: verses 29-30)

The seldom quoted last part may be understood as sharply pointing to the stigmatization often suffered by the socially deprived.

There is another formulation taken from American health service research – though not presented in the form of a law:

> The goodness of justice may be blind, but she smells, and particularly class differences. (Hollingshead and Redlich 1958, p 192):

Of relatively recent formulations we could include one directly related to the administrative system:

> It is not by accident that some pass through the system as if helped by an invisible hand, while others are met by its invisible clenched fist". (Jacobsen et al 1982, p 41).

Thus we have a series of formulations summarizing different forms of social maldistribution and showing that the historically rather new "welfare system" has not been capable of reversing the logic. These are general statements referring to a law which deals with certain mechanisms underlying social maldistribution. A possibly important dividing-line between them is that some are sufficiently general to suggest that maldistribution is a kind of natural law (the 'Matthew effect', or the presentation given in Hollingshead and Redlich 1958), while others imply that the effect is due to a particular shaping of the public administrative system (Hart 1972, Eskeland and Finne 1973, Dahl Jacobsen et al. 1982). The inverse care law belongs to the latter category. The formulation links the law to a particular shaping of the health care system, as do the arguments presented. Moreover, it is characteristic that the form of Hart's law is less general – the law explicitly points to a pattern which is typical of the way health care systems are organized.

In its logical form the law conforms to a long series of statements on society which summerize empirically observed tendencies with several possible causes. The law stating the downward tendency of the profit rate is an interesting comparison (Hellesøy 1988). According to at least one interpretation that law can be summarized as the contention that a series of underlying circumstances make it such that we will normally find a tendency of the kind in the society for which the law is valid. The tendency is due to socially defined causes that can thus be counteracted through action, even though the connection is normally observable. In the closing passage of his article Hart indicates that we have to regard the law as a general tendency in our type of society, albeit a tendency that we are able to counteract through political processes and system changes.

It follows that the inverse care law applies to a limited sector of society, and reflects different underlying causal mechanisms. Since both these causal mechanisms and the sector to which the law applies are man-made, this is no "natural law", but a highlighting of certain relations or laws which are, undoubtedly, subject to human intervention.

5. Generality and testability. Critique

Having briefly and precisely formulated the law as the interrelationship between a few factors, it would seem reasonable to assess some precise interpretations and strict graphic presentations of the law. The simplest and most direct interpretation is the assumption of a linear connection where health care facilities – in terms both of quantity and quality, directly and absolutely – decrease in proportion to increasing demand.

Figure 1 shows such a simple, curvilinear connection, where supply, understood as an absolute value, is reduced with increase in demand. Several geographic indications given in Hart's article allow an interpretation of the kind, and it is in terms of such an interpretation that the law presents a brutal and dramatic deviation from the expressly stated main principles of public health care policy.

But we could also present a less strict interpretation of the law by saying that it points to a tendency characteristic of most distributive efforts within the welfare state: that the availability of good services increases less than would correspond to the increase in demand. Such a relation is presented in figure 2. Here, the law represents merely a systematic deviation from an expectation that the availability of health care should increase in proportion to demand. The light curve shows increase in availability following increase in demand, the dark curve shows the decrease in the extent to which needs are met. The considerable discrepancy between figures 1 and 2 indicates that when we are imprecise in defining the relations we are looking for, the result is a multitude of very different conclusions all of which fit in with the law. There is a risk that many empirical findings would fit in with the less strict interpretation as presented in figure 2, while the argumentation might easily evoke the dramatic situation presented in figure 1. As a

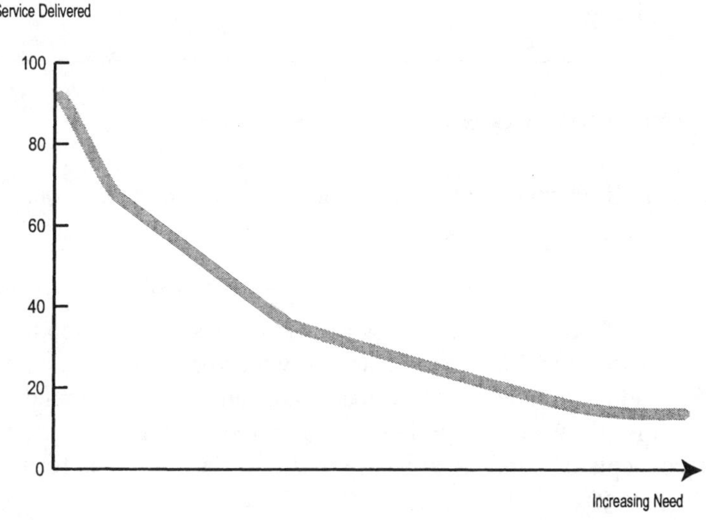

Fig. 1 Hart's Inverse Healt Care Law – strict interpretation.

simple, testable hypothesis the first alternative is clearest and easiest to examine, while the relative interpretation reflects primarily a general underlying tendency of many public distribution systems. Alternative 2 is therefore the most general, but also the least precise. In the less categorical interpretation it would seem justified to interpret the law (provided it is valid) as a problem of adjustment, organization or implementation, rather than as a fundamental shortfall in the provision of public health care.

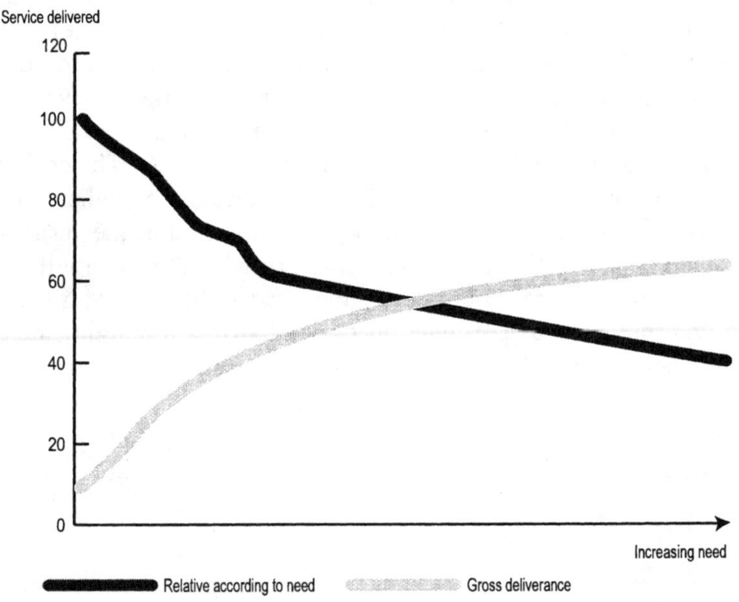

Fig. 2 Hart's Inverse Health Care Law – relative interpretation.

As has already been noted, the law can also be seen in relation to social status and social maldistribution, and may thus be interpreted as implying that bad health and poor health care are caused by low social status. Here the implications of the law can be directly related to one of the basic concepts of public health care in the welfare state, as formulated by Asa Briggs:

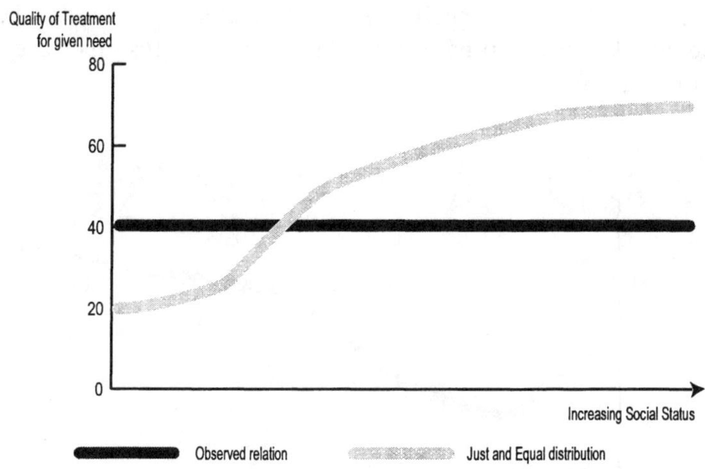

Fig. 3 Hart's Inverse Health Care Law: Social Inequality Interpretation.

[...] to secure for all citizens, regardless of class or status, the availability of
health care of the best possible standard within an established level of social care
(quoted in Seip 1981, p. 35).

The public health care system is one of those sectors where an offen-
sive objective such as this has the greatest legitimacy. Even though
"best standards available" cannot always be complied with, to establish
service quality priorities on the basis of social status is clearly illegitimate. A version of the law which emphasizes a connection between social status and the availability of good health care might be presented
as in figure 3. Expectations are shown by the dark curve, indicating
equal treatment quality regardless of social status. The light curve indicates improvement in quality in proportion to increased social status,
which accords with Hart's law. Here we should mention a few reasonable and qualifying concerns. First, there is the possibility that at least
some particular low-status groups avail themselves of health care services to a considerable extent, e.g. institutionalized and/or handicapped
people with visible and "worthy" defects. Secondly, the real situation is
indisputably such, that a minimum health service lies within everybody's reach, and a maximum, where public funding achieves as much
as might realistically be expected. Thus we can modify the law as
shown in figure 4. Here the services offered are reasonably good for

some weak groups with specific needs ("formal needs"), but for the rest of the population it still holds that higher social status gives access to better health care.

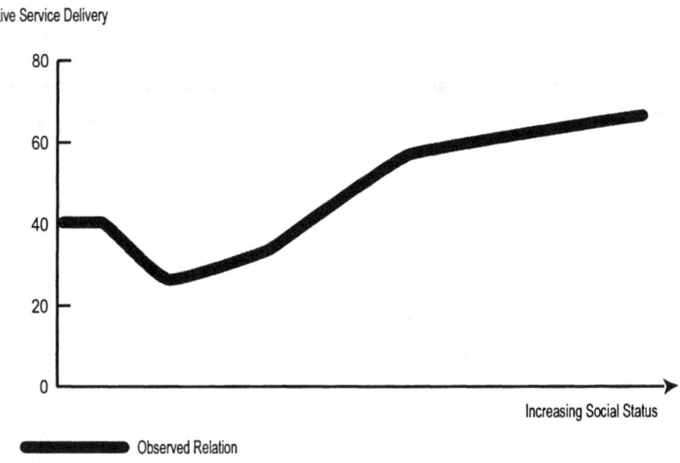

Fig. 4 Hart's Inverse Health Care Law – a realist interpretation of social inequality?

Such illustrations can be made in many ways. Our point has been to indicate that a formalization of the law may easily suggest differing interpretations and can thus prove an inspiration for the formulation of prolific hypotheses to which the law is an invitation. On the other hand, it would apply to this law as it does to others, that an empirical illustration may be less useful than a knowledge of the mechanisms which inspired the law. But we shall always face some difficulty in trying to account for such knowledge in terms of simple two-dimensional and linear presentations.

Basic causes

Hart's intention in formulating such a law is presumably twofold. It is partly descriptive, insofar as he wants to point out that reality is systematically different from the formally acknowledged aims of official policy. Secondly, his intention is normative; he is of the opinion that the situation can and should be changed. If attempts to change something are to be successful, thorough knowledge of the causes is required, and it is precisely the causes, and strategies for change, which Hart discusses in his article. In Hart's view the general cause is quite clear: "The inverse care law has its maximum validity in sectors where market forces have the strongest influence on health care, and its minimum where such influence has been reduced".

This market influence is both direct – through the possibility of buying health care – and indirect, in as much as the economic and social strength of the individual heightens his/her chances of obtaining good public health care, individually as well as collectively. Hart's article was written partly to warn against the increasing market emphasis within public health care, a trend that was visible at the time when the article was written. Direct market mechanisms mean that health care can and must be bought, and are bought by those who are economically strongest, who are best motivated and best informed. In this way health care services acquire a marked social bias, which again results in a pattern that conforms to the inverse care law. There were clear and direct features of the market in Great Britain in the 1970s, and to a somewhat lesser extent we see them in today's Norway. Patients' contributions and private specialists are such elements. The wave of privatization in the 1980s triggered an extensive discussion of the danger that the health service might come to reflect the distribution of economic strength and not the needs for such services. As noted already, several analyses indicate that the maldistribution of health and health care in Western countries has become worse since the wave of privatization of the 1980s.

Indirect market mechanisms are nevertheless of greater interest in societies with health care systems that have, in principle, abandoned the free and private market as a mechanism for the distribution of care, or which at least apply a principle of distribution according to needs to health care as a whole. Hart discusses several indirect market mechanisms, the most central being that related to the market in doctors and doctors' preferences. When doctors are broadly free to choose where to live and work, and when, as is generally the case, they themselves belong to the upper social strata, they will tend to feel attracted towards regions which can ensure them a good working situation and high status, and where they will be among people who share the same background.

It is worth noting that in this sector our societies have attached great importance to the freedom of the profession. In other sectors where geographic distribution is important, quite another professional culture applies. The telecommunications firms Televerket/Telenor, the postal services Postverket/Posten, and the national defense services, for example, all employ a combination of postings by order and on request from the personnel employed. Free choice of profession is subordinate to the need for the postal service or the defense forces to cover the entire national territory.

Hart's exposition concerning Great Britain bears resemblance to what we find in Norway. When there is a critical shortage of qualified personnel, e.g. when there are too few doctors, the decisive factor in finding the required staff will reflect the private preferences of the personnel in question, a situation which contrasts sharply with the line of thought prevailing in the more substantial and classic public service branches, where personnel shortages might be dealt with e.g. by a practice of more extensive postings, or by exploiting the scarce resources available. We have already commented on the general wish for a good life in a high-status environment. Hart further stresses the importance of the collective medical ideology, which now pays considerable attention to the interaction between doctor and patient. The wish for the best possible working conditions and an ideal doctor-patient relationship lead to a situation in which social care is given lower priority, and Hart arrives at the harsh conclusion that:

> The ambition to practice such an ideal medicine under ideal circumstances still makes doctors all over the world leave the people in greatest need of them, to go to those needing them least.

The circumstances that create this effect have already been examined under the title "The Efficiency Threshold". There are several practical and normative circumstances that cause high-status patients and regions to be seen as the most natural and attractive tasks (Jacobsen et al. 1982).

A theme not discussed by Hart is the basic planning system that allocates health care resources and distributes these within the medical sector. It would seem reasonable to search for causes here too. Different county councils, provinces and State authorities constitute innumerable arenas where patient and professional groups can present and negotiate their claims, and where values and needs beyond the ambit of the health sector also have some weight. Even the very simplest assessments that consider relative negotiating strengths and the interplay between the respective participants would seem to indicate that there must be far more processes involved than just the allocation of health care according to needs. If for example the richest county councils can use their resources in the negotiating process and professional associations support the private interests of their members, we have more reason to expect that the system will favor places of high status and limited needs. The people who are potentially most liable to counteract this, i.e. the patients and the population of under-privileged areas, hardly have any say in these arenas. Insofar as patient and population interests are at all represented in this game, there will be strong and weak groups also on this side, and the strong ones may easily become dominant.

Many studies have been made of hospital planning and other allocation processes The frequent conclusion of studies of decision-making and implementation processes is that ideal and formal aims of distribution and equality of rights are transformed into something different through the political systems that implement them.

On the macro level many comments have been made regarding the general and problematic tendency to define priorities according to criteria other than needs, such as for example geographic considerations and the relationship between the larger, specialized hospitals and regional health services (Fuggeli 1982).

Some of the causes that underlies the inverse care law can be related to health services seen as a complicated structur of access to health care. We would be justified in comparing the availability of health care, and not least the best services and those at the highest level of specialization, with an obstacle race where the client has to overcome a number of difficulties, e.g. inconvenient office hours, periods of waiting, requirements for articulacy and documentation, and more subtle mechanisms relating to one's ability to make a good impression and to present oneself as a deserving applicant (Jacobsen et al. 1982).

On the basis partly of the information provided in Hart's article and partly of other health service research we thus find a set of interconnected factors, all of which tend to support the inverse care law. Seen as a totality, these factors can prevent public health care from satisfying the ideal and the formal objective of meeting real needs.

6. Empirical assessment – conclusion

Empirical evidence

Hart opens his article by pointing out that in his district health standards as gauged by mortality rates have deteriorated compared with averages for Great Britain. In 1931 the mortality rate in his district was 128% of the national average, and in 1968 it increased to 131%. In a later article (1972) he provided even clearer numbers: a mortality rate that rose from 111% of the national average of 1931 to 143% of the 1959 average. The development of infant mortality was along the same lines. As already mentioned, socially biased health distribution – and even increasing social differences – have been confirmed by numerous studies in Great Britain (Blaxter 1976, Townsend and Davidson 1982). In the 1970s evidence was produced that among the lowest social strata the risk of certain diseases was approximately double what it was among the highest, a finding which was confirmed by various methods of computation. For certain diseases (e.g. Bronchitis) the variation was even greater (Williams 1977). In the words of Titmuss:

> 15 years of experience with the National Health Service have taught us that high income groups know how health services can best be exploited. They more frequently are treated by specialists, occupy a greater number of ward beds in better equipped and better staffed hospitals, receive more surgical treatment, have better maternity care and get psychiatric assistance and psychotherapy more easily than do low income groups, and quite particularly those representing unskilled labor (Titmuss 1968).[1]

A general statement of this kind must be empirically verified. There are two elements in the statement: it contends partly that people belonging to higher social strata interact more efficiently with the system, and partly that a better health service has been established in their local environments. Concrete analyses are difficult, since members of higher social strata are healthy, and corrections must be made to allow for the lower needs of these strata. A further complication arises from the fact that high-status people demand more, both in terms of their own health and from public services (Jensen 1983). The assessments of Titmuss have been confirmed insofar as it has been possible to effect concrete and reliable analyses (Jensen et al. 1982, Jensen 1983, Townsend et al. 1990, Pappas et al. 1993). For Great Britain analyses exist which indi-

---

1   Quotation from Hart's article.

cate that consultation rates at the bottom of the status hierarchy – with corrections made for needs – are only half of what they are at the top (Blaxter 1976). The registered data is complex and tends to spawn erroneous inferences concerning levels, but we should note that the difference between high- and low-status groups is greatest in terms of preventive health care (Collins and Klein 1980). If we focus on specific diseases and not on the general pattern, the methodological problems become fewer and the results clearer. To give some examples from England we can mention that the number of vaccinations is inversely related to need, that in abortion cases among the lower social strata twice as many go to hospital too late, and that the frequency of home visits during fatal complaints is almost five times higher at the top of the status pyramid (Williams 1977).

In the Norwegian health care system we find built in mechanisms that automatically modify such imbalances and which render services more easily accessible (enterprise health care, state health examinations, housewife examinations, infant checkups, vaccination programs etc.).

But systems of this kind have now lost some of their importance and have partly been replaced by more ordinary systems which depend on the initiative being taken by users.

Developments within quantitative health services distribution patterns constitute just one aspect of the maldistribution problem, yet it is this aspect which provides the basis of Hart's inverse care law. It is also possible to identify some indicators which demonstrate the quality of health care, and Hart makes a survey of several such indicators: in working class areas 80% of operation rooms were built before 1900, and only 5% had been built after 1945, compared to 25% new operation rooms in middle class areas, and only 50% from the time before 1900. As for doctors engaged in public service, we can look at the number of potential patients in their individual lists. In middle class areas there were far more doctors with lists comprising less than 1000 patients, and fewer with lists exceeding 2500, compared to working class areas. Also, clear quality differences were registered between doctors and the equipment at their disposal. In middle class areas four times as many doctors had studied at Oxford or Cambridge, and five times as many in London. They had more X-ray equipment, and five times as many were in a position to offer physiotherapeutic services. During the first period of the National Health Service (NHS) there occurred perceptible improvements in the standards and redistribution of doctors, but during the 1960s there was a shift back towards earlier conditions.

Nearly all doctors who began service in 1968/69 in medically under-staffed areas were imported, and there occurred a general increase in the percentage of the population living in areas with too few doctors. If one were to develop a measure which contrast this maldistribution with the far greater need for health care among the lower social strata, there is little doubt that one would find sufficient empirical evidence to support Hart's inverse care law, also with regard to quality.

As might be expected, given the rather dramatic formulation of the law in a brief article, some critics have claimed it to be too general and oversimplified, yet very few have doubted the basic law-like relationship (Williams 1977).

Does the law apply to Norway, and today?

Since Hart's law is now rather old and refers to a Great Britain where class distinctions are far more pronounced than they are in Norway I might be supposed that the law will hardly apply in today's Norway. Yet there is no systematic documentation available that could unequivocally refute an optimistic hypothesis of this kind. One reason for the lack of documentation and research is the fact that there are no simple and generally accepted criteria of social strata nor indicators of demand.

Unfortunately however, the indications are that the law is valid also here and now. A systematic review of the research results available indicates that there is undoubtedly a social maldistribution of health care in Norway, and this maldistribution is most conspicuous among men (Dahl 1988). On the other hand it is more difficult to assess whether there has been a progressive relative deterioration, despite the assumption that there has been one in terms of the principal cause of death among males, namely heart and vascular diseases (Jensen 1983). On the other hand circumstances suggest that maldistribution and relative deterioration are likely to be less pronounced in Norway than in England and USA (Dahl 1988, Pappas et al. 1993).

Geographic maldistribution of health care is a well-known phenomenon that has worried Norwegian health officials for much of the post-war period (Hansen 1979). These geographic differences tend to correlate with social dividing-lines and also reflect available knowledge concerning the frequency of health complaints. Hence on a regional level there is evidence to support Hart's law: the higher the frequency of health complaints, the poorer the health care. The most obvious instance of an area where health care services are insufficient and overstretched is the county of Finnmark, whereas certain areas of

Eastern Norway are examples to the contrary. On a more local basis, we find that in urban areas of low social status the available health care is poorer. In the case of Oslo this is fairly well documented. In a report on Oslo, Otterstad (1988) shows that, with adjustments made for health condition (mortality rate), the number of consultations registered by doctors was far higher in Western than in Eastern districts (e.g. in the Western districts, people aged 50-59 were 1.39-2.25 times more likely to receive a home visit from a doctor).

Otterstad summarizes as follows:

> (...) the connection between high mortality as an indication of poor health, and low use of health care services. Current patterns of mortality and figures for the use of health care services could indicate that the health care system contributes to a widening of the differences between social groups (Otterstad 1988, pp. 8-9).

The gravity of the maldistribution of health care facilities in the Eastern and Western Oslo districts must bee seen in the light of dramatic overrepresentation of fatal heart attacks among men in the low-status East regions of Oslo. (Holme 1982, Otterstad 1988, Dahl 1988). There are also significant indications that a well-developed health care system and frequent utilization of its facilities leads to a greater emphasis on preventive measures. The health care resources are thus used for checkup purposes, counseling and early contact, which in turn influence health standards (Jacobsen et al. 1982, Aarø 1986, Elvebakken 1994).

These clear indicators – mortality rates and the number of doctor consultations – seem to suggest that the inverse care law is valid in the social hierarchy of Oslo. In an analysis of more prosaic data – the number of inhabitants and people's own assessments of the need for health care – differences between parts of Bergen have been found which unquestionably corroborate Hart's law. The least well-established health and social services were those of the most problem-ridden parts of the town (Jensen et al. 1991).

In studying the connections between various population groups and the health services, we also notice significant differences along social dividing-lines. General surveys of the Norwegian health care system have been published, which underline social differences, including unequal development of the said services (Fuggeli 1982). The poor health care facilities for patients suffering from chronic diseases, and particularly from such as are typical for the working class (e.g. muscular- and skeletal complaints due to wear and tear) should also be noted as indicative of the system's failure to help those of the lowest social ranks.

Thus we see that, when taken together, many different circumstances confirm the general validity of the inverse care law. If we were to conduct a systematic test of the law, we would have to study the rather extensive basic material now available concerning health and health care in relation to geography and social status, and develop indicators suitable for the purpose. An approach along these lines would probably furnish systematic documentation to show that actual distribution does not satisfy requirements for how demands are to be met, for equal treatment, and for the elimination of differences in provision of health care.

We should also bear in mind that Hart's political point was to warn against market mechanisms in health care. From the mid-1980s onwards this worry about the social consequences of the health care sector being converted into a market has also been apparent in the Norwegian situation. But in addition to these clear and simple circumstances, research in mechanisms of public service deliversy systems points to an even grater challenge, namely that public health system seems to promote uneven distribution, despite all ideals of equal rights and the intention to provide most care to those who need it most.

Conclusion

The inverse care law is worrying , in that it concentrates on mechanisms wholly contrary to the priorities assigned to public systems of health care. Sufficient studies have been made to confirm the tendencies indicated by Hart, but in Norway the general pattern has not been discussed or made an object of research to the same extent. Although in recent times several good studies have been published (Dahl 1988, Otterstad 1988), few projects have focused specifically on Hart's inverse care law. Future research projects should endeavor to establish, e.g. whether the social distribution of health complaints in Norway accords with Hart's law, and whether the expansion of the health system should follow the needs of the population.

One person who has for many years been closely involved with the English system, the sociologist Margaret Stacey, is of the opinion that a "Phase 2" should be defined for the development of public health. "Phase 1", now concluded, was aimed at the allocation of sufficient general resources and personnel for health care. Phase 2 would aim at the creation of an organisation and a culture which guarantee the establishment of priorities according to needs and included in this; the solution of the problem of social maldistribution (Stacey 1986).

Interest in the inverse care law may be based on an implicit desire to take seriously the political and formal objectives of the welfare state and the public health system. The law (and my interpretation) also originate from a commitment to social equalization, admittedly rooted in a civil right, human right socialist or social democratic ideology. From a more cynical and pragmatic liberal point of view the law is less interesting. It simply shows that the strongest individuals in a society are not only the healthiest, but also that they manage to get the best health care, just as they manage to get the best of practically everything. If we go beyond such cynical pragmatism and adopt an active liberal, social Darwinist outlook, we would regard the law as a confirmation of our having a well-functioning society where the strong and healthy get most, this being in accordance with universal laws and values, and in society's best interests.

Since the law represents a tragic problem in the light of the objectives of public health care, it would seem reasonable to conclude our review by discussing the possibilities of "abolishing" the law or of mitigating its consequences. Several types of reform can restrain market mechanisms and introduce regulation or affect the strength of the participants in order to "mitigate the effects of the law". We shall give just a brief sketch of five different steps in such a process:

- The first step is a fully developed public health system where private market elements are minimal or regulated so as to promote the aims of the public system.
- The second step is to minimise the right of health personnel to establish themselves freely, linked to a sufficient training capacity adjusted to needs.
- The third step is to furnish each and every inhabitant with a clear legal right to easily available and high quality health care.
- The fourth step is the alteration of the central political decision making processes so that they focus on health values in a way that has for many years been lacking in Norwegian politics. (Jensen 1994).
- The fifth step is to promote high formal and informal professional standards which emphasize public health needs in a stronger way.

Even an optimistic view of the possibilities of implementing such changes must lead to the conclusion that, for many years to come,

Julian Tudor Hart's inverse care law is likely to remain a central tendency in Norwegian health care, albeit one which is variable and can be manipulated.

7. Literature

Angell, M. 1993: "Privilege and Health - What Is the Connection?", *New England Journal of Medicine* nr. 2, pp. 126-127.

Blaxter, M. 1976: "Social Class and Health Inequalities", in Carter and Peel (eds.): *Equalities an Inequalities in Health*, Academic Press.

Bomann-Larsen, P. and T.Ø. Jensen 1992: "Pasienterfaringer med helsevesenet" (Patients' Experiences with the Health Service), in Piene (ed.): *Helsevesent i klemme* (Health Service in trouble), Ad Notam.

Botten, G. and T. Bjerkedal 1988: "Ulikheter i helsevaner i Norge" (Inequalities Health Customs in Norway in 1985, *Tidsskrift for den Norske Lægeforening*, nr. 108, pp. 157-62.

Collins and Klein 1980: "Equity and the NHS: Self-Reported Morbidity, Access and Primary Care", *British Medical Journal* nr. 281, pp. 1111-1115.

Dahl, E. 1988: *Sosial ulikhet i helse,* (Social Inequalities in Health), SIFF, Gruppen for helsetjenesteforskning, (Group for Health Care Research), report nr.7.

Elvebakken, K. T., S. Fjær, T.Ø. Jensen 1994: "Forebygging og politikk: historie, dilemma og grenser", (Prevention and Politics: History, Dilemmas and Limits), in Elvebakken, Fjær and Jensen (eds.): *Mellom påbud og påvirkning. Tradisjoner, institusjoner og politikk i forebyggende helsearbeid* (Between Command and Influence.Traditions, Institutions and Politics in Preventive Health Work), Ad Notam.

Ekeland, S. and J. Finne 1973: *Rettshjelp* (Legal Aid), Pax Forlag.

Fuggeli, P. 1982: *Det medisinske klassesamfunnet* (The medical Class Society), Universitetsforlaget.

Hart, Julian Tudor 1972a: "The Inverse Health Care Law", in *The Lancet* 27. February 1972 (also published in Cox and Mead (eds.): *Sociology of Medical Practice*, Collier/McMillan 1975).

Hart, Julian Tudor 1972b: "Data on Occupational Mortality", *The Lancet* 22. January 1972, p.192.

Hansen, F.H. 1979: "Kjempevekst og fordelingskrise" (Gigantic Growth and Distribution Crisis), *Tidsskrift for Samfunnsforskning*, nr. 20, p. 21ff.

Hellesøy, A. 1988: "Profittratens fallende tendens" (The Falling Trend of the Rate of Profit), in Ugelvik Larsen (ed.): *Lov og Struktur* (Law and Structure), Universitetsforlaget.

Hollingshead and Redlich 1958: *Social Class and Mental Illness*, John Wiley.

Holme, I. 1982: "Coronary Risk Factors and their Possible Role in the Development of Heart Disease. The Oslo Study", *Journal of Oslo City Hospital* nr. 32, pp. 79-105.

Hurowitz, J.C. 1993: "Towards a Social Policy for Health", *New England Journal of Medicine,* nr. 2, pp. 89-101.

Jacobsen, K.D., T.Ø. Jensen and T. Aarseth 1982: "Fordelingspolitikkens forvaltning" (The Administration of the Distribution Policy), in *Sosiologi i dag,* nr. 3.

Jensen T.Ø. 1983: *Helsevesen og sosial skjevfordeling* (Health Service and Social Unequal Distribution), publication nr. XX from "Forvaltningen og svakstilte brukere" (Administration and Vulnerable Users), Bergen 1983 (in distribution at SEFOS, UiB).

Jensen, T.Ø. 1994: "Forebygging og helse i politikken – den nære fortid" (Prevention and Health in the Politics – the Near Past), in *Mellom påbud og påvirkning. Tradisjoner, institusjoner og politikk i forebyggende helsearbeid,* (Between Command and Influence. Traditions , Institutions and Policy in Preventive Health Work), Ad Notam.

Jensen, T.Ø. 1992: *Pasienterfaringer med helsevesen* (Patients' Experiences with the Health Service), SEFOS, note nr. 57, Bergen.

Jensen, T.Ø., Ø. Venneslan and Vaage 1991: *Desentralisering som administrativ reform* (Decentralisation as Administrative Reform), SEFOS, report nr. XX 1991.

Lindblom, C. 1976: "Another State of Mind" in *American Political Science Review,* nr. 1, pp. 9-21

McKeown, T. 1976: *The Role of Medicine. Dream, mirage or nemesis*, Nuffield Provincial Hospital Trust, London.

Otterstad, H.K.: 1988: *Helsetjeneste er best for de friske* (Health Care is best for the Healthy), SIFF, Group for Health Care Research, report nr. 2.

Pappas, G. et al. 1993: "The Increasing Disparity in Mortality between Socioeconomic Groups in the United States, 1960 and 1986", *New England Journal of Medicine,* nr. 2, pp. 103-109.

Seip, A.L. 1981: *Om velferdsstatens fremvekst* (On the Growth of the Welfare State), Universitetsforlaget

Townsend, P., Davidson and M. Whithead 1990: *Inequalities in Health*, Penguin Books, London.

Williams, F. 1977: *Why the Poor Pay More*, Mamillian Press / National Consumer Council UK.

Aarø, L.E. 1986: *Health Behaviour and Socioeconomic Status*, doctoral thesis, University of Bergen

12
The Tragedy of the Commons Common Resources and Individual Interests

ØRNULF GULBRANDSEN

Original quotation

Freedom in a commons brings ruin to all (Hardin 1977, p. 20).

2. Brief explanation

In brief, the thesis is that when individual users of a commons (i.e. a limited basis of common resources) are not subjected to any kind of restrictions, the result of their total exploitation will be excessive and ultimately detrimental to all.

3. Background

In many areas of social life tensions exist between people's efforts to satisfy their individual interests by means of exploiting common resources and the higher order need to maintain the resource base. This kind of tension was recognized already by Aristotle, who asserted that:

> For that which is common to the greatest number has the least care bestowed upon it. Everyone thinks chiefly of his own, hardly at all of the common interest; and only when he is himself concerned as an individual. (Politics, Bk. II: Ch. 3)

Basically, what we are dealing with here is the tensions that exists between the actions of different decision-making units to safeguard their interests, and the overall consequences of these actions. Such tensions are found in a great many areas of society, albeit with considerable variation in terms of how they are culturally perceived and socio-politically managed. Garret Hardin's formulation of the "law", known as the "The Tragedy of the Commons" (1977), represents a generalization of these variations.

The timing of the law's publication and Hardin's use of common grazing land to exemplify the theses of the tragedy of the commons are important in understanding the huge interest the thesis aroused in the 1970s. In that decade the world's attention was for the first time directed towards extensive ecological catastrophes, such as the expansion of the deserts in the Sahel region. Cultural ecologists, anthropologists and other social scientists took Hardin's thesis as their starting point in explaining that the desert expansion was not caused by natural factors alone, such as climatic variations, but was exacerbated by human overexploitation of the available resources.

4. Formalization – precise definition

Hardin clarified the statement "freedom in a commons brings ruin to all" by establishing a thesis about the central underlying mechanism. For this purpose he used as his example the exploitation of unregulated common grazing lands by cattle/sheep farmers:

> As a rational being, each herdsman seeks to maximize his gain [...] He asks, "What is the utility *to me* of adding one more animal to my herd?" This utility has one negative and one positive component.
>
> 1. The positive is a function of the increment of one animal. Since the herdsman receives all the proceeds from the sale of one more animal, the positive utility is nearly +1.
>
> 2. The negative component is a function of the additional overgrazing created by one more animal. Since, however, the effects of overgrazing are shared by all the herdsmen, the negative utility for any particular decision-making herdsman is only a fraction of -1.
>
> Adding altogether the component partial utilities, the rational herdsman concludes that the only sensible course for him to pursue is to add another animal. And another; and another ... But this is the conclusion reached by each and every rational herdsman sharing the commons. Therein lies the tragedy. Each man is locked into a system that compels him to increase his herd – in a world that is limited. (Hardin 1977, p. 20)

The main point can be elaborated as follows: while the entire profit of putting one more animal onto the commons falls to the individual farmer, the costs which this animal represents in terms of increased pressure on the grazing land, are shared by all users of the commons. Assuming the people involved are individually motivated to maximize their own returns, there is a strong incentive in this kind of situation for each user to avail himself of the opportunity and increase his stock, an incentive which results from the following *system constraint*: even if *I* do not use the opportunity to increase my herd – because I want to participate in the preservation of this common resource – I have no guarantee that *others* will behave likewise. And if they set no limits on themselves, the pastures will deteriorate, while I will have failed to increase the yield of my own herd – a yield which is furthermore endangered because of the reduced grazing land. By increasing my herd I would at least reduce the danger of being marginalized, while at the same time spreading the costs of the increase among all the herdsmen who use the commons.

Logically speaking, it is probable that the tragedy effect is triggered in a situation where 1) a certain number of *independent* resource users endeavor to maximize their individual profits by 2) using a *limited* common resource which 3) is not subject to any collective control or other regulations. Such a situation is potentially tragic in the sense that it is progressive in character: as pressure on the pastures increases, so the process will accelerate, with each herder impelled to maximize his stock in order to maintain the herd in the face of increasing mortality.

Hardin's concern was to alter this 'game' of the commons by specifying conditions which can prevent the tragic process from ever starting. Initially his polemic was directed against those who supposed that *technical* solutions to the problem could be found, meaning solutions "presupposing only changes in techniques of a scientific nature, but only to small, if any, extent calling for changes in human values and moral ideas" (1977, p. 16). The great challenge is, he claims, "to find the correctives needed to make guardians remain honest. We must find methods of legitimizing the necessary authority of the guardians as well as that of the correctives" (1977, p. 23). In the meantime he has formulated this problem as a question of transforming what he calls a "private profit – communalized costs" game (PP-CC), logically leading to the tragedy of the commons, into a "private profit – privatized costs" game (PP-PC) (Hardin 1986; cf. Håland 1991).

5. Generality and testability. Critique

The logical structure of Hardin's thesis has proved highly resilient to the many critical voices that have been raised against it over the years. But to some extent the critique has helped to clarify where and when the thesis is applicable and to query the solutions suggested by Hardin. I shall briefly summarize some of the major points.

Anthropologists in particular have attempted to limit the extent of the thesis' applicability by presenting a series of examples in which commons do not necessarily result in excessive exploitation and the destruction of resources. For example, on the basis of studies made in rural districts of the Alps, Netting has maintained that:

> [c]ommunal tenure promotes both general access to and optimum production from certain types of resources while enjoining on the entire community the conservation measure necessary to protect these resources from destruction. The persistence of communal rights should not be dismissed as a historical anachronism or credited solely to external domination of the closed corporate society. (Netting 1976, p. 145)

In this case, Hardin's assumption of "freedom on the commons" does not apply, and it proves that users of commons can be controlled by limitations – a fact that is well known to us from Norwegian commons. This means that such examples are irrelevant in relation to Hardin's thesis. Moreover, they show that it is in fact possible to establish control systems for commons. Anthropologists have accordingly endeavored to make constructive contributions to the development of collective resource administration, often regarding as a special task the identification of the cultural and organizational conditions needed to establish such control measures. But the optimism that has occasionally resulted in recommendations of this kind has encouraged naivety about the ability of such 'traditional' systems of collective regulation to resist individual acquisitive ambitions in contexts where market forces and other external factors apply.

In his original article Hardin maintained that "the commons, if justifiable at all, is justifiable only under low-population density. As the human population has increased, the commons has had to be abandoned in one aspect after another" (1977, p. 28). On this point it might be noted that Hardin fails to consider the possibility of population regulation on the basis of law-like connections that also apply in the relationship between population and the resource base, also known as the Malthus effect.

Fredrik Barth's classic study of a group of nomadic pastoralists in the Middle East provides a suitable illustration. This group, known as Basseri are sheep-keeping nomads who move seasonally between the lowlands and mountainous regions of Southern Iran (Barth 1964). Even though the sheep flocks have considerable growth potential, the overall strain on pastures is generally kept well within carrying capacity. However, this is not a result of collective administrative decisions, but is due to particular processes that directly limit the number of herd-owning units. On the one hand, strong growth in a herd means that sooner or later a limit will be reached where the flock becomes difficult to manage. In such cases there are strong incentives to convert the animals into more secure forms of capital. Consequently, owners sell their flocks to buy agricultural land and settle down as sedentary farmers. In this way they reduce strain on pastures in that they sell the sheep out of the area.

On the other hand, for a household to function as a viable unit, a certain minimum number of sheep are needed. In falling beneath this lower limit the flock's reproductive capacity will be too low to meet the household's own consumption requirements. Thus, for units that fall beneath this limit, flock size necessarily diminishes towards zero, and the families are compelled to abandon their pastoralist lifestyle. Barth points out that when strain on pastures exceeds carrying capacity, mortality tends to increase, while fertility decreases, with the result that the reduction mechanism is accelerated and the ecological balance gradually recovers (Barth 1964, p. 113 ff).

It can therefore be said that the Malthus effect influences the herd (and indirectly humans), which in turn serves to maintain the ecological balance. In some pastoralist societies, population increase and over-exploitation have directly influenced fertility and mortality in the population itself, thus restoring the ecological balance. Thus, Hardin's thesis does not apply in areas where Nature is capable of "hitting back" and thereby restoring the balance between resource reproduction and resource use.

In later works Hardin's concern has been that "to escape the tragedy, the unmanaged commons must be abandoned" (Hardin 1986, p. 93), and he points out that "[a] commons is a resource to which a population has free and unmanaged access; it contrasts with private property (accessible only to the owner) and with socialized property (access to which is controlled by managers appointed by some political unit)" (1986, p. 90). According to Hardin, the problems related to unregulated commons can be overcome either by 1) privatizing the resources or by 2) appointing some political unit to control access to the resources.

Critics have stressed that the privatization suggestion has a serious political-ideological aspect in that any privatization of common resources will be exclusive and thus create class differences, particularly by converting the resources into a market commodity. One of the best-documented examples where this has happened is the English "enclosure movement" (cf. Thompson 1976). From Northern Somalia Håland reports on an attempt to introduce exclusive rights, which provided:

> a basis for establishing a stable and more productive resources exploitation. [...] On the other hand it is inevitable that a privatization like this will influence the reduction of the pastoral niche in a way creating new problems, particularly when individual units can gain control over great parts of a pastoral migration area (Håland 1991, p. 112).

An important limitation to Hardin's thesis is its inability to reflect the socio-economic and political implications of a situation involving competition for resources. A frequent political consequence of such competitive situations, is that privatization is often represented as a compelling ecological – and therefore *natural* – requirement if carrying capacity is not to be exceeded. In Botswana the President himself once put forward precisely this type of argument in a campaign which aimed to set the scene for a nationwide privatization of extensive grazing lands via the establishment of fenced-in ranches. Among other things he said that:

> [t]he trouble is that as things stand it is in no ones interest to do something about it. If one man moves his cattle off a piece of land someone else moves his cattle on. The problem cannot be solved unless livestock numbers are somehow tied to a specific grazing quota. Only then will farmers have a clear incentive to control grazing [...] Under a new grazing land policy [...] groups and individuals will be given exclusive rights to specific areas [...] Ranch development will be encouraged. (Khama 1980: 321-2).

It is not only in Botswana that the belief in privatization as advantageous to natural resources has proved deceptive (Gulbrandsen 1994, pp. 316-52). A general objection to Hardin's thesis has been that privatization of common resources does not necessarily stimulate those concerned to exploit natural resources in accordance with carrying capacity. In an early critique Fife put forward the notion of "killing the goose", arguing that "in certain situations [...] 'industrial self-regulation' is not merely questionable, it is farcical" (Fife 1971, p. 27). Numerous examples have shown how business enterprises consider it most profitable to make *short-term gains* by over exploiting potentially renewable resources.

This means that we must add the following assumption to Hardin's thesis on the advantages of a so-called PP-PC game (see above) for it to have the desired ecological result: the *economic costs* of *ecological over-exploitation* must exceed the total economic advantages that can by these means accrue to the unit in both the short- and the long-term.

As indicated in the above quotation, Hardin suggests superior political control as an alternative to privatization. It is not quite clear what "some political unit" should mean, but I assume that Hardin is thinking primarily of some external coercive power, and not a community-based administrative organ originating among the resource users themselves. Such a solution has been formulated in straightforward terms by Ophuls, wherein he stresses that "because of the tragedy of the commons, cannot be solved through cooperation ... the rationale for government with major coercive powers is overwhelming " (1973, p. 228). Similarly, Carruthers and Stoners argue that public control is required, without which "overgrazing and soil erosion of communal pastures" will be the necessary consequence (1981, p. 29).

The idea that such an external coercive authority is needed to regulate the use of a commons has been criticized by anthropologists on the basis of examples such as those mentioned above, i.e. instances showing that resource users can constitute communities which are capable of managing the available resources (cf. e.g. several articles in McCay and Acheson 1987). One aspect of this critique has been aimed at Hardin's allegedly ethnocentric starting point, i.e. his assumption that every unit which uses the resources is governed exclusively by the urge to maximize individual interests. The critics present examples intended to show that those who use the resources might well uphold an *ethic of collective resource management*. This kind of argumentation has occasionally been pushed to such extremes that it has been criticized as naively romantic and lacking in realism (McCay and Acheson 1987, p. 10). However, this controversy is aimed not so much at the logical structure of Hardin's thesis, as at a particular empirical condition which the thesis happens to imply: that the urge to maximize individual interests overrides any consideration one might feel for the ethics of collective resource management.

A related critique of the thesis of the need for external coercive authority focuses on people's inherent ability to experience, communicate and co-operate. It is argued that such abilities often degenerate when an external coercive authority attempts to take over administrative control. Such a shift in control has occasionally led to a worsening of the ecological situation rather than to improvement. Ostrom is one of the most constructive critics of the idea that external coercive authority is needed to avoid the tragedy effect. She emphasizes the need to learn more from people's own experiences, and asks: "Why have some efforts to solve commons problems failed, while others have succeeded?" (1990, p.14). And furthermore: "What differences exist between those who have broken the shackles of the commons dilemma and those who have not?" (1990, p. 21). On the basis of such questions she makes a laudable attempt to identify the principal conditions for the establishment of autonomous commons, concluding with "a complex array of variables as a framework rather than as a model" (1990, p. 214). But she offers no theoretical clarification of the conditions necessary to enable resource users to manage resources both rationally and collectively, or, alternatively, of the conditions that would render necessary an external coercive authority to attain this objective.

A far more serious attempt to make a game-theoretical clarification of the preconditions for collective processes is found in Axelrod's works, where it is asked "under what conditions will cooperation emerge in a world of egoists without central authority?" (1981: 306, cf. 1984). Thus, Axelrod's assumptions about the nature of the participators and the absence of a superior authority are the same as those of Hardin. However, he imagines the possibility of overcoming the apparent system constraints implied in Hardin's logical model through cooperation initiated by the participators themselves – an initiative prompted not by ethical or moral assessments, but by their own interests. Axelrod pursues this idea focusing on a situation:

> in which narrow self-maximization behavior by each person leads to poor outcome for all. This is the famous Prisoner's Dilemma. Two individuals can each either cooperate or defect. No matter what the other does, defection yields a higher payoff than cooperation. But if both defect, both do worse than if both cooperated. (1981, p. 306).

On this basis it could be claimed that Hardin's thesis describes one of several possible games originating in a situation where the participants are caught in a "prisoner's dilemma". And here we discover the crux of our endeavor to delimit the scope of Hardin's thesis. As suggested in the above quotation, there are (at least) two fundamentally different ways of solving such a commons dilemma where resource use is not initially regulated: either one can accept the absence of regulation as a fact, thereby accepting also the need for a maximizing strategy such as that of Hardin's thesis, or alternatively, one could make an effort to mobilize the other units in an endeavor to establish such regulations, i.e. to alter the game itself.

Generally speaking, some of the criticism against Hardin's thesis can be ignored because it regards his argument – which is based on particular and explicitly stated assumptions – as an empirical conclusion that the tragedy of the commons is inevitable. Moreover, Hardin's thesis has been criticized as being "Western" and therefore culture-specific, because of Hardin's assumption of resource users who seek to maximize their individual rewards. Although this critique has drawn attention to a problem among Hardin's central assumptions, and thus helped to clarify the limits of the applicability of his thesis, it has occasionally been over-simplified, insofar as it regards the thesis as a generalized theory about how all commons actually work, and ignores the important *premise* of the thesis: individualized herd owners who operate under the conditions of *freedom* on the commons. Hardin's thesis can only be properly appreciated if we regard the problem of the socio-cultural nature of the units – in terms of the relationship between self- and communal interests – as an *empirical question*. The utility of Hardin's thesis lies in linking the answer to this question with specific processes of importance for resource administration.

In my opinion the most fruitful approach is to view Hardin's argument as a tool that can *trace specific processes and tendencies potentially active in any commons situation, and that would have destructive consequences for the resources*. We shall then find that in some situations they will encounter no obstacles, while in others they are modified or even blocked by processes that enable collective resource management to dominate over individual resource use.

Such use of the thesis prompts an analysis of the comparative strength of the individual resource users with that of the collective resource management. In this context I can only suggest what the outcome of such an exercise would be. *Firstly*, we have to assume that the power relationship will shift to the disadvantage of collective resource management when market forces are allowed to operate, i.e. when the units acquire greater opportunities for individual capital accumulation and, consequently, increased economic interest in – and technical capability for – a more intensive resource exploitation. *Secondly*, there is probably a connection between social scale and the tragedy effect: the greater the number of resource users, the greater also the difficulty – other things being equal – of opposing the establishment of an external control authority with the power to halt excessive exploitation. *Thirdly*, we would expect the tragedy effect – other things being equal – to depend on the extent to which reduction mechanisms are active. This in turn is a question of a) Nature's capacity to fight back and b) the range of means at the disposal of the unit to safeguard its economic viability. *Fourthly*, local sociocultural conditions represent an important set of variables that determine inter-unit communication and co-ordination which, in turn, influence the possibilities of the resource users to develop a community that promotes responsible resource use.

Hardin's thesis is based on the assumption that the resource base exploited by a certain group is limited, and that its ability to renew itself is incontrovertibly diminished when use exceeds a certain level. It may be objected that an assumption of this kind distracts us from recognizing processes which in many circumstances confer elasticity on the resource base. In what follows I shall point out how the notion of "carrying capacity" in itself has been critically examined. Here, I would like to emphasize that the framework of the group's resource base is not a mere question of the relationship between the group and its resource base (e.g. Sandford 1983). It is also a question of the group's relation to its socio-political environment, as demonstrated by Barth in his theoretical development of the niche concept in cultural ecological analysis (Barth 1956). In Botswana I have seen for myself how the political supremacy and capacity for economic accumulation among the cattle-owning Tswanas have furnished the basis for a huge expansion of the ecological conditions for cattle-farming by forcing the majority of hunters and gatherers (Bushmen) out of their own habitat.

6. Empirical assessment – conclusion

Hardin's examples have inspired many people to apply his thesis in the study of human-ecological aspects of nomadic cattle-keeping. In their article "A tragedy of the Commons in the Sahel" (1976), Picardi and Seifert present solid demographic and ecological data to show how population increase among cattle-keepers – with a consequent increase in cattle stock – results in the carrying capacity of pastures being exceeded. Eventually this causes a reduction in carrying capacity, which, if serious enough, will lead in turn to a reduction in cattle fertility and an increase in their mortality. The inevitable consequence is that the cattle stock declines and the population is afflicted by famine or forced to abandon its nomadic cattle-keeping existence.

Already in the early 1970s, Georg Henriksen, in his studies of the Turkana, a nomadic people in Northwest Kenya, discovered such connections (Henriksen 1974). He pointed to the basic dilemma which sooner or later arose for all good Western forces that wanted to help the suffering populations: how could the individual families be helped in a way that would not exacerbate ecological destruction? For obvious reasons any initiative that contributed to the recovery of impoverished and destitute cattle nomads exerted additional pressure on pastures. On the basis of extensive statistical material from the Sahel region, Picardi and Seifert simulated the effects of different technical "development programs", such as veterinary services, breeding assistance, well-digging programs and assistance in building up cattle stock. A trend forecast of these effects is sketched in the following diagram:

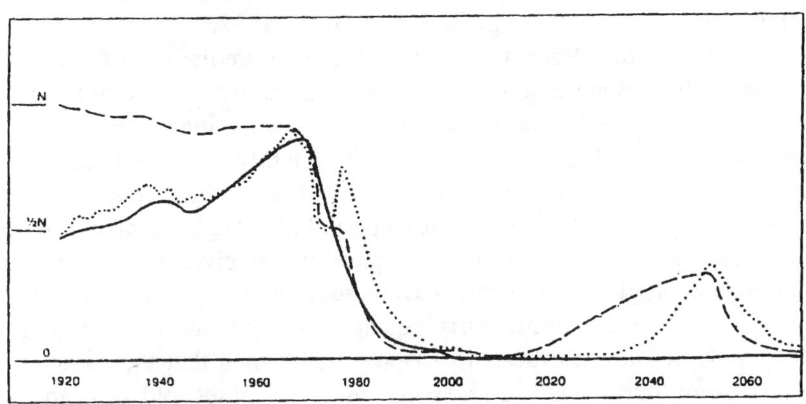

Extrapolation analysis: livestock, population and carrying capacity

Livestock   *Population*   *Carrying capacity*

Fig. Extrapolation analysis: cattle stock, population and soil yield (Source: Picardi and Seifert 1976)

Here we see that from around 1960 population and cattle stock exceeded carrying capacity. The implication is that there is a constant overtaxation in relation to carrying capacity. The large-scale increase in cattle stock during the late 1970s represents the simulated effect of the "development programs" referred to. The ecological implications are obvious. Carrying capacity is expected to increase as a result of cattle stock being forced down to a very low level. In such a situation carrying capacity is expected to exceed the degree of exploitation around the year 2010, after which it will increase rather rapidly – even if remaining far below the level of 1960 – before reaching a new point at which the cattle stock will once again exceed carrying capacity. Development programs are not the only force behind such a development: another is the increased possibility of cattle-keepers to reduce herd taxation by means of external economic alternatives (Henriksen 1974). The apparent paradox is that in cases where alternative opportunities for economic income are found, strain on pastures is increased rather than reduced. The simple reason is that households which exploit such possibilities do not necessarily give up cattle-keeping. If anything, the opposite is true: the herd acquires a further growth potential, as it often represents an attractive investment object for the surplus drawn from other sources of income (e.g. Gulbrandsen 1994: 223 ff.).

However, in the 1980s it became evident that predictions of the kind presented by, among others, Picardi and Seifert, in the wake of the Sahel drought disaster of the 1970s, proved somewhat inaccurate (cf. e.g. Sandford 1983). The question was subsequently raised whether the ecological analyses of carrying capacity had taken due account of the capacity of pastures to recover after a period of drought combined with the pressure of heavy grazing. This question has given momentum to intensive ecological studies that have gradually produced considerably better-founded estimates of carrying capacity. However, these findings do not affect Hardin's thesis in any way other than that the estimates are of some importance in assessing where the threshold lies, above which the tragedy is triggered.

A further empirical point important in assessing the breadth of the thesis' relevance is the fact that, although nomadic cattle-keepers often have only limited direct control of pasture exploitation, they can exercise *indirect* control in terms of how they manage the use of water resources. What might at first sight appear to be enormous, open and uncontrolled grazing areas might in fact be managed by minor, territorially delimited groups, who govern the use of pastures by restricting access to water sources (see e.g. Storås 1995). In such cases the main premise of the thesis – "liberty on the commons" – has only limited validity.

Another empirical field where Hardin's thesis has been extensively applied, and where we can draw on Norwegian examples, is that of marine fisheries (cf. Brox 1991). The study of fishermen and fisheries from a commons perspective is interesting for two reasons: firstly, fishermen find themselves in a situation of potential competition in the fisheries, a situation which is likely to assume the character of a what Hardin has conceptualized as PP-CC game (see above). Secondly, only very few fishermen produce merely to support themselves: on the contrary, they are greatly dependent on a market. The market can also be conceived as a PP-CC game. When a single participator increases the supply of fish in order to increase his profit, this affects the price level in keeping with a simple supply and demand mechanism. The ground rent is reduced, i.e. the economic yield from increased fishing decreases. It is, however, an open question whether this constitutes negative feedback in the PP-CC fisheries game. Jentoft has said that "fishermen are not necessarily poor because they catch so much fish." It might just as well be the other way round:

> They catch so much fish because they are poor. If one depends on a certain level of income without having alternative income sources, a natural reaction to price reduction will be an effort to increase one's catch, which in turn is likely to result in even lower prices due to increased quantities of raw material being brought onto land. It was in an effort to break this vicious circle that Norwegian fishermen at one time took action to obtain an organized first-hand trade, the result being the 1951 raw fish law. (Jentoft 1987, p. 377).

However, it is obvious that the raw fish law has been inadequate to prevent over-fishing in Norwegian fisheries. To a large extent this is due to the appearance of operators based on capitalistic rather than family-based principles (cf. Brox 1966), which, combined with developments in the processing industry and new markets, has resulted in a huge increase in the volume of fish produced, and consequently over-fishing.

As in the case of common pasture exploitation it is relevant here to ask whether an external coercive authority is necessary and expedient to bring fisheries under control. With reference to Kristiansen (1985) and others, Jentoft has suggested that control already exists on the basis of local sanctions. Kristiansen "describes for example Norwegian fisheries as a 'communications center' where fishermen obtain and exchange information relevant to the efficient management of fish resources, and where the infringement of established standards of reciprocity are subject to moral sanctioning" (Jentoft 1987, p. 381).

However, such local sanctioning systems have proved utterly insufficient, not least in Norwegian fisheries. To an ever-increasing extent the state has intervened as a force to regulate both quotas and the size of the fishing fleet. Fisheries of large social scale, where participants lack local connections, together with expansive methods of capitalistic production, have undermined the conditions necessary for internal co-operation on the management of fisheries. The development of state control and monitoring authorities has therefore become increasingly necessary.

This development would seem to suggest that, as the scale increases (in terms both of size and complexity), the only way to avoid the tragedy effect is to establish strong, external controlling authorities. In most cases this means state authority.

However, in some cases not even the state is capable of imposing sufficient limits to the exploitation of a commons. I witnessed this myself in Botswana, where state authority is fully controlled by the great cattle owners. Thus whenever the relevant technical-agronomic expertise proposes regulatory policies to halt the increase and serious over-exploitation of common pastures, the proposals do not receive the necessary political support (Gulbrandsen 1996).

The situation among the Sami reindeer-herders of Northern Norway is an excellent illustration of how problematic state regulation of a commons can be, both for the state authority itself and for those who exploit the commons. In this case the state has introduced an extensive regulatory system. The pastures are divided into districts governed by district boards. A limited number of production units is fixed for each grazing area, based on an assessment of the capacity of the areas and on the standard number of a breeding unit, as worked out by the state in conjunction with the Norwegian association that represents the reindeer-herding Sami (Norske Reindriftsamers Landsforbund). The number has been fixed at 300 animals, i.e. the stipulated basis for a man-labor year. In this case we see that both the number of units that use a commons and the size of these units are regulated by state agencies.

From an administrative point of view this is not a non-regulated commons. But this doesn't automatically mean that the situation is unproblematic. From time to time pastures are heavily over-exploited due to strong pressure from below to increase the number of breeding units and for permission to build up large herds. When we attempt to clarify this aspect of the situation, Hardin's thesis is useful in identifying the processes that underlie this pressure. One thing is that society has a higher order interest in avoiding over-exploitation, which ought in principle to be supported by all reindeer-herding Sami. A quite different question concerns the factors governing the strategies of each family. These latter are guided e.g. by strong cultural attitudes which encourage the accumulation of large herds as indicators of success and influence (cf. Henriksen 1991). The fact that such considerations often become very powerful, with over-exploitation being the result of their applying to so many units, reflects the type of assessment made by Hardin in the quote on page (200) above. This illustrates an important analytic point: to a large extent "freedom on the commons" will be a relative matter. Considering such situations from the point of view of process, we can conceive the degree of over-exploitation as a consequence, on the one hand, of the relative strength of the relationship between regulation processes, and on the other, of processes originating in the urge to maximize individual interests. This example shows that it is one thing to take the abolishment of non-regulated commons as one's program, as Hardin recommended (Hardin 1986, p. 93), but quite another to ensure that users show sufficient concern for the higher order, long-term aims regarding exploitation of the commons.

In designing strategies to handle situations of this kind, the most plausible measure available to the state will for obvious reasons be the intensification of control activities. Another strategy which has been tried in recent years involves reducing the number of new units which are established by creating opportunities for alternative economic careers. Considerable resources have been allotted to education and labor market initiatives, although the effect has been very limited.

In other regards, circumstances are favorable for the state to ease pressure on common resources so as to expand the resources themselves. A good example is the public road system, particularly in densely populated areas. Public roads can be seen as a commons which all users have considerable liberty to exploit, resulting in some areas in traffic congestion. We could account for this by saying that each driver is guided by ideas such as those sketched by Hardin in the quotation on page (200). In this case, the those who manage public road systems rarely react by regulating them, or by trying to meet transport demands by means of collective measures. The typical way of handling the problem has been – and is – to expand the commons by enlarging the road system. What this leads to, however, is that drivers change the assessments they make – according to Hardin's thesis – in ways that encourage an ever-greater use of this common resource, since it reduces the negative effect of total car use. Once again, the consequence is traffic congestion. This dynamic has proved to have truly expansive potential, since political authorities react repeatedly by enlarging the road network.

7. Literature

Aristotle 1988: *The Politics*, ed. Stephen Everson, Cambridge University Press, Cambridge.

Axelrod, R. 1981: "The emergence of cooperation among egoists," *The American Political Science Review*, 75: pp. 306-18.

Axelrod, R. 1984: *The Evolution of Cooperation*, New York: Basic Books.

Barth, F. 1956: "Ecological relations of ethnic groups in Swat, North Pakistan," *American Anthropologist*, 58(6).

Barth, F. 1964: *Nomads of South Persia. The Basseri Tribe of the Khamseh Confederacy*, Universitetsforlaget, Oslo.

Brox, O. 1966: *Hva skjer i Nord-Norge?* (What happens in the North of Norway?), Pax, Oslo.

Brox, O. 1991: "The common property theory. Epistemological status and analytical utility," in R. Grønhaug, G. Henriksen and G. Håland (eds.), *The Ecology of Choice and Symbol. Essays in Honour of Fredrik Barth*, Alma Mater, Bergen.

Ciriacy-Wantrup, S.V. and R.C. Bishop 1975: "'Common property' as a concept in natural resources policy," *Natural Resources Journal*, 15(4), pp. 713-27.

Carruthers, I. and R. Stoner 1981: "Economic aspects and policy issues in groundwater development," World Bank Staff Working Paper No. 496, The World Bank, Washington DC.

Fife, D. 1971: "Killing the goose," *Environment*, 13(3), pp. 20-7.

Gulbrandsen, Ø. 1980: *Agro-Pastoral Production and Communal Land Use. A Socio-Economic Study of the Bangwaketse*, Botswana Government Press, Gaborone.

Gulbrandsen, Ø. 1986: *When land becomes scarce. Access to Agricultural Land and Communal Land Management in Eastern Botswana*, Bergen Studies in Social Anthropology, No. 33, Department of Social Anthropology, University of Bergen, Bergen.

Gulbrandsen, Ø. 1991: "On the problem of egalitarianism: the Kalahari San in transition," in R. Grønhaug, G. Henriksen and G. Håland (eds.), *The Ecology of Choice and Symbol. Essays in Honour of Fredrik Barth*, Alma Mater, Bergen.

Gulbrandsen, Ø. 1994: *Poverty in the Midst of Plenty. Socio-Economic Marginalization, Ecological Deterioration and Political Stability in a Tswana Society*, Norse Publications, Bergen.

Hardin, G. 1977: "The tragedy of the commons," in G. Hardin and J. Banden (eds.) 1977 (first published in *Science*, 162: 1243-8).

Hardin, G. 1986: *Filters against folly: how to survive despite economists, ecologists, and the merely eloquent*, Penguin Books, New York.

Hardin, G. and J. Baden (eds.) 1977: *Managing the Commons*, W.H. Freeman and Company, New York.

Henriksen, G. 1974: *Economic Growth and Ecological Balance: Problems of Development in Turkana, North-West Kenya*, Bergen Studies in Social Anthropology, No. 11, Norse Publications, Bergen.

Henriksen, G. 1985: "Norwegian administration and the Sami community in Helgeland," in J. Børstad et al. (eds.), *Native Power. The Quest for Autonomy and Nationhood of Indigenous Peoples*, Universitetsforlaget, Oslo.

Henriksen, G. 1991: "The experience of social worth as a force in inter-ethnic relations," in R. Grønhaug, G. Henriksen and G. Håland (eds.), *The Ecology of Choice and Symbol. Essays in Honour of Fredrik Barth*, Alma Mater, Bergen.

Håland, G. 1977: "Pastoral systems of production: the socio-cultural context and some economic and ecological implications," *African Environment*, Special Report, 5.

Håland, G. 1991: "Pastoralsamfunn og utnyttelse av fellesbeite: En humanøkologisk ramme" (Pastoral society and the use of the commons: A human-ecological framework), in Nils Chr. Stenseth et al. (eds.), *Forvaltningen av våre naturressurser* (Regulation of our natural resources), Ad Notam, Oslo.

Jentoft, S. 1987: "'Allmenningens tragedie' – statens ansvar?" ('The tragedy of the Commons' - a responsibility for the State?), *Tidsskrift for samfunnsforskning*, 28, pp. 369-90.

Khama, Sir Seretse 1980: *From the Front Line. Speeches of Sir Seretse Khama*, edited by G.M. Carter and E. Ph. Morgan, Rex Collings, London.

Kristiansen, A. 1985: "Fiskerireguleringen i historisk- og krysskulturelt perspektiv"(Regulations of the fisheries in a historical- and cross-culturalt perspective), Mimeographed, Institutt for fiskerifag, Universitetet i Tromsø, Tromsø.

Leeuw, P.N. de, and J.C. Tothill 1990: "The concept of rangeland carrying capacity in Sub-Saharan Africa – myth or reality," *Pastoral Development Network*, Paper 29b, Overseas Development Institute, London.

Manger, L. 1993: "Managing pastoral adaptations in the Red Sea Hills of the Sudan: challenges and dilemmas," paper presented at Technical Meeting on 'The New Directions in African Range Management and Policy' at Wodburn, UK, 31 May- 4 June, 1993.

McCay, B.J. and J.M. Acheson 1987: "Human ecology and the commons," in B.J. McCay et al. (eds.).

McCay, B.J. et al. (eds.) 1987: *The Question of the Commons. The Culture and Ecology of Communal Resources*, The University of Arizona Press, Tucson.

Netting, R. 1976: "What Alpine peasants have in common: observations on communal tenure in a Swiss Village," *Human Ecology*, 4 (2): pp. 135-46.

Ophuls, W. 1973: "Leviathan or oblivion," in E.E. Daly, *Toward a Steady State Economy*, Freeman, San Francisco.

Ophuls, W. 1977: *Ecology and the Politics of Scarcity*, Freeman, San Francisco.

Ostrom, E. 1990: *Governing the Commons. The Evolution of Institutions for Collective Action*, Cambridge University Press, Cambridge.

Picardi, A.C. and W.W. Seifert 1976: "A tragedy of the commons in the Sahel," *Technology Review*, May, pp. 42-52.

Sandford, S. 1983: *Management of Pastoral Development in the Third World*, Wiley, London.

Storås, F. 1995: "Being a Nomad in Turkana, Kenya," Dr.philos. Thesis, Department of Social Anthropology, University of Bergen, Bergen.

Thompson, E.P. 1976: "The grid of inheritance: a comment," in J. Goody et al. (eds.) *Family and Inheritance*, Cambridge University Press, Cambridge.

13
Durkheim's Suicide Hypothesis

KNUD KNUDSEN

1. Original quotation

Nous arrivons donc á cette conclusion générale: Le suicide varie en raison inverse du degré d'intégration des groupes sociaux dont fait partie l'individu. [...] C'est donc que, dans le milieu commun qui les enveloppe, il existe quelque force qui les incline toutes dans ce même sens et dont l'intensiteé plus on moins grande fait le nombre plus ou moins élevé des suicides particuliers. (Durkheim 1912 pp. 223 and 343).

2. Translation and brief explanation

We arrive, thus, at this general conclusion: there is an inverse correspondence between suicide and the degree of integration of the social groups of which the individual is a member [...] There must, therefore, exist some force in their common environment inclining all in the same direction, whose greater or lesser strength causes the greater or lesser number of individual suicides.

The sentences quoted represents the essence of Durkheim's theory, which we shall here coin his Suicide Hypothesis. In one of the most widely read English translations (Durkheim 1951) of the original version *Le Suicide* (1897), the corresponding quotations are found on pages 209 and 305.

The basis of this suicide hypothesis is his assumption that the suicide rate is a result of the stronger or weaker connection that exists between single individuals and their social environment and society at large. The suicide rate is to be understood here as the number of suicides per year per 1,000,000 persons in a given population.

Durkheim argued that there are different socially conditioned causes for why people take their own lives. *Egoistic* suicide results from a too weak integration of the individual in the family and close social groups, while so-called *altruistic* suicide comes from of the opposite, that is, too strong integration, or mechanical solidarity. Durkheim moreover postulated that the suicide rate will increase when traditional norms appear unclear and are under rapid change. He termed this suicide type *anomic* suicide. He further suggested that very rigid regulation of the individual on the part of society is likely to result in higher suicide numbers. This type he called *fatalistic* suicide. All four types are involved in his general suicide hypothesis.

3. Background

Emile Durkheim (1858-1917), born of Jewish parents in the French town of Epinal, is looked upon as one of the great pioneers of modern sociology. In his early years he was a student at the École Normale Supèrieure. In 1887 Durkheim obtained the first French professorship in sociology at Bordeaux, and later became professor at the Sorbonne in Paris.

In his works Durkheim concentrated particularly on collective consciousness and solidarity, and on the relation between the collective and the personality of the single individual. His most central works are *The Division of Labor in Society* (1893), *The Rules of Sociological Method* (1895), *Suicide* (1897) and *The Elementary Forms of the Religious Life* (1912).

Suicide was, in part, a continuation of *The Division of Labor in Society*, and deals with all aspects of the problem of social order, and the conditions that lead to the 'bad' – as opposed to the 'good' – society. Durkheim's suicide study did not originate from an interest in the phenomenon of suicide in itself. He saw the suicide rate as an *indicator* of what really interested him, namely the general *condition of society*, i.e. the extent to which society was either bad or good. A low suicide rate would supposedly indicate a healthy society, while a relatively high suicide rate would indicate a sick society, where the individuals had no roots, were unhappy and dissatisfied. Durkheim chose the suicide rate as an indicator primarily for methodological reasons. He regarded the suicide rate as the simplest and most reliable way of gauging "the temperature of society".

From a methodological point of view *Suicide* was a highly advanced study for its time. Durkheim's method implied gathering all statistical information available about suicide and social groups, and then comparing suicide rates across specific groups. He focused on characteristics such as nationality, religion, age, sex, marital status, family size and economic conditions. His aim was to prove that, by means of such a comparative method – based on existing data – it would be possible to refute several theories of the time (for instance theories suggesting that suicide could be explained by certain climatic conditions, race or inheritance). At the same time Durkheim demonstrated that suicide statistics supported his own hypothesis.

Durkheim held the view that traditional theories about the causes of suicide – such as some based on the mental condition of the individual – were unsuitable for his sociological approach, and therefore introduced the four main types mentioned of what he considered to be socially conditioned forms of suicide. Durkheim's typology is based on the relation of the individual to the close group and the society to which she or he belongs. Following Durkheim's ideas, the two first types, *egoistic* and *altruistic* suicide, come from deviation from an adequate or ideal integration of the individual into the social environment, such as the family and close friends. Durkheim explained the two other types, *anomic* and *fatalistic* suicide, as deviations from an adequate or ideal relation between social standards and the adaptation of the individual to these standards. Anomic suicide originated in a lack of standards, i.e. society's expectations of the citizens seem unclear and absurd to the individual. Fatalistic suicide, although not further elaborated in Durkheim's work, was caused by society's having a too strict and rigid grip on individual, leaving no space for autonomous action. Although it could be found that the individual suicide was of many different types, all cases of suicide should, in principle, be classifiable under *one* of (or as a combination of) the four main forms.

4. Formalization – precise definition

As already noted, Durkheim held the opinion that society became unhealthy or sick due to inadequate adaptation of the individual to the collective. This could mean deviation from an assumed ideal degree of integration into the local environment, but also from an ideal stability of social standards. He saw the suicide rate as an indicator for society's health. Thus, one could suggest that Durkheim regarded the suicide rate as a function of two fundamental relations, as represented by the following equation:

$$S = f\,(\,|\,I - I^+\,|,\,|\,N - N^+\,|\,)$$
$$S > K \text{ for } |\,I - I^+\,| \text{ not equal } 0 \text{, and/or } |N - N^+| \text{ not equal } 0$$
$$S = K \text{ for } |I - I^+| = 0 \text{ and } |\,N - N^+\,| = 0$$

where f = unspecified function form

           S = suicide rate, i.e. number of suicides per year per 1,000,000 persons in a given population

           I^+ = adequate or ideal degree of solidarity and integration

           I = degree of solidarity and integration observed

           N^+ = ideal degree of stability and clarity of society's standards

           N = degree of stability and clarity of society's standards observed

           K = theoretical minimum size of suicide rate in an ideal society, i.e. where $|\,I - I^+\,| = 0$ and $|\,N - N^+\,| = 0$

Bracketing with vertical bars indicates that the operating factor is the size of the deviation, not the negative or positive sign applied.

It is not clear whether Durkheim considered K as equal to zero or greater than zero. He may have regarded as inevitable a certain incidence of suicides. Moreover, his conceptual apparatus appears less precise (integration, lack of standards etc., see Douglas 1967, pp. 37-41). It is particularly difficult to realize how he imagined the different degrees of integration and lack of standards *operationally defined*. We shall not go into the problem of operationalization here. It seems likely that Durkheim assumed that $S > K$ for $|\,I - I^+\,|$ not equal 0, and $|\,N - N^+|\, = 0$, and that $S > K$ for $|\,N - N^+|$ not equal 0 and $|\,I - I^+\,| = 0$. Hence suicide typically is related to one type of imbalance, particularly egoistic suicide, although other types of deviation would influence the suicide rate too. Neither did he address the question of whether empirical evidence could be found for all conceivable combinations of the two types of deviation from the ideal. In this respect Durkheim's suicide hypothesis is in need of clarification.

Durkheim discussed altruistic, egoistic, anomic and fatalistic suicide separately. However, he did not go into the question of what could be the combined effect on the suicide rate, in a society characterized for instance by both altruism and anomie, or by egoism and fatalism.

It appears, however, that Durkheim regarded the rising suicide rate of France and the rest of Europe as a result of lower integration (egoistic suicide) and a decrease in the stability of norms (anomic suicide), in other words, a *combination* of the two basic forms of imbalance. But he did not explicitly discuss what influence different combinations of the two kinds of deviation would have on the suicide rate. One way today to specify Durkheim's suicide hypothesis in a simple, pedagogic form, could be as follows:

$$S = a + b_1 \, | \, I - I^+ \, | + b_2 \, | \, N - N^+ \, |$$

Here the suicide rate is understood as an additive, linear function of the two fundamental forms of disturbance or imbalance. This linear specification is, however, only one of many possible specifications, and should be seen as an approximate, first approach. We could also imagine other potentially testable definitions of the suicide hypothesis, for example in a multiplicative form, but here we will not go into further elaborations. For a recent discussion, see Pampel (1998).

5. Generality and testability. Critique

Durkheim imagined that a good balance between the individual and the collective would result in a healthy society, consisting of content and happy members. The individual should not be too loosely integrated, but she or he should not be over-integrated either. Moreover, a healthy society would be the result of a certain degree of clarity and stability of norms felt by the individual, suggesting an optimal social regulation of society.

Durkheim's hypothesis points out that groups and societies that depart from an ideal degree of integration and of stability in terms of its standards will have a relatively high suicide rate. And he demonstrated that his suicide hypothesis was supported by available data. He argued that Protestants were less integrated (in his terminology more "egoistic") and experienced less solidarity than Catholics. Protestants should, therefore, have a higher suicide rate than Catholics, both on a national and on group level. Official suicide statistics supported Durkheim's predictions. One of the tables from *Suicide* (p. 150) is reproduced below, showing that the suicide rate decreased with increasing percentage of Catholic's in different provinces of Bavaria.

Catholicism and Suicide Rate. Bavarian Provinces (1867-75)

Provinces with Catholic minority (under 50%)	Suicides per 1,000,000 inhabitants	Provinces with Catholic majority (50-90%)	Suicides per 1,000,000 inhabitants	Provinces with more than 90 % Catholics	Suicides pe 1,000,000 inhabitants
Rhenish Palatine	167	Lower Franconia	157	Upper Palatine	64
Central Franconia		Schwabia		Upper Bavaria	
Upper Franconia	207		118	Northern Bavaria	114
	204				19
Averages	192	Averages	135	Averages	75

As noted Durkheim also argued that *too strong* integration (with individuals characterized by blind obedience and submission) should result in a relatively high suicide rate, as should also too weak integration. He saw some social classes in Japan and certain military groups as representing such over-integrated social environments, and claimed that a relatively high suicide rate was found for these categories.

Durkheim further stated that divorce implied a disturbance of the individual-society balance, indicating a *normless* or anomic situation. Consequently this should justify the expectation that the suicide rate among divorcees should be higher than among married people. Also for this hypothesis he found support in official statistics.

The excerpts given above are but a small section of the various methods employed by Durkheim to test his theory. Systematically comparing his own postulates with official statistics, he invalidated competing theories, at the same time rendering more plausible his own suicide hypothesis.

What in many respects gave originality and strength to Durkheim's analysis was at the same time its weak point. Durkheim regarded the suicide phenomenon as *exclusively* due to social circumstances. He was neither oriented towards nor interested in the psychological side of suicide. In his view individual psychology was of little relevance in a sociological study. It was Freud who, in 1916, presented the first important psychological study of suicide. Part of today's criticism of Durkheim is therefore aimed at the *too narrow scope* of his approach, which focuses exclusively on social forces. Psychological causal factors that can occur *independently* of social circumstances are not integrated into Durkheim's hypothesis. If one wanted to defend Durkheim against such criticism, it could be argued that he may have taken for granted that this psychological component was constant from one society to another. But the *differences* between different societies should be explicable with reference to social circumstances, as sketched already.

Another type of criticism questions specific aspects of Durkheim's theoretical reasoning, and claims that his observations can probably be explained better by alternative *theories*. Douglas (1967) particularly insists that the first thing to look for when explaining variation in suicide rates across societies, should be how a particular group defines suicide, or in other words: to what extent suicide is looked upon as morally acceptable or reprehensible.

Other social scientists, such as Gregory Zilborg (1935) have drawn attention to the poor reliability of Durkheim's basic data, mainly the suicide statistics. The official definition of suicide employed in the statistics is not the same from one country to another, and it is a fair assumption that there exist considerable variations in suicide registration. We have already drawn attention to the problem of gauging the variables integrated in the analysis. Today it is clear, therefore, that relevant objections to Durkheim's suicide hypothesis can be made.

6. Empirical assessment – conclusion

Norwegian suicide studies have traditionally used a psychological approach. Nils Retterstøl (Retterstøl 1970) summarized theoretical arguments and findings already thirty years ago, attaching particular importance to psychological factors behind suicides and suicide attempts. He demonstrated the validity of international results also for Norway. Then and now this holds for such patterns insofar as more men than women commit suicide, rates are higher among the elderly, suicide is more frequent among unmarried and divorced than among married people, and the urban suicide rate is higher than that of rural areas. In a more recent work (1990) Retterstøl shows that these pattern are fairly stable. Nonetheless, since 1970 there has been a striking change: there has been a doubling of the number of suicides. The most dramatic increase has been registered among younger groups, and particularly among young men. Retterstøl and his research group undertook a special study to get a better understanding of the problem (Retterstøl et al. 1985). This study shed light on the complicated patterns and combined causes behind the high suicide rates among youngsters.

One third had previously undergone treatment in psychiatric institutions, and another third had suffered from alcohol or drug problems. Approximately one quarter had written farewell letters, most of these directed to father and mother. Thus, it seems as if Durkheim's main argument may be relevant as a general explanation also in this respect.

Herbert Hendin (1964) tries to explain differences in the suicide rates between the Scandinavian countries, where Denmark and Sweden have traditionally had conspicuously higher suicide rates than Norway. Hendin believes the explanation is to be found in cultural differences, particularly concerning the education of children. He suggests the low Norwegian suicide rate can be explained in terms of upbringing; competitiveness and expectations of success in one's career and social standing are given less emphasis in the way children are brought up in Norway than in, say, Sweden. Therefore, Norwegians do not experience difficulties and defeat as so negative as do the Swedes, with the result that Norwegians in such situations are less inclined towards suicide. A supplementary explanation of the low Norwegian level has been offered by Faber (1968), who focuses on Danish and Norwegian family relations. He claims Norwegian mothers are more preoccupied with giving their children love and care. He further argues that Norwegian fathers hold a stronger and more central position in the family than Danish fathers. Faber's main point is that there is more warmheartedness and care in primary groups and within the family in Norway than in Denmark.

In recent years some strands of suicide research have focused on the consequences of the changing position of women in modern nations. Some researchers have put forward hypotheses postulating that women's liberation has resulted in greater difference between male and female suicide rate, while others have claimed the traditional gap to have been reduced. On the basis of data from 18 countries in the years 1953-92 Pampel (1998) demonstrates that the pattern is in fact highly differentiated. During the initial stages of women's liberation the results tend to be a smaller differences between the sexes, as regards suicide rate. At later stages, after various institutional adaptations, the tendency is once again towards greater difference. A striking difference is also the considerable variation that has been recorded with regard to sex differences between different countries. Pampel suggests that an essential part of this variation can be related to different degrees of collective orientation in these countries.

Most of the sociological studies available deal with the suicide phenomenon within the framework of Western industrialized societies.

Studies from other continents and other types of society appear to have been undertaken in most cases by social anthropologists, such as the early studies by Devereux (1937) and later by Bohannan (1960). It seems that the logic of Durkheim's suicide research has been applied in only limited analyses of Asian and African societies. It would be particularly interesting to look into the long-term consequences for the suicide rate after fundamental social changes such as the upheavals experienced in China in the decade preceding the year 2000. In all probability such studies are now underway.

We have already stated that relevant objections can be made to Durkheim's suicide hypothesis. The studies referred to which have been undertaken in a Norwegian or Scandinavian context, represent examples of alternative approaches in an effort to explain the suicide phenomenon. The reason why Durkheim's suicide hypothesis still holds such a strong position, is expressed in a classical formulation by Douglas (1967):

> Nevertheless, *The Suicide* is the best sociological work on suicide, in the first place due to the scientific research ideal for social phenomena on which it is based, and because the investigation in its final analysis broke down the positivistic tradition in suicide research, – a tradition strongly contrasting with an understanding of suicide as a socially meaningful act. (p.76)

Douglas' statement from a generation ago is still valid today.

7. Literature

Bohannan, P. (red.) 1960: *African Homicide and Suicide*, Princeton University Press, Princeton, N.J.

Devereux, C. 1937: "Mohave Soul Concept", *American Anthropologist* Vol. 39.

Douglas, J. 1967: *The Social Meaning of Suicide*, Princeton University Press, Princeton, N.J.

Durkheim, E. 1912: *Le Suicide*, Libraire Felix Alcan, Paris.

Durkheim; E. 1951: *Suicide. A Study in Sociology*, the Free Press, New York.

Freud, S. 1949: "Mourning and Melancholia", in *Collected Papers*, Vol. IV, Hogarth Press, London (originally written in 1916).

Gibbs, P. and W. T. Martin 1961: *Status Integration and Suicide*, University of Oregon Press, Eugene, Oregon.

Hendin, H. 1964: *Suicide and Scandinavia*, Anchor Books, New York.

Pampel, F.C. 1998: "Nation, social change and sex differences in suicidal rates", *American Sociological Review* Vol. 63, pp. 744-58.

Retterstøl, N. 1970: *Selvmord. Et personlig, sosialt og samfunnsmessig problem* (Suicide. A personal, social and societal problem), Universitetsforlaget, Oslo.

Retterstøl, N. 1990: *Selvmord* (Suicide), Universitetsforlaget, Oslo.

Retterstøl, N. H. Ekeland and R. Hessø 1985: "Selvmord hos unge. Utviklingen i Norden. Et syv års materiale fra Oslo" (Suicide among young people. The development in Scandinavia. Material collected over seven years in Oslo), *Tidsskrift fra Den norske lægeforening* 105, pp. 119-22.

Zilborg, G. 1935: "Suicide among Civilized and Primitive Races", *American Journal of Psychology*, Vol. 95, pp. 1361-62.

14
The Cross-Pressure Hypothesis On Influences and Voting

LARS SVÅSAND

1. Original quotation

People who are exposed to cross-pressure delay their □nal vote decision. (Lazarsfeld, Berelson and Gaudet 1968, p. 58)

The attachment of a particular group to the party which on the whole may be regarded as representing the groups most closely, rises with the strength of the group within the area. (Tingsten 1937/1963 p. 230)

2. Brief explanation

The cross-pressure hypothesis is one of the most common explanations of why some voter groups show a low rate of election participation, or are not consistent in their party choice. Cross-pressure is a situation in which the voter a) has several roles which might in some cases be in conflict with one another, and b) has several preferences which cannot always be satisfied by choosing just one of the available alternatives.

In any society, every individual will play several roles. Each and every one of these roles involves certain expectations, both of the person who fills the role, and of the environment. In a situation where someone has to choose between the candidates, or parties, A and B, he/she will endeavor to do so in a way that avoids conflict between his/her roles.

In the USA there is evidence that Catholics tend to vote for the

Democrats, while the upper middle class tends to vote for the Republicans. If an American voter is a Catholic belonging to the upper middle class, a conflict may arise between these two roles when he has to vote for a candidate in a presidential election. Conflicting expectations about behavior may thus be expected from two opposing roles, as already described. The result of this kind of cross-pressure might well lead the person to delay his decision as to which of the candidates he will choose, or to refrain from voting altogether. Such a situation may be described as a socially-based cross-pressure.

Another type of cross-pressure arises when the individual is persuaded that one of several election alternatives implies the fulfilment of *one* of his preferences, while another alternative would fulfil *another* preference. When the individual is faced with choosing among various "policy packages", e.g. between party programs, a conflict of this kind may arise. If a voter favors the domestic policy of the A party, and at the same time the foreign policy of the B party, and both preferences are equally strong, then he faces a *psychologically-based cross-pressure situation.*

Tingsten's hypothesis is concerned more with the actual election alternatives than with election participation, as analyzed by Lazarsfeld et al. In Tingsten's view a party's share of the votes in an area will depend on the size of the social group with close ties to the party. This means that in a region where group A constitutes a very small part of the electorate, the party nearest to A will register an even smaller percentage of the votes cast. On the other hand, if in a certain region the social group that identifies with party A is dominant, then the party of this group will receive an even larger proportion of the votes.

A possible interpretation of this is that in the first case the social pressure felt by the voter to vote in conformity with his own social group is negligible, in other words, other factors will also influence his choice. In socially homogeneous areas, on the other hand, conformity pressure will be strong, spreading also beyond the predominant social group, and causing members of minority groups to vote in conformity with those belonging to the majority group.

This hypothesis has been termed "the law of the social center of gravity" (Tingsten 1963, p. 250).

3. Background

It was above all the classic study of the 1940 US presidential election, *The People's Choice*, that made the cross-pressure hypothesis known. This research initiated an American research tradition which later spread to Europe. *The People's Choice* marked the transition from the analysis of aggregated data to individual data and was the first of its kind to use panel data, i.e. the same persons were interviewed several times, in this case seven times between May and November 1940. One of the objectives of the enquiry was to find out *when* the voters made their final choice for one of the two candidates for the presidency. This allowed researchers to study when voters made their choice, and whether they changed their opinion in the course of the election campaign.

Tingsten's book *Political Behaviour* was published for the first time in 1937, and is quite different in character from that of Lazarsfeld et al. In *Political Behaviour* Tingsten examines election statistics from several European countries, and he was the first to point out the interdependence and variety of connections between factors such as party strength, election participation and different social groups among the electorate. The book has become a classic in the study of the relationship between social structure and political behavior at an aggregated level. In this book Tingsten formulated not only "the law of the social center of gravity", but also "the law of disparity", which claims that differences in election participation of different groups increase in inverse proportion to the general level of election participation.

4. Formalization – precise definition

The cross-pressure hypothesis as formulated by Lazarsfeld et al. postulates a relationship between the influences which the individual receives from the environment, and the point of time when he makes his final decision on how to vote. In Tingsten's case the analysis focused not on individuals, but aggregates. At an aggregate level it is not possible to analyze the data in the same way as one would on the individual level, but Tingsten's findings can be interpreted in the light of the cross-pressure hypothesis.

It is difficult to gauge cross-pressure, at any rate it has not yet been done. Cross-pressure exists only to the extent that an individual feels there to be a conflict between two or more of his reference groups, or between two or more of his own preferences. But the relationship that has been found to exist between, on the one hand, a late decision on whether or not to vote and, on the other, membership of a social group whose party preference is not stable, renders possible an interpretation such as that presented by Lazarsfeld et al. In their terminology the time required to decide whether or not to vote will be a function of the exposure to cross-pressure.

Formally the cross-pressure situation can be illustrated by means of four equations. In its most general form:

1) c (cross-pressure) = f $\left(\frac{A}{B}\right)$	
2) c max when $\left(\frac{A}{B}\right) \longrightarrow 1$ i.e. A≈B	In cases where there is equal pressure to vote for the two alternatives, the cross-pressure will be approximately equal to 1. This is the cross-pressure maximum, and the voters will delay their choice up to the last moment, or abstain from voting.
3) p(a) = A/B p (a) max. when A$\rightarrow \infty$ and B $\rightarrow 0$	The probability of voting for alternative A, p(a), increases as pressure to vote for A approaches infinity. Cross-pressure approaches 0.
4) p(b) = B/A p (b) max. when B $\rightarrow \infty$ and A $\rightarrow 0$	Here the situation is inverted: the probability of voting for alternative B, p(b), increases as B approaches infinity. Cross-pressure approaches 0.

Tingsten's law is so formulated that there is a curvilinear relationship between his two variables – party strength and social group – making it possible to express the relation between the variables as:

$$y = a + bx^2$$

We can illustrate this as in fig. 1. When the independent variable, i.e. the part of the electorate made up by the social group, surpasses a certain level, just a slight increase is required to cause a massive increase in the quantity of votes cast for the party that best represents this group. Even if there is no necessary connection, it is often the case that, in the absence of cross-pressure, the individual is subjected to pressure from one side only, namely the pressure to conform. Inversely, the absence of pressure to conform usually implies the presence of a cross-pressure situation.

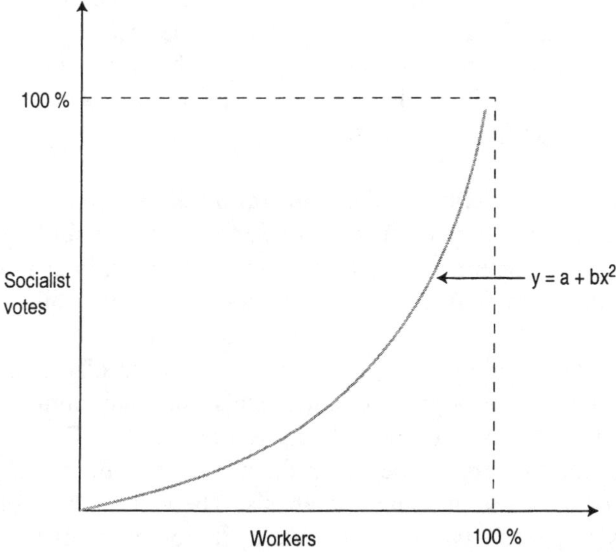

Fig. 1 Relationship between party strength and social group

5. Generality and testability. Critique

General considerations

The cross-pressure hypothesis was formulated in connection with re-search on a presidential election, and it has been cited primarily in the context of later political elections. However, the problem is known also from psychology, where several models and theories have been elabo-rated regarding the behavior of individuals subjected to pressure. The best-known of these are the dissonance-, balance- and congruence theo-ries. The dissonance theory focuses on the problem of the relationship between the conscious behavior of an individual and the knowledge that individual might have that contradicts such behavior. Research has also been done on situations where individuals have the choice between sev-eral election alternatives and where dissonance exists between what the individuals know about the negative aspects of the chosen alternative, and the positive aspects of the alternatives which were rejected (Festing-er 1975). The balance and congruence theories confine themselves to the study of attitudes. The subject here has been the problem of whether people who assess interrelated objects do so in the same or in different ways (Zajonc 1960). A survey of these models in relation to the cross-pressure hypothesis is to be found in Hellevik (1975).

Criticism of the cross-pressure hypothesis has been directed at the assumptions behind its application, and at the problems encountered in attempting to gauge cross-pressure.

Assumptions for application

The cross-pressure hypothesis has been applied to explain, among other things, why some people take less interest in political issues than others. The argument is that, due to the apparent impossibility of making a decision, people lose interest in the issue. However, this does not mean that the people who do participate in, say, an election, must be greatly interested in politics. Casting one's vote may simply imply a conformity with social norms: "Voting is a civil duty". Those who cast their votes might therefore be just as disinterested as the cross-pressure people. For the cross-pressure hypothesis to be valid it therefore seems necessary to specify two assumptions: a) the outcome of the relevant decision must be emotionally important to the person making the decision, and b) the result of the election must be uncertain. The latter assumption refers to the question of why some groups of the electorate refrain from voting. The reason might be a) they judge the situation to be hopeless – there is no point in voting because the voter belongs to a minority, or b) the outcome is certain – there is no need to vote because others will take care of one's interests.

Another criticism of the hypothesis concerns its validity within different political systems. The cross-pressure hypothesis was formulated in a political system where the voters generally face only two alternatives. In this system allegiance to parties is often weak, and the personalities of the contenders play an important role. In a system with strong party loyalties and many alternatives, low election participation may be due to a passing disenchantment with the party the voter would normally vote for. Party loyalty may be strong enough to rule out any possibility of the individual voting for another party, and he therefore prefers not to vote at all.

The gauging of pressure

Even if the assumptions for applying the cross-pressure hypothesis are met, there remains one important objection: how can one measure cross-pressure? This problem is still unsolved. It is impossible to say anything about the precise strength of different kinds of pressure, nor about what would happen if the strength of one of the conflicting pressures should decrease. Moreover, voting behavior is not determined by social and psychological pressure alone: the political system itself might have an influence. For example, the way in which seats are allocated may affect a voter's choice (Allardt and Littunen 1967, p. 139).

6. Empirical assessment – conclusion

It is above all in studies of the many American elections that the cross-pressure hypothesis has been tested. Berelson, Lazarsfeld and McPhee (1966, pp. 284-285) found that increasing pressure in the course of the election battle resulted in an increasing tendency towards consistency, i.e. attitudes inconsistent with the policy of the two American parties dwindled considerably as election day approached.

In a study of the US presidential elections of 1952 and 1956, voters were classified as Democrats or Republicans on the basis of their answers to six different questions. Only a few cases were registered where the voters were consistent with one of the parties on all six questions. The research demonstrated that, as the number of attitudes which diverged from one of the parties increased, so too did the percentage of voters who were late in deciding which of the candidates they would vote for (Campbell, Converse, Miller and Stokes 1964, pp. 40-46). This is an instance of psychological cross-pressure, where the voters find it difficult to reconcile voting behavior with their attitudes to political issues.

Using survey-data from the US presidential election of 1964, Eitzen (1964, p. 284) examined variations in election participation among different status groups. The starting point for the research was the cross-pressure hypothesis, which implies, among other things, that people whose status differs when assessed in terms of different criteria (such as occupation, income, and in some cases also sex, race and religion), will participate in elections less than those whose status is consistent across several criteria. However, Eitzen found that it was only those who were consistently high-status, i.e. those who were high-status according to several criteria, who showed a higher rate of election participation than the inconsistent category. The consistently low-status category showed the lowest rate of election participation. On the basis of this material he concludes that the hypothesis on status inconsistency and low election participation has to be rejected.

Himmelstrand (1970, p. 80) found that election participation differed between voter groups which were instrumentally oriented towards election participation, and those which were expressively oriented. For those who were instrumentally oriented, voting meant a means of achieving an objective, whereas for those who were expressively oriented, it was an act of intrinsic value. When confronted with cross-pressure situations, voters who were instrumentally oriented refrained from voting more often than those with an expressive attitude towards election participation, even though the instrumentally oriented generally took more interest in, and knew more about politics than the expressively oriented category.

Valen (1973) found that the low rate of participation in Norway's EU referendum was due to the fact that many voters felt a cross-pressure between the parties with which they identified and between their opinions regarding EU membership. The most important factor influencing the rate of participation seems to have been local community conditions: the more consistent the opinions, the higher the rate of participation. The greatest decrease in voter turnout relative to the foregoing government election was registered in areas where the two alternatives were equally strong.

In Norway, the EU referendum was the first political situation to resemble the US presidential election, involving just two alternatives and a very intense electoral campaign. In such a situation it should be far easier to gauge cross-pressure than in the case of normal elections, where a lot of other factors play a part.

In his analysis of the EU referendum, Hellevik (1973, p. 105) has shown that voters felt there was cross-pressure between local environment factors and the political parties, which promoted their arguments largely through the mass-media.

It seems that cross-pressure also played a part in voter participation in the 1994 referendum on EU membership. Turnout for this referendum was considerably higher than for the referendum of 1972, and also higher than it was for the parliamentary election of 1989. In a 1994 analysis at municipality level, Valen and Pettersen (1995) found that the increase in voter participation between the government election of 1989 and the referendum of 1994 was connected with the decisiveness with which the residents of an area voted yes or no to EU membership. A considerable increase in referendum participation could be noted particularly in areas where the no-party was strong. In constituencies where opinion was more equally divided between yes and no, the increase in turnout was much lower. The connection is clearly illustrated in figure 2.

In more recent research on political participation and political be-

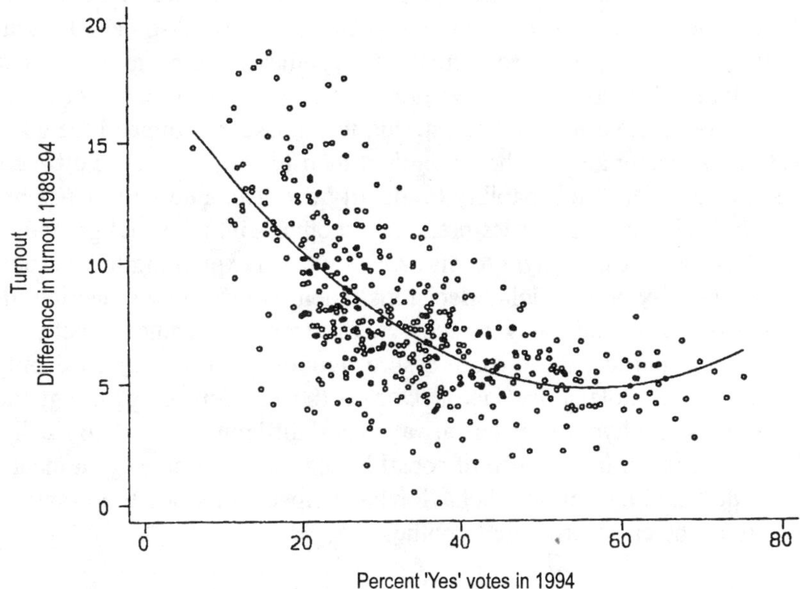

Fig. 2 Difference in turn-out 1989–94 and Yesvote at the EU-referendum in 1994 (Source: Valen and Pettersen 1995).

havior, the cross-pressure hypothesis is conspicuous in its absence. References to, or use of, the cross-pressure hypothesis can be found neither in analyses of participation and behavior in individual countries (Nie et al. 1976, Valen 1981, Särlvik and Crewe 1983) nor in textbooks that take a broader view of these subjects (Butler et al. 1981, Dalton et al. 1984, Rose 1980).

We can only speculate on the causes for this. A possible cause might be a growing mistrust of socio-economic variables as possible predictors of voting behavior. This has proved true particularly in the USA, where the cross-pressure hypothesis originated, but the tendency can be registered in other countries as well. A reduction in the reliability of these variables as a means of predicting behavior, will influence their reliability as predictors of participation rates. In its most common form, the cross-pressure hypothesis builds on the importance of the norms that apply in different social environments, such as class or religious affiliation. It goes without saying that when such factors lose their reliability as predictors, the cross-pressure idea is also affected.

The traditional background variables have been replaced by a shift of focus towards the voters' views on political issues or so-called "issue voting". Here too the cross-pressure hypothesis seems to have been abandoned. Methodological development in election research has supplied more precise tools for registering *which* issues command the interest of the electorate, and the *strength* of their feelings about the different issues. An improved capability to identify the electorate's *priorities* has also helped to push the cross-pressure hypothesis into the background.

The cross-pressure hypothesis proved vital in explaining low participation or why people delay decisions when they face two election alternatives. In multi-party systems with strong attachments between voters and parties, the cross-pressure hypothesis has been used only rarely as an explanatory factor. Due to the problem of gauging, the cross-pressure hypothesis has always been difficult to use empirically. The decrease in importance of social background variables as a means of understanding political behavior has helped to reduce the practical utility of the cross-pressure hypothesis.

7. Literature

Allardt, E. and Y. Littunen 1967: *Sociologi* (Sociology), Stockholm.

Allardt, E. and Stein Rokkan 1970: *Mass Politics*. New York

Berelson, B., P. Lazarsfeld and W. McPhee 1966: *Voting*, Chicago.

Butler, D., H.R. Penniman and A. Ranney (eds.) 1981: *Democracy in the Polis*, AEI Publications, Washington DC.

Campell A., P. Converse, W.W. Miller and D. Stokes 1964: *The American Voter*, New York.

Alton, T., J. Scott, C. Flanagan, and P.A. Beck (eds.): *Electoral Change in Advanced Industrial Democracies*, Princeton University Press, Princeton, N.J.

Eitzen, D.S. 1972: "Status Inconsistency and the Cross-Pressure Hypothesis", *Midwest Journal of Political Science* vol. XVI (May 1972), no. 2.

Festinger, L. 1957: *A Theory of Cognitive Dissonance*, New York.

Hellevik, O. 1973: *Endring i standpunkt til norsk EF-medlemskap: Betydningen av nærmiljø og politisk parti analysert ved hjelp av en kryss-press modell* (Change in point of view on EU-Membership: The Importance of Local Environment and Political Party analyzed by a Cross-Pressure Model), Oslo (preliminary ed.).

Himmelstrand, U. 1970: "Depoliticization and Political Involvement: A Theoretical and Empirical Approach", in E. Allardt and S. Rokkan (eds.): *Mass Politics*, New York.

Lazarsfeld, P., B. Berelson and H. Gaudet 1968: *The People's Choice*, New York

Nie, N.H., S. Verba, and J.R. Petrocik 1976: *The Changing American Voter*, Harvard University Press, Cambridge, Mass.

Pinner, F. 1968: "Cross-Pressure", in *International Encyclopedia of the Social Sciences* vol. 3, New York.

Rose, R. (ed.) 1980: *Electoral Participation*, Sage, London.

Särlvik, B. and I. Crewe 1983: *Decade of Realignment*, Cambridge University Press, Cambridge.

Tingsten, H. 1963: *Political Behaviour*, Totowa.

Valen, H. 1973: "Norway: No to EEC", *Scandinavian Political Studies* vol. 8.

Valen, H. 1981: *Valg og politikk* (Elections and Politics), NKS-forlaget, Oslo.

Valen, H. and P.A. Pettersen 1995: "Rekordhøy valgdeltagelse" (Record in turnout) in *Brussel midt imot. Folkeavstemningen om EU* (Against Brussels. The Referendum on the EU), Ad Notam Gyldendal, Oslo.

Zajonc, R.B. 1960: "The Concepts of Balance, Congruity and Dissonance", *Public Opinion Quarterly*.

15
The 'Two-Step-Flow-of-Communication' Hypothesis

HELGE ØSTBYE

1. Original quotation

[...] ideas often ⊏ow from radio and print to the opinion leaders and from them to the less active sections of the population. (Lazarsfeld, Berelson and Gaudet 1968: p. 151)

2. Brief Explanation

The *'two-step-flow-of-communication' hypothesis* or the law of *opinion leaders* is central for the understanding of the relation between personal communication and mass communication. It calls attention to one of the central themes in mass communication research, viz. the question of how strong is the effect on the recipients of a message brought by mass media: what are the conditions necessary to influence the recipient strongly enough to make them change their opinion?

The hypothesis deals with three types of participants: *mass media, opinion leaders* and *"plain" recipients* ("the less active sections of the population"). The novelty presented by the two-step flow of communication hypothesis was the discovery of the middle group called opinion leaders. This group acts as agents transmitting mass media information to the "plain" recipients.

The idea of the two-step flow of communication hypothesis can be illustrated as shown below:

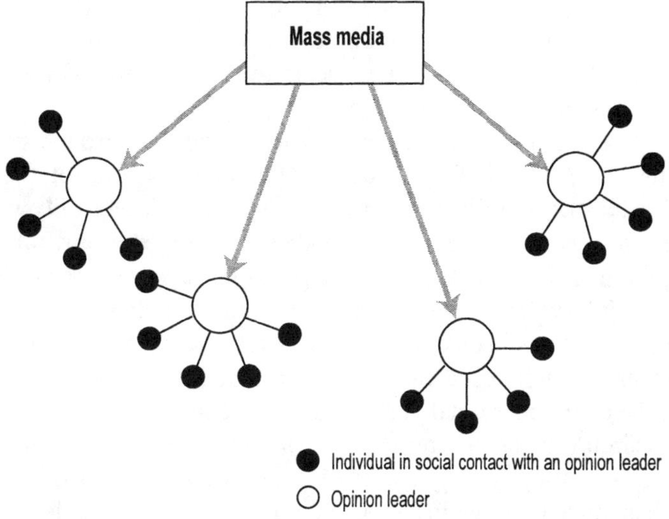

Fig. 1

The arrows indicate the communication "getting through", i.e. that it has an effect on the recipient.

3. Background

Before the introduction of the two-step flow of communication hypothesis (the book was published in 1944) the prevalent theory was that there was a direct influence from the media to the public. Innate psychological dispositions or the individual's social standing might certainly modify such effects, but only a few doubted the existence of a direct effect from mass media to the "masses". The earliest media effects model has sometimes been called *The hypodermic needle model*: the effect of the media effort to influence the public was regarded as roughly comparable to the direct injection of opinions and attitudes into a vein. (DeFleur, 1970, p. 115.)

The name that is inextricably associated with the development of the two-step flow of communication hypothesis is that of Paul F. Lazarsfeld. Lazarsfeld left his native country, Austria, for the USA in 1933. His professional background was in European social psychology. In the USA he was attached to Columbia University for a long time.

On the occasion of the 1940 US presidential election he and a number of other researchers at Columbia University worked on a project which studied the factors that were decisive for the electors' voting patterns. The research was reported in the book *The People's Choice* (Lazarsfeld, Berelson and Gaudet, 1968), from which the introductory quotation has been taken. This study turned out to be one of the most fruitful pieces of empirical research ever conducted. Not only was the two-step flow of communication hypothesis presented as a result of the investigation, it was also the first great *panel research* (i.e. the same persons were interviewed several times over an extended period). Since then the method has been employed in a great many investigations, e.g. Norwegian election research undertaken since 1957 (see e.g. Valen, 1981 and Valen and Aardal, 1983). Another concept introduced in the 1940 research was the *cross pressure hypothesis* (see chapter 14).

Thus it was not primarily a study concerning the effects of the mass media. But since these were supposed to be important in understanding why people changed their opinions, it was deemed necessary also to include some questions concerning the use of the mass media. It was certainly clear that the mass media alone were not sufficient to explain people's choice of party. During the 1932 election campaign Roosevelt faced considerable opposition in American mass media, and was nevertheless elected.

The data collected by Lazarsfeld and his collaborators at an early stage of the election campaign showed that only few changed their opinion, and among those who did, only very few claimed their change had been influenced by information in the mass media. On the con-

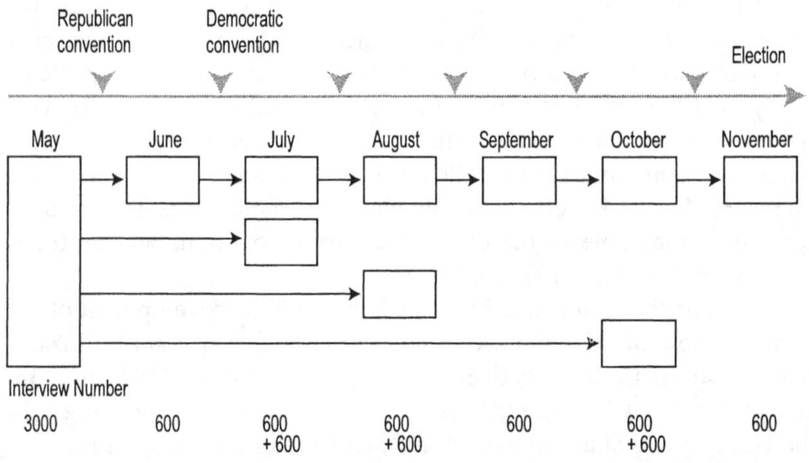

trary, the reason given by a majority was *personal communication*. In the later parts of the project more attention was given to this point, and the answers of those interviewed indicated that a message transmitted by the mass media was interpreted for the "masses" by opinion leaders. (Lazarsfeld, Berelson and Gaudet, 1968.)

Almost simultaneously with Lazarsfeld's research Robert K. Merton embarked on a project originally conceived as a readership study for an American magazine. This study gradually acquired a more general perspective. Merton did not use the term "opinion leaders", but "influentials", which was pretty much the same. Also Merton established the importance of the social structure for understanding how a mass media message gains the necessary impact to change the opinion of the receivers. (Merton 1949.)

4. Formalization – precise definition

Going back to the introductory quotation we note that the subject is *ideas*, not *news*. Ideas can be more complex messages. In *The People's Choice* the theme was influence with the aim of making people vote for a certain party. Further, the quotation says "often". The hypothesis is not an overruling theory to explain why people change their mind. The hypothesis could supplement other theories, and points at a certain aspect of the transmission, namely, the connection to the social environment of the recipient. The two-step flow of communication hypothesis or the theory of opinion leaders can be used to explain why changes of attitudes etc. are brought about when messages are "filtered" through opinion leaders, and why changes do *not* occur as a result of a message directly received from mass media.

The participants can be depicted as follows:

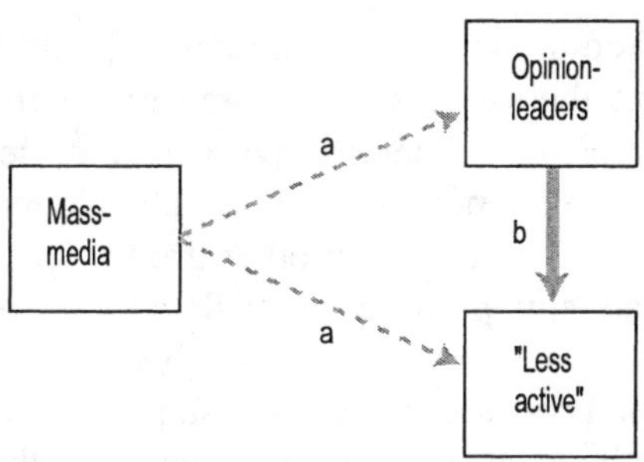

Here, *a* denotes the mass media message, which can reach opinion leaders as well as "plain" recipients. *b* denotes the message from the opinion leader to the "plain"-recipients. The opinion leader may have changed the content of the message, making it different from that transmitted by the mass media. The change may imply a total inversion, the same message with a certain addition, an emphasis of certain aspects of the original message, or a simple presentation. Even when the opinion leader redistributes the message in an unchanged form, it will be interpreted differently from how it would be when received directly from the mass media. The opinion leader adds his prestige to the message, in addition to the prestige that the mass media have conferred on it.

The hypothesis says nothing clear as to the probability of a direct influence from a mass media message, only that the probability of such a message being accepted is greater when conveyed by an opinion leader. Nor does the hypothesis say anything as to whether opinion leaders change their own opinions as a result of the mass media message. This will vary from one field to another. In a field where the objective is to keep up with certain changes, the opinion leaders will probably be the first to change their mind. However, in a field where the connection to fundamental values is concerned, we could expect there to be only a small probability that the opinion leaders will be swayed to change their opinion.

Since the model does not make clear whether *b* – the opinion leader's message – has the same direction as *a* – the media message – we are not able to tell in which direction the change of attitude will take place. This again contributes to reduce the direct importance of the mass media in bringing about a planned change of public opinion.

5. Generality and testability. Critique

The two-step flow of communication hypothesis should be regarded as a reaction against the theory of a strong and direct influence of the mass media on its recipients. Generally speaking, theories of such simple, direct and strong influences have been abandoned by most researchers, but still keep a firm hold on other groups, e.g. politicians (it would suffice to read any parliamentary debate on television programs).

This does not mean, however, that all one-step hypotheses have been abandoned. Attempts have been made, for instance on the basis of Festinger's theory of *cognitive dissonance* (see any introductory work on social psychology), to explain why not all messages conveyed via mass media have the same effect. (Troldahl 1967.)

The most common critique of the two-step flow hypothesis in its original wording is, however, that it suggests the existence of a *permanent set of opinion leaders*, and that the idea of *two-steps* is too simple.

Different people are opinion leaders in different sectors. Person A may very well be the opinion leader of – as regards politics, while – is the opinion leader of A regarding clothing fashions.

It is probable also that opinion leaders may be found on different levels within one and the same sector. Person A may be the opinion leader of – regarding politics, but B, can, in his turn, be the opinion leader of C in this same field.

These two types of critique do not really undermine the core of Lazarsfeld's statement, but are rather to be regarded as extensions and clarifications of the original hypotheses, and partially as a supplement which Lazarsfeld himself has taken care to document. (See below.)

The British media researcher Denis McQuail has summarized the actual status of the two-step flow hypothesis approximately as follows :

> Firstly, subsequent research, while confirming the importance of conversation and personal contact as accompaniment and perhaps modifier of media influence, has not clearly demonstrated that personal influence always acts as a strong independent or 'counteractive' source of influence normally affected by mass media. [...] Secondly, it has become clear that the division between 'leaders' and 'followers' is variable from topic to topic, that the roles are interchangeable, and there are many who cannot be classified as either one or the other. Thirdly, it seems probable that the flow is as likely to be multi-step as two-step. Finally, it seems clear that direct effects of the media can occur without 'intervention' from opinion leaders, and highly probable that personal influence is as likely to reinforce the effects of media as to counteract them. (McQuail 1983, pp. 193-194.)

Regarding *generality* we can say that the hypothesis is conceived to cover all situations where mass media convey a message intended to make people change their opinion. It would also appear reasonable to say that it covers situations where mass media do not consciously aim to influence.

An important condition for the possibility of *testing* the hypothesis (i.e. of falsifying it) is the possibility of identifying opinion leaders. Rogers and Shoemaker point out three methods of identifying opinion leaders in empirical research:

> The *sociometric method* consists of asking questions of respondents as to whom they sought (or "hypothetically" *might* seek) for information or advice about a given topic, such as technological innovation or news events. Opinion leaders are those members of a system who receive the greatest number of sociometric choices. [...]
>
> An alternative to sociometry is the selection of *judges or key informants* who are especially knowledgeable about the patterns of influence in a system. [...] The judges or key informants are asked to identify the opinion leaders for a given topic or topics.
>
> The *self-designating technique* asks the respondents to indicate the tendency for others to regard them as influential. [...] An advantage of the self-designating technique is that it measures the individual's perceptions of his opinion leadership, which is actually what affects his behavior. (Rogers and Shoemaker 1971, pp. 215-217.)

A disadvantage of all these methods is their tendency to produce differences in the material thus obtained, regardless of whether such differences actually exist or not. They are well suited *if*, in some way, the two-step flow of communication hypothesis holds good, but they are not so well suited to testing out whether it really does.

6. Empirical assessment – conclusion

Lazarsfeld did his work on the two-step flow hypothesis and the opinion leadership theory in research conducted in co-operation with Katz. This research resulted in a new book – *Personal Influence* – in 1955. The object of the second study was not how political information is spread, but the question whether or not opinion leadership existed, and if so, how it functioned in areas such as people's knowledge about the market for ordinary household goods, fashion, public affairs, and movies. Three important facts were established in *Personal Influence*:

Firstly, opinion leaders have much the same *social status* as those led by them (the "influencees"). When opinion leaders and influencees differed in status, the opinion leader was usually of a higher status. (Katz and Lazarsfeld 1964, p. 237)

Secondly, opinion leadership was found to be *specific to a certain topic* i.e. a person acting as an opinion leader in one field would not necessarily hold this position in other fields. (Katz and Lazarsfeld 1964, pp. 333-34)

Thirdly, opinion leaders turned out to be, as a rule, far *more exposed to the mass media* than the influencees. (Katz and Lazarsfeld 1964, p. 312 ff.)

In addition to these three characteristics of opinion leaders, Rogers and Shoemaker note that opinion leaders have a more cosmopolitan outlook and more social intercourse, and are more innovative than the influencees. (Rogers and Shoemaker 1971, pp. 378-80)

The hypothesis has been tested in a lot of other studies. The two instances given below have been taken from non-Western cultures. Their conclusions differ regarding the validity of the two-step flow of communication hypothesis. A Cambodian study concludes that

> information itself is considered sterile by the individual villager until someone of status has interpreted it. The individual does not see it as his role to judge the news. (Gude 1961, p. 14, – here the main conclusion quoted from Pool 1967, p. 244.)

On the other hand, a Nile Delta study has:

> shown that the mass media reach the people in a direct and effective way. (Harik 1971, p. 731)

Both of these inquiries are concerned mainly with the transmission of information, rather than of ideas.

But it has been shown that personal influence is of great importance also with regard to the transmission of new ideas. The object in one study was the spread of the use of a new drug among doctors. Evidence was presented that doctors integrated in a network of other doctors started using the new medicine far earlier than did others. Personal contact was important to bring about the spread of knowledge and to deliver a push to start using the new and better drug. (Coleman, Katz and Menzel 1966, pp. 95-112)

Studies from the Nordic environment are relatively few. In a Finnish research project Piepponen found a far greater overlap of opinion leaders in different fields compared to the results published by Katz and Lazarsfeld. This may be explained, however, by the fact that the fields studied in the Finnish research were more closely related than those studied in the Personal Influence project (Piepponen 1960, pp. 72-75, quoted from Allardt and Littunen 1968, p. 37).

In his studies of the Swedish parliamentary elections in 1960, Rune Sjödén found television to have been the most important source of information for the majority of voters. Sjödén used a self-designating technique to distinguish between opinion leaders and the influencees. For opinion leaders newspapers were the most important source of information. In all kinds of political activity described in the inquiry, opinion leaders were more active than those "led". (Sjödén 1962, pp. 35 and 78)

With regard to elections it is worth mentioning that the idea of backing up messages conveyed by the mass media by means of personal communication is actively used in election campaigns. The first time this was systematically done in Norway was in the 1965 election campaign for the Liberal Party in Akershus county, where Halfdan Hegtun was elected even though in earlier elections his party had been far from achieving a mandate in this constituency. Several Norwegian social researchers, well acquainted with Lazarsfeld and his theories, participated in the planning of Hegtun's campaign.

In Østbye's research on the spread of television in Norway no significant differences were established between opinion leaders and influencees (on the basis of self-designation) regarding the time when they bought a television set. But here the object of the dissemination process was a material good, not an idea. (Østbye 1972, p. 147)

On the other hand, research has proved personal contact to be important for the success of a health campaign (Eriksen ct al. 1984).

7. Literature

Allard, E, and Y. Littunen 1968: *Sociologi*, Almquist and Wiksell, Stockholm (1. ed. 1962).

Blumler, J.B. and E. Katz 1974: *The Use of Mass Communication*, Sage, Beverly Hills.

Coleman, J., E. Katz and H. Menzel 1966: *Medical Innovation*, The Bobbs-Merril Co., NY.

Curran, J. 1990: "The New Revisionism in Mass Communication Research: A Reappraisal", *European Journal of Communication*, vol. 5, no. 2-3 1990, pp. 135-164.

DeFleur, M.L. 1970: *Theories of Mass Communication* (2. ed.), McKay, N.Y.

Eriksen , R., G. Henriksen and L. Hjulstad 1984: *Evaluering av Trim-Glad. En aksjon for økt fysisk aktivitet i Sogn og Fjordane høsten 1983*. (Evaluation of 'Trim-Glad'. A movement for increased physial activity in Sogn og Fjordane Autum 1983) Universitetet i Bergen. 1984.

Gebner, G. et al. 1994: "Growing up with Television: The Cultivation Perspective" in Jennings Bryant, J. and D. Zillman (eds.): *Media Effects*, Hillsdale, J.J., Lawrence Erlbaum..

Gude, E. W. 1961: *Buddhism and the Political Process in Cambodia*, manuscript.

Hardt, H. 1992: *Critical Communication Studies: Communication, History and Theory in America*, Routledge, London

Harik, I.F. 1970: "Opinion Leaders and the Mass Media in Rural Egypt", *American Political Science Review*, vol. LXV (September 1970), pp. 731-740.

Høst, S. 1979: *Moderne bruksstudier – snarvei eller blindspor?*(Modern applied studies – quick path or blind track), Oslo: Institutt for presseforskning.

Jensen, K.B. 1986: *Making Sense of the News*, Aarhus University Press, Århus.

Katz, E. and P.F. Lazarsfeld 1964: *Personal Influence*, Free Press, New York (1. ed. 1955).

Klapper, J.T. 1960: *The Effects of Mass Communication*, Free Press, New York.

Lazarsfeld, P.F., B. Berelson and H. Gaudet 1968: *The People's Choice (3. ed.)*, Columbia University Press, New York (1. ed. 1944).

McQuail, Denis 1983: *Mass Communication Theory. An Introduction*, Sage, London.

Merton, R.K. 1949: "Patterns of Influence" in P.F. Lazarsfeld and F.N. Stanton (eds.): *Communication Research 1948-1949*, Harper & Row, New York.

Piepponen, P. 1960: *Ilarrastusen valinta*, Helsinki.

Pool, I. de Sola: "Mass Media and Politics in the Modernization Process", pp. 234-253 in Pye, L. W. 1976: *Communication and Political Development*, Princeton University Press, Princeton, N.J.

Rogers, E.M. and F.F. Shoemaker 1971: *Communication of Innovations*, Free Press, New York.

Schwebs, T. and H. Østbye 1995: *Media i samfunnet*, (Media in socity) Samlaget, Oslo.

Sjödén, R. 1962: *Sveriges första TV-val* (Sweden's first TV-election), Sveriges Radio, Stockholm.

Svåsand, L. 1987: "Krysspresshypotesen", (The Cross Pressure Hypotesis) pp. 54-61 in S.U. Larsen (ed.): *Lov og struktur*, (Law and Structure), Bergen: Universitetsforlaget.

Teigen, H. 1997: "Sosialpsykologi" (Social psychology), ch. 24 in G. Nielsen and K. Raaheim (eds.): *En innføringsbok i psykologi for universiteter og høgskoler*, (An introductory Text in psychology for universities and colleges), Cappelen, Oslo.

Troldahl, V.C. 1967: "A Field Test of a Modified Two-Step Flow of Communications Model", *Public Opinion Quarterly*, vol. XXX, pp. 609-623.

Valen, H. 1981: *Valg og politikk*, (Elections and Politics), NKS-forlaget, Oslo.

Valen, H. and D. Katz 1964: *Political Parties in Norway*, Universitetsforlaget, Oslo.

Waldahl, R. 1989: *Mediepåvirkning*, (The effects of media), Ad Notam, Oslo.

Whyte, W.F. 1955: *Street Corner Society*, The University of Chicago Press, Chicago (1.ed. 1943).

Windahl, S. and B. Signitzer 1992: *Using Mass Communication Theory*, Sage, London.

Østbye, H. 1972: *Om innføring av fjernsyn i Norge* (On the introduction of TV in Norwy), NAVF's Sekretariat for Mediaforskning, Bergen.

Aardal, B. and R. Waldahl (eds.) 1994: *Valg og velgere: utvalgte bidrag fra 40 års norsk valgforskning*, (Voters and elections: selected contributions from 40 years of Norwegian electoral research), Oslo: Institutt for samfunnsforskning.

PART III

The Theoretical Challenge: Working with Laws and Theories

16
The Theoretical Challenge

Stein Ugelvik Larsen

How do theories represent
a challenge to society?

The role of science in society is not unproblematic, even though science enjoys high prestige and the State contributes large sums of money to scientific activity. The prestige springs from the belief that science reveals truth and that scientific theories are true. Scientific knowledge is regarded as neutral and above political strife. Such knowledge acquires a special position in all societies, a status that is consequently accorded also to those who represent this knowledge, – i.e. the scientific institutions. Thus the social and political position which is implied when something is defined as science becomes an important aspiration.

Scientific activity has certain consequences, relating to how scientific findings are utilized, of which both scientists and the general public are scarcely aware. In the boxes below I have illustrated various dilemmas caused by the use of science.

There is no clear dividing line between science and research. Much research is of great value in itself, but cannot be termed science in the strict sense of the word, its object being to furnish the answers to concrete problems, and not to invalidate or establish general theories. It is true, however, that the observations made can form the basis of empirical generalizations. Moreover, all research starts from a more or less explicit theoretical basis. Therefore, research without theory is inconceivable, just as science without a view to empirical confirmation will prove abortive. Thus what we are dealing with is two contrasting positions, but the priority assigned to one of them can also raise political questions: should theoretical work on nuclear physics be continued without making atomic bombs? To what extent should the development of quantum theory be promoted with the aim of using it in the microprocessor industry?

Basic research: research aimed at producing fundamental theories on social life.

Applied research: research based on known theories, aimed at the solution of practical problems.

Action research: political initiatives where a researcher uses his knowledge and theories to attain practical aims.

Task research: applied research where an employer outside the research environment finances the research and defines its goals.

These different types of research highlight dilemmas of research policy. In their competition for research funds both the so-called research centers outside the universities and the universities themselves have at times endeavored to erase the dividing line between basic research and applied research. Research centers try to become more academic, while the universities search for practical commissions. Basic research is then sure to be the loser.

The Norwegian sociologist *Johan Galtung* (born 1930) has become increasingly concerned with the problem of "sociological imperialism" towards underdeveloped countries. On the basis of his experience with Western sociologists who have carried out research in such countries, he calls attention to the way in which Western researchers set the standards for the self understanding of the inhabitants.[1] In this way they take Western attitudes as the only applicable standard, and "colonize" the Third World anew. There is a need for symmetry in the contact between Western researchers and the people in the countries they visit. In many cases there even ought to be an asymmetry in favor of the underdeveloped countries. For they themselves ought to formulate the problems at which research is directed, and interpret the results, while Western researchers should be at their service.

---

1. Galtung, Johan 1977: "Science Assistance and Neo-Colonialism", in *Methodology and Ideology*, Vol. II, 1977.

Another political consequence of science has to do with *the theory of comparative advantages*, developed by David Ricardo in the early years of the 19th century. Ricardo demonstrated why it is profitable for each country to manufacture the goods the country is best qualified to produce. England, for instance, was in a more favorable position than others to produce clothing, while Portugal was in a better position to produce wine. Intuitively we all understand that specialization and the exchange of goods is profitable. The theory has therefore legitimized the general development of international trade.

But the theory is commendable only in the short-term perspective. In the longer-term, instrumental use of the theory is, for many countries, destructive. As in the case of countries that produce raw materials, wine producing countries suffer from the disadvantage that their production provides little knowledge of technological development. In the long-run countries that produce low technology goods will drop behind, compared with countries that produce high technology goods, i.e. countries that utilize their "comparative-advantages". Hence the paradox that the theory is "true" in a short-time perspective, although it does not take into account the long-term effects of international trade, which happens to be based on short-term profit considerations. The main reason is that the theory doesn't take into account the *type of goods* in terms of which the "comparative advantages" of different countries are identified.

At the main entrance of the Central Party High School in Beijing there is a statue of Mao Zedong (1893-1976) with the inscription: "Seek Truth through Facts".

Mao emphasized that politics and thought (theory) should be connected with practical circumstances (empirical observation). He aimed to prove his policy as "right" by referring to actual circumstances in China. But his subordinates did not provide him with the "facts" about life in China, since they were concerned to give their dictator positive feedback, rather than reveal how critical the country's situation really was. The main problem is a difference between the "use of facts" and the "interpretation of facts". In themselves, facts have no sense when not seen in the light of a general theory, and it is here that Mao, availing himself of Marxist scientific terminology, made his great mistake. He interpreted facts in the way that suited him best, and formulated political guidelines for China's development based on desired ends and not on scientific theory.

I have presented these examples to illustrate the social and political consequences of theoretical work. The conflicts of science and the choice as to what kind of theoretical work should be given priority are far from unproblematic.

The challenge to develop new theories

The theories dealt with in this book are old, inasmuch as some of the original formulations are found in publications from as early as around 1700. In selecting the theories it has been important to highlight how 'classic theories' survive and still remain of current interest. However, the more recent theories, such as Hart's inverse health care law (chapter 11) or the Finitism thesis (chapter 4) also indisputably have their roots in older theories. The impression might therefore arise that theoretical innovation is rare, in the social sciences as well as in other scientific disciplines. What is the explanation for this? Is it because scientists are conservative and prefer to depend on theories they know, or is it because these known theories themselves have proved to have explanatory potential which is strong enough to force us to admit them as inevitable components of our future knowledge?

In all science there is a progressive dynamic which is sustained by our search for answers to new questions and the need to enlarge our knowledge. Therefore, science is characterized by a constant unrest that would seem to safeguard it against the all too easy acceptance of what has already been discovered. Yet the force of existing paradigms is often active in counteracting innovation (see the article on Thomas Kuhn, chapter 2). Thus, in scientific work both conservative and progressive elements are to be found. The question is: what is the key to the invention of new theories, and how should we go about finding them?

The most usual answer is that the theory will emerge through the observations made. Theories emerge when scientists are engaged in empirical observation. "nother answer is that the theory element is introduced from the "list" of known theories within the discipline concerned. The theories are already there, and it is impossible to make empirical observations without a theoretical background, because we have to know what it is we are looking for.

> The concept of "serendipity" was formulated in 1945 by the well known sociologist Robert Merton in *American Journal of Sociology*, vol. 50:469. Merton refers to the fact that in the same year Walter B. Cannon, in his *The Way of the Investigator*, New York, had found several phenomena which he describes as follows: "fruitful empirical research not only tests theoretically derived hypotheses; it also gives rise to new hypotheses. This might be termed the "serendipity" component of research, i.e. the discovery, by chance or sagacity, of valid results which were not sought for". See also "The Serendipity Pattern" p. 157-62 in Merton 1968: *Social Theory and Social Structures*, New York. (The concept was first used by Horace Walpole in 1754).

Karl Popper is the foremost advocate of the view that the theories are already there and that the task consists in subjecting them to the most challenging tests possible, i.e. testing the theory against real circumstances with the expectation of seeing it falsified. But even after the most challenging test we have no certainty that the theory is "true", since new situations may arise in the future, which suggest new tests that might falsify it. There is no use in turning first to the facts in search of patterns and theory, because facts acquire a meaning only in relation to a theory.

This view is fairly uncontroversial. More controversial is Popper's answer to the question where theories come from. His answer is that theories belong to "World 3", meaning a collective basis of public knowledge where "true" knowledge is integrated with attempts to sort out falsified knowledge. There is no one who governs this knowledge base, and nobody can know its total extent. Everybody is born with a certain "World 3 luggage", in that we all inherit the possibility to take in theories from "World 3"; we all participate in it and indeed anybody can influence its contents. When preoccupied with a problem, a researcher must allow "World 3" to influence the perspective of theoretical meaning connected to the problem. In this way it will be possible to include one or more theories in the project and make them a guideline for the research.

In sociological circles is *Karl Popper* (1902-1994) is known particularly for the demarcation criterion, his critique of historicism, and the "World 3-theory".

With the *demarcation criterion* he establishes a dividing line between science and non-science. A scientific theory is characterized by its suitability for being tested against reality and falsified ("the falsification criterion"), i.e. the theory can be refuted, or proved false.

In his *historicism critique* he criticizes Plato, Hegel, Marx and (between the lines) Nazism. These take as their starting points prophecies of the future which cannot be tested against reality. Yet they are presented as scientific truths, and demand, moreover, total submission. These theories are not susceptible to falsification, and the consequence of believing in them will be a "closed society" governed by demagogues. Popper therefore advocates an "open society" with competing theories that can be falsified.

The "*Worlds 1, 2 and 3 -theory*" is the most ambitious aspect of Popper's theoretical work. *World 1* is the material part of existence (body, subsistence and biological interaction), *World 2* is constituted by individual consciousness (experience, emotions, intentions, memory), while *World 3* is the objective knowledge that exists outside the single individual, and the result of many generations of thinking. It is from this accumulated knowledge base that we derive our theories for research. Through scientific work we also furnish "World 3" with new material, but without being able to control it.

Popper's view of theories as a potential arsenal of knowledge at the disposal of every human being has its background in two circumstances. On the one hand a theory is needed to make facts meaningful. On the other, Popper refutes as impossible the construction of a general theory based on observation, since one cannot know what kind of knowledge will be produced in the future. Generalizations as predictors of the future are at best mere conjectures that do not deserve to be defined as scientific theories. Therefore, Popper adopts an idealized view which entails the existence in "World 3" of a reservoir of theories that constitute something more than a "list" of theories already known.

Popper offers few examples that resemble *social science* theories.[1]

produce results which are quite the opposite of what is predicted by the theory. One instance is large monopolies which do away with all price competition and thus lead to total price and production control. Another thing that is sometimes ignored in connection with the functioning of the free market is the need for a powerful state. If the State is not powerful enough to guarantee the conditions mentioned – in addition to other institutional conditions, such as a system of laws, methods for policing and a rational administration – the invisible hand will not work. Yet according to Adam Smith's theory it was the very absence of State control (against mercantilism and for free trade) that would set free the liberating powers of the market mechanism.

In Askildsen's discussion we therefore find many indications of the weaknesses of the theory, but he also shows how the theory is robust enough to explain important developments in the world. The fact that objections can be made to a theory does not imply that it is useless and therefore not worth retaining. On the contrary, fruitful theories are not either true or false, as Popper contended, but embody an arsenal of ideas which tend to furnish new perspectives on social relations/conditions. The invisible hand is a good illustration of how assumptions have to be made explicit, and how this facilitates the understanding of what happens when they are missing or perverted. Scientific efforts along these lines are therefore of great value.

In his discussion of von Thünen's theory of how agricultural production is spread across a landscape (chapter 10), Peter Sjøholt has expounded a theory which is in principle very similar to the invisible hand theory, although it deals with something entirely different. Von Thünen was one of the great pioneers of geography, and the theory is a good example of how, on the basis of one variable (transport distance from market; X, the "independent"), we are able to explain the production of agricultural goods within the whole area (Y, the "dependent"). The assumptions required for the theory to apply are:

1. The area must be a homogeneous plain, i.e. the soil must be of identical quality from closest to the market to its outermost parts.
2. All production costs must be constant, except transport costs which vary in relation to distance from the market.
3. There must be only one market, i.e. one trade center (see the "isolated state" concept).

Provided these assumptions are met, agricultural production will vary according to distance to the market; the nearest areas will be intensively exploited (vegetables, milk etc.), whereas the most distant will be exploited extensively (grazing ground, i.e. meat/wool etc.). If one of the assumptions is left out or "perverted", the theory will no longer apply with the same precision. When, for instance, a new transport technology is introduced, or more than one trade center are established, "corrections" have to be made for altered assumptions to make the prediction of (rational) agricultural production in a given area come true. When the soil is not homogeneous but rather of highly differing quality (e.g. due to a river running through the area), calculations must be made to assess how this assumption will effect the outcome. Von Thünen's isolated state is therefore a good example of an empirical theory from which we can derive testable hypotheses, and the theory applies to all areas and all types of agricultural production. Moreover, the theory offers the possibility of generalizing upwards so as to account for the use of space in cities and to predict optimal location for industry. Even though the theory "belongs to" the discipline of geography, most social scientists find it a useful example, not least due its formal structure: the explicit assumptions and the co-variation between the independent variable and the dependent variable.

Levels of analysis: the small and the large deduction/induction

In the "Generality and testability" section (5), each author has discussed the position held by the theory in a hierarchy of other possible theories. When we have to decide whether or not a test falls under a hypothesis, and a hypothesis falls under a theory, the question must be asked: *of what is this test an example, and from which theory has this hypothesis been deduced?* In other words, an inductive question is posed to identify the test and hypothesis levels. Likewise, the question must be asked whether a theory can be an example of some more general theory.

As mentioned in the introduction, Hart's inverse health care law (chapter 11) may be called an example of *the Matthew effect* (pp. 179-80), which can also be found in several other fields. Jensen demonstrates that where goods are distributed equally there is a tendency towards accumulation. Those favored with initial advantages will increase their lead. Those in greatest need of help lack both the ability and the knowledge required for the formulation of their needs. Social institutions reinforce maldistribution.

Moreover, we can discuss whether Hart's theory is an instance of the *status theory*, which maintains that social status will always reproduce itself, and that differences will increase if nothing is undertaken to counteract this trend (pp. 179–80). Does this mean that the Matthew effect should be conceived as covering all these circumstances, and is it therefore a highest-level theory? Or are both Hart's law and the Matthew effect instances of the market mechanisms that were formulated by Adam Smith, i.e. on a higher general level?

> How can we ascertain whether one theory is more general than another? And what will be the correct level for our endeavors? Robert Merton is of the opinion that the most useful method for social science is to concentrate on "middle range theories". These theories "of course imply abstraction, but are near enough to observed data to be built into hypotheses intended for empirical testing, they are related to more limited social phenomena. Instances are reference group theory, theories on social mobility, role conflict and price theory, theories on bacteria causing infection, kinetic gas theory".[1]
>
> Merton warns against "total system theory" – "the upper range" – because of the risk of losing oneself in useless speculation. But it is not clear where the borderline between middle and upper range should be located. I would advise students not to be afraid of thinking widely, even though they are writing on more limited subjects.

1.   Robert Merton 1957/1968: "On Sociological Theories of the Middle Range", in *Social Theory and Social Structures*, p. 39-72.

Similar questions can be asked regarding Durkheim's suicide hypothesis (chapter 13). Which theory of a higher generality level is exemplified by the suicide hypothesis? Durkheim was searching for the higher order paradigm that could explain the extent of suicide as well as of criminality, divorce and other types of deviation which characterize weak societies. Knudsen's discussion of the suicide hypothesis is a good illustration of the alternation between theoretical generalizations and deduction to empirical tests. Durkheim called attention to the forces that contribute to the shifting of "society temperature" from "warm" to "cold" societies. Durkheim defined the (independent) social-integration variable operationally (rendering concrete) from no-integration (absence of norms) to over-integration (excessively norm-controlled), with an intermediate form constituting "the best temperature". He further defined the dependent variable – the state of society – in terms of the incidence of suicide cases. Several hypotheses can be deduced from the theory, such as the contention that, in societies where integration is either too feeble or too thorough, more suicides will occur than in areas of "medium" integration. The suicide types (anomic, egoistic, altruistic and fatalistic) will also vary according to the degree of integration.

A scrupulous theorist is always bound to ask himself whether the tests are fairly and reasonably inferred from the hypotheses such as they are formulated. In scientific literature the concept of *validity* is used to refer to questions such as: is the test a fair and reasonable way of testing the hypothesis concerned?

In jurisprudence the same problem arises concerning general rules, single case questions and actual decisions. Lawyers avail themselves of the "subsumption" concept (inclusion under a rule), "analogous interpretation" (search for parallel cases on the same level) and "extended interpretation" (search for higher levels of generality). Jurisprudence is not an empirical science, but does, like social science, shift between higher and lower levels of interpretation.

In jurisprudence there is no logic that determines correct interpretations. Some interpretations derive their authority from tradition, while other decisions are made by judges in court.[1]

This is also much the same in empirical social science. Whether an induction or deduction is fair/reasonable is a matter to be decided by specialist circles in the course of time. In the subsequent round another group may reject the decision and repudiate the validity of the test. This is how science develops, though it is a widespread belief that the operations of deduction and induction are based on much stricter, more formal rules. In such cases the part played in the development of scientific knowledge by inventiveness, intuition and different types of argument is neglected.

---

1.   The English lawyer A.G. Guest illustrates how judges wander "upwards" and "downwards" when having to state the reason for actual decisions. "It has often been said that the judge first finds his result, as it were, by intuition, thereafter shaping the logical grounds for the result. As a psychological phenomenon this is, per se, not all too peculiar. All the numerous aims the legal order is intended to promote and with which the judge is, through his professional activity, well acquainted, can have become part of his own nature. He succeeds in finding a rational result, without having beforehand made clear to himself all the arguments that can by deductive reasoning give the reasons for and legitimate the outcome." (Quoted from Frede Castberg: *Forelesninger over Rettsfilosofi* (Lectures on Philosophy of Law), 1965, p. 79).

A clever social scientist is capable of realizing the theoretical implications of the connection between theory and empirical finding and of moving – "upwards" or "downwards" – between the different types/levels of inferences.

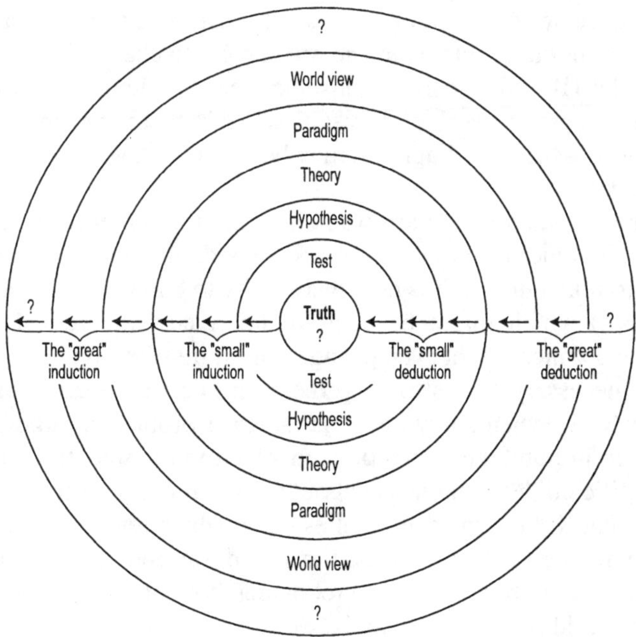

Fig. 1: From world-view to test: the "great" and the "small" deduction. From test to world-view: the "great" and the "small" induction.

In fig. 1 I have endeavored to illustrate the different levels from test to world view and the interaction between the levels. At the top I have placed a question mark to indicate that we do not know what governs our world-view. The "great" deduction is the subsumption of the theory under paradigms, which in turn fall under the world-view. Our world-view determines what sort of knowledge we seek, and what is important to us. A fundamental change in our world-view will render necessary new paradigms and new theories. This facilitates our understanding of, e.g. the Weber/Merton thesis, according to which the altered framing contexts of modern science give rise to new paradigms and theories. Likewise, the theory of relativity altered Newton's mechanical world-view, which had long dominated natural science. The "great" deduction is therefore rare, but of a very fundamental nature.

The "small" deduction is the way from theory to test, i.e. the deduction commented on in the introduction of this book, from theory to concrete hypothesis and to empirical test. I have also placed a question mark at the center of the figure to indicate that the criteria for approving a test are not unproblematic and are subject to change in the course of time. The HIV diagnosis, for instance, came a long time after the disease had begun its work of devastation. So in fact not even "truth" is fully obvious – the HIV diagnosis may be a test for a very new hypothesis of disease.

In terms of *induction* the arrows point from the center to the periphery, from the innermost question mark towards the outermost. This is intended to illustrate that it is not always easy to know how we arrive at "fins" (tests) which might be decisive for a new theoretical breakthrough, and which might even change our entire world-view.

It isn't necessary for us to keep the entire deductive and inductive context in view when studying social science problems, although we should keep in mind the interactions involved in the scientific process. E.g. scientific circles feel uneasy about tests that don't harmonize with theory – what Kuhn termed anomalies – and which result in theoretical changes with upward effects for the paradigm and the world-view. What is most important is that we recognize both how fragile and how robust the world of science really is.

Identifying the core of theories:
the four incompatible hypotheses

My reason for attributing so much importance to theory in social sciences is that theories reveal patterns of enduring stability and sure identification. Stability and patterns are necessary for our mutual understanding and for the functioning of social life. We form expectations about how others will act and about the structure of society, which enable us to predict in some degree the consequences of our own and of other people's actions.

Many people believe that what characterizes social life is not so much pattern and stability, but variation, multiplicity and instability. Hence it is futile to look for general theories, and we ought instead to regard social life as a welter of individual "narratives". A belief in the value of theories and stability might preclude the genuine experience of what actually happens.

This criticism of the search for theories and of the belief in stability is, to a large extent, connected with the fact that there are no "good" theories which easily allow the deduction of certain and testable statements. On the contrary, it is easy to falsify almost any established piece of general knowledge about social life. It might therefore seem safer to "establish facts" without elevating them to the level of theory. Over the years this view has left its mark particularly on the discipline of history.

Yet the postmodern emphasis on individual "narrative", and on the unique in traditional historical research, leaves us with a problem: in researching single cases, and in emphasizing the unique, one still needs general notions and comparisons in order to ascertain how a narrative is conveyed and the ways in which it is unique. Hence patterns are just as involved in this line of thought, even if one would prefer to ignore them. But postmodern criticism and the uniqueness trend of thought oblige social science to aim at still greater clarity concerning the implications of thinking in terms of theory and pattern.

To identify the core of a theory it may be useful to consider different types of mutually exclusive hypotheses. The purpose is *to formulate explicit hypotheses* as though they were deduced from the theory in question. These are the four hypotheses:

Theory: $X \rightarrow Y$	
1. *Basic hypothesis*:	$X \rightarrow Y$
2. *Contradictory hypothesis*:	$X \nrightarrow Y$
3. *Inverse hypothesis*:	$Y \rightarrow X$
4. *Alternative hypothesis*:	$Z \rightarrow Y$

Use of this simple logical apparatus in the examination of theories can be helpful in deciding the most reasonable identification of a theory's core. There are endless ways of formulating the four hypotheses, but the logic must be the same for all four. We can illustrate the method with reference to Lars Svåsand's discussion of the cross pressure hypothesis (chapter 14):

Theory: cross pressure (X) Late decision as to party choice (also possible abstention) → (Y)	
1) *Basic hypothesis* (deduced from theory):	Catholics in high status areas (X) → take a long time in deciding which party they will vote for (Y)
2. *Contradictory hypothesis*:	Catholics in high status areas (X) → immediately decide which party they will vote for (Y)
3. *Inverse hypothesis*:	It is the time required to make up one's mind (Y) → that decides who Catholics will vote for in high status areas (X)
4. *Alternative hypothesis*:	It is the efficacy of party propaganda in an area (Z) → that decides whether the voters of that area take a long time in making up their minds (Y)

Which is the correct identification of the cross pressure hypothesis as presented in chapter 14? In our case it is number 1, since this was deduced from the classical theory. One implication of our example is then that the other three hypotheses cannot be correct. But scientists who are either skeptical to the cross pressure hypothesis in general, or who wish for an even more solid foundation for further research, can formulate the other three to see if they appear reasonable in terms of the realities offered by election analyzes. If for instance the *alternative hypothesis* (4) seems to be supported by the available material, this may result in the invalidation/falsification of the cross pressure hypothesis. The *contradictory hypothesis* (in its statistical version also known as the 0 hypothesis) cannot be correct if the basic hypothesis is judged reasonable, and if it can be formulated as a clear antithesis to the basic hypothesis with the purpose of illustrating what the implications of the opposite would be. The *inverse hypothesis* should be formulated to ascertain the most reasonable causal direction when there is a high degree of covariance between X and Y, and when it is uncertain which variable can be independent (X) and which dependent (Y). I shall give some further examples to clarify the method.

In Helge Østbye's discussion of the two-step hypothesis (chapter 15) we can localize a *contradictory hypothesis*, e.g.: during an election campaign there are as many people who claim to change their party allegiance (Y) because they have been personally influenced (X) as there are people who claim to change allegiance (Y) because they have been influenced by TV and newspapers/mass media (the *contradictory hypothesis* here formulated as a 0 hypothesis).

Another formulation of a *contradictory hypothesis* (also contradicting the two-step hypothesis): during an election campaign there is no difference between the number who claim to change party allegiance (Y) because they have been personally influenced (X) and the number who claim to have been influenced by newspapers and TV (X).

An *alternative hypothesis* to the two-step hypothesis might be this: the reason why people change the party they support (Y) during an election campaign is that they move from one area to another (X). In other words, it might be the fact that a voter moves from a low-status area to a high-status area or vice versa, that determines a shift in party allegiance at an election, and not the influence of opinion leaders in the new environment.

An *inverse hypothesis* can be formulated thus: the decision to change party during the election campaign (Y) makes the individual in question more personally exposed to opinion leaders (X). On first view this hypothesis appears quite unreasonable due to the chronological sequence of the causes (opinion leaders are expected to have an effect *before* the change of party), but it could be pointed out that, at the next round, it is the waverers (insofar as they are known) whom opinion leaders concentrate on trying to influence. A strategy for managing an electoral campaign might in fact be to devote a minimum of time to influencing "safe" voters, and those who are "obviously unsafe". Thus conceived the *inverse hypothesis* is not without interest, although what we then face is a *different* hypothesis, not the two-step hypothesis. Yet the purpose of formulating the *inverse hypothesis* was to find solid confirmation of the causal direction implied by the two-step hypothesis, but in the same operation we have "discovered" an interesting new hypothesis.

The tragedy of the commons (chapter 12) provides an example of how a *contradictory hypothesis* can be formulated: individual expansion (X) in an area where resources are shared has no influence on the ecological balance (Y) of the area. However, this hypothesis does not deal specifically with restrictions, and a more reasonable formulation might be the following: heavy restrictions (X) in an area where resources are shared have no influence on the ecological balance (Y) of the area.

If this hypothesis is reasonable, it would seem natural to follow it up with an *alternative hypothesis*: decisive in disturbing the balance of an area (Y) is the capability of that area for biological resistance and renewal (Z), and not restrictions imposed by society.

An *inverse hypothesis* might look like this: decisive for the extent of restrictions (X) for an area is the balance of resources in that area (Y). This hypothesis is interesting in relation to the tragedy of the commons, because it tackles the problem of how regulations might be brought about: prior to the introduction of regulations (X), the balance (Y) must be disturbed or threatened. It is doubtful whether it is reasonable to call this an *inverse hypothesis* of the tragedy of the commons, but in our context the point is to show how the formulation of *inverse hypotheses* can lead to new theoretical ideas – ideas that can be fruitful in further research on, for instance, resource balance. But it is also possible that some other *basic hypothesis* – comparable to the *inverse hypothesis* – could be deduced from the theory, which might furnish an even better understanding of the "tragedy effect" on areas with balanced resources.

In this way we could examine all the social science theories in this book and other publications, and write out all the reasonably deducible hypotheses we can find – of the four types referred to above – and carefully consider which hypothesis seems most reasonable in relation to the theory (valid deduction).

The purpose of this method is to furnish students and researchers with the tools to "open up" or "dissect" theories and hypotheses in terms of clear formulation in different directions. In other words, it is a method for becoming more aware of theory, and of how to identify their essence, and consequently it is a method for improved science and research. This process is by no means straightforward and simple, but it provides a necessary heightening of awareness which is often ignored in traditional books on method.

Concluding remarks

If the impression you are left with is that theoretical work is difficult and that theories are far from unambiguous and obvious, you are not far from the truth. But the greater one's awareness of such difficulties, the easier it is to take them into account in research, thereby avoiding the risk of becoming trivial and superficial.

There are many amorphous and uncertain transitions in the various steps involved in theoretical explanation which might prompt pessimism. It is no easy task to distinguish between assumptions and the theory itself – or the different levels of theoretical hierarchy. At the same time, defining the problem and testing the essence of the theory/ hypothesis might offer so many scenarios that the entire project can appear hopeless.

But it is in this very tension between difficulties, fruitful answers and solutions to theoretical complexities that we find the challenge of theoretical work. It is no easy undertaking; one must grapple with it without sweeping the difficulties under the carpet. Knowledge of the nature of theories, an acquaintance with the difficulties of theoretical work, critical sense, optimism, a wealth of ideas and curiosity – these are the qualities I would encourage you to cultivate and which are vital to an enjoyment of this work.

Contributors

Jan Erik Askildsen (1954) is associate professor at the University of Bergen. "Regulating Monopolies with Worker Participation" in *Economic Analysis* 1/1998. "Human Capital, Property Rights and Labour Managed Firms" (with N. J. Ireland) in *Oxford Economic Papers* 45/1993. "Allocation of Capital and Labour-Owned Firm Consisting of Heterogeneous Workers" in *The Scandinavian Journal of Economics* 90/1988. "Medarbeiderstyre eller kapitalstyre?" (Coworker Rule or Capitalist Rule?) in Sandmo and K. P. Hagen (eds.): *Offentlig politikk og private incitamenter (Public Policy and Private Incitements)*, 1992. "Assymmetrisk informasjon i kredittmarkeder" (Asymmetric information credit markets) in G. Torsvik (ed.): *Informasjonsproblem og økonomisk styring (Problems of Information and Economic Control)*, 1998.

Ole Jacob Broch (1940) is professor in pharmacology at the University of Bergen. He has worked on the central nervous system, essentially metabolism of serotonine and dopamine, and the regional distribution of these substances and enzymes in the brain. *Studies of catechol-O-methyl transferase in nervous tissue of the rat*, 1974. *Atferdsfarmakologi for psykologer (Behavioural Pharmacology for Psychologists*, 1992.

Tom Colbjørnsen (1951) is professor in organization theory at the Norwegian School of Economics and Business Administration in Bergen. *Mangfold, medvirkning, tillit: Ledelse og nye organisasjonsformer (Diversity, Participation, Confidence: Management and New Forms of Organization)*, 1997. *Development Coalitions in Working Life* (with B. Gustavsen and Ø. Pålshagen), 1998. *Reisen til markedet (The Journey to the Market)*, 2. ed. 1995.

David R. Doublet (1954-2000) was professor in general theory of law at the University of Bergen. *Trancendentalfilosofi og historisisme (Transcendental Philosophy and Historicism)* 1988. *Die Vernuft als Rechtsinstanz (Reason as Judicial Authority)* 1989. *Rett, Vitenskap og fornuft (Law, Science and Reason)* 1995. *Retten og vitenskapen (The Law and Science)* (with J. Bernt), 1992. *Juss, samfunn og rettsanvendelse (Law, Society and Application of the Law)* (with J.

Bernt), 1996. *Vitenskapsfilosofi for jurister (Philosophy of Science for Lawyers)*, (with J. Bernt), 1998.

Nils Gilje (1947) is professor in philosophy at the Centre on Theory of Science, University of Bergen. *Anomalier i moderne vitenskapsfilosofi* (Anomalies in Modern Philosophy of Science), 1987. *Hermeneutikk i vitenskapsteoretisk perspektiv* (Hermeneutics in Scientific Theoretical Perspective), 1987. *Samfunnsvitenskapenes forutsetninger* (The Assumptions within the Social Sciences) (with H. Grimen), 1993. *Hans Nielsen Hauge og kapitalismens ånd* (Hans Nielsen Hauge and the Sprit of Capitalism), 1994, *Filosofihistorie I-II* (History of Philosophy), (with G. Skirbekk), 1996.

Harald Grimen (1955) is professor in philosophy at the University of Tromsø. "Fornuftige usemjer og epistemisk resignasjon" (Sensible disagreements and epistemic resignation), in E. O. Eriksen (ed.): *Den politiske orden (The Political Order)*, 1994. "Causally inefficient knowledge and functional explanation" in *Social Science Information* 33/1, 1994. "Starka värderingar och holistisk liberalism" (Strong assessments and holistic liberalism) in C. Taylor: *Identitet, frihet och gemenskap (Identity, Freedom and Fellowship)*, 1995. "How conditions of adequacy for text-interpretations depend on practices for explaining actions" in K. S. Johannessen and T. Nordenstram (eds.): *Wittgenstein and the Philosophy of Culture*, 1996. "Consensus and Normative Validity" in *Inquiry* 40/1, 1997.

Ørnulf Gulbrandsen (1946) is professor in social anthropology at the University of Bergen. Has earlier worked on themes of industrial anthropology. *Samarbeidsideologi og interessekonflikt (Ideology of Collaboration and Conflict of Interests)*, 1976. Later extensive studies in Botswana with several articles and books on politic-religious issues, kinship/marriage and economic-ecological problems. The last lager work is *Poverty in the Midst of Plenty*, 1996.

Thor Øivind Jensen (1951) is associate professor in public administration at the University of Bergen. Has worked on health- and consumer related issues. *Håndbok i publikumsundersøkelser* (Manual for public research investigations) (with Bomann-Larsen), 1986. *Mellom påbud og påvirkning, Tradisjoner, institusjoner og politikk i forebyggende helsearbeid* (Between command and influence, Tradition, Institutions and Policy in Preventive Healthcare), (with Evebakken and Fjær), 1993. *Product Safety in the Field and Services*, 1997. *Den europeiske unions utfordringer: ny organisasjon og kultur omkring avhenghetsskapende substanser* (The European Union's Challenges: New Organisation and Culture around Dependence Creating Substances), 1996. "Designing the good life: Nutrition and Social democracy in Norway" in Sulkunen et al. (eds.): *Constructing the new Consumer Society*, 1997.

Jan Erik Karlsen (1942) is professor at Stavanger University College and research manager at Rogaland Research. Has written several books within both economic organisation theory and health, environment and safety management. Research on technological- and environmental ethics and on robust forms of organisation for use of new technology.

Knud Knudsen (1944) is professor in sociology at Stavanger University College. *Lithuania in a period of transition*, 1995. "Scandinavian Neighbours with different character?" in *Acta Sociologica*, 1997, "Reactions to global processes of change: Attitudes towards marriage and gender roles in modern nations" (with Kari Wærness) in *Comparative Sociology Yearbook*, 1999.

Stein Ugelvik Larsen (1938) is associate professor at the Department of Comparative Politics at the University of Bergen. *Who were the fascist? Social Roots of European Fascism* (ed. with B. Hagtvet and J. P. Myklebust), 1990. *Fascism and European Literature* (ed. with B. Sandberg), 1991. *Nazismen og norsk litteratur (Nazism and Norwegian Literature)*,ed. with B. Birkeland, L. Longum and A. Kittang), 1995. *I balansepunktet. Sunnmøres eldste historie 800-1600 (In the point of balance. Sunnmøre's oldest history 800-1600)* (ed. with J. Sulebust), 1994. *Modern Europe after Fascism* (ed.), 1998. *Krigen og i krigens kjølvann (The War and in the Wake of War)* (ed.), 1999, *Meldungen aus Norwegen* (SD/SIPO-Reports from Norway) (ed. with B. Sandberg and H. Paulsen), 2001.

Peter Sjøholt (1925) is professor emeritus at the Norwegian School of Economics and Business Administration in Bergen. *– og bygda ble by. Strindas historie 1946-64* (- and the village became a town. The history of Strinda 1946-64), 1971. *Systemet av sentrale steder og omland* (The System of Central Places and Surrounding Country) 1981. "Vil varene vare?" (Will the Goods Last?) in *Det moderne Norge* (The Modern Norway) vol. 3, (ed. with D. Bjørnland and H. F. Dahl) 1982. "Norge i verden" (Norway in the World) in Cappelen: *Norge* (Norway), vol. 3, 1985. *Tropical colonization. Problems and achievements*, 1988. *Nasjonalatlas for Norge. Innenriks varehandel* (National Atlas for Norway. Domestic Commodity Trade), 1992. *Internationalisering af service og regional udvikling i Norden* (Internationalisation of Service and Regional Development in the Nordic Countries), 1992.

Lars Svåsand (1947) is professor in comparative politics at the University of Bergen. The field of research is political parties. *Challenges to Political Parties: The case of Norway* (with K. Strøm), 1997. *Partier uten grenser?* (Parties without Boundaries?) (ed. with K. Heidar), 1997.

Gaute Torsvik (1963) is professor in economics at the University of Bergen. "The ratchet effect in common agency: Implications for regulation and privatization" in *Journal of Law, Economics and Organizations,* 9/1993. "Collusion and renegotiation in hierarchies; the case of beneficial corruption" in *International Economic Review,* 1998. "Incentives and Discretion in Organizations" in *Journal of Labor Economics,* 1999. *Informasjonsproblem og økonomisk organisering (Problems of Information and Economic Organization,* 1997. All publications is in co-operation with T. E. Olsen.

Helge Østbye (1946) is professor in media science at the University of Bergen. Worked on the first report on power (*NOU 1982:3* and *NOU 1982:30*). Contributor to several books from The Euromedia Research Group. *Sosialpolitikk eller sosialpornografi? (Social Policy or Social Pornography?)* (with R. Puijk and E. Øyen), 1984. *Mediepolitikk (Media Policy)* 2. ed. 1995. *Metodebok for mediefag (Methods for Media Studies)* (with K. Helland, K. Knapskog and T. Hillesund), 1997, *Media i samfunnet (Media in Society)* (with T. Scwebs), 4. ed. 1999.

Index